Fields of Nourishment

Plant-Based Recipes with
Their Nutrient Profiles

By

Janet M. Lacey, DrPH, RD

INFINITY
PUBLISHING

Copyright © 2011 by Janet M. Lacey, DrPH, RD

ISBN 978-0-7414-6488-0 Black & White
ISBN 978-0-7414-6489-7 Partial Color
ISBN 978-0-7414-6860-4 Full Color

Printed in the United States of America

Published August 2011

INFINITY PUBLISHING
1094 New DeHaven Street, Suite 100
West Conshohocken, PA 19428-2713
Toll-free (877) BUY BOOK
Local Phone (610) 941-9999
Fax (610) 941-9959
Info@buybooksontheweb.com
www.buybooksontheweb.com

Fields of Nourishment
Plant-Based Recipes with Their Nutrient Profiles

TABLE OF CONTENTS

ACKNOWLEDGEMENTS

Most of these recipes are my favorites. Over the past 35 years, I have been fortunate to have attended classes by some of the pioneers in whole foods cooking. I have saved several recipes in their original formats, modified some of them, and used them over the decades. This book is a way of sharing these wonderful dishes with all of you, and a way of saying "Thank you!" to those who have helped me along the path to health.

In the mid-to-late 1970's, I was one of many students working and studying with Michio and Aveline Kushi. I met countless people seeking healing, dietary approaches and witnessed their renewal of health and hope as they returned to a more natural way of life. I attended as many seminars as possible on complementary medicine, yin and yang and their applications to everyday phenomena. I am grateful to Michio for his tireless, pioneering efforts in teaching Oriental Philosophy and Integrative Healing Practices. The Order of the Universe will continue to open new worlds to me, with precious principles that can be applied so uniquely to everyday life. I also had the wonderful opportunity to cook alongside Aveline and to learn her traditional style of home cooking, as she shared her wealth of knowledge in the kitchen. I am very appreciative of her kindness and invaluable education.

I am indebted to the amazing cooking skills of friend and teacher Gretchen DeWire. I continue to use her recipes, many of which are included in this book, and I remember fondly the time spent in her study-house kitchen. I extend sincere appreciation to teachers Hiroshi Hayashi, Evan Root and Michael Swain, as well as for the culinary contributions of Lima Ohsawa, Cornelia Aihara, Wendy Esko, Deborah Madison, Christina Pirello, Annemarie Colbin, and Marilyn Waxman.

I am grateful for the training I received in whole foods recipe and nutrient data analysis under the guidance of Frank Sacks, M.D., at Channing Laboratory in Boston. I would also like to thank my dear friends in Kobe, Japan who so generously invited me into their homes and shared their cooking styles and exquisite food with me.

Thank you to all my students from Simmons College, the University of Delaware and West Chester University of Pennsylvania, who have joined in the exciting studies of food and nutrition throughout the years. You have challenged my thinking and helped me to see things in many new ways. I am grateful for the sabbatical support from West Chester University, which gave me the creative time and energy to complete the recipe testing and data analysis for this book.

Heartfelt thanks to my dear friends and mentors, Simmons College emeritus professors, Drs. Kathleen (Kay) Dunn and Richard B. Lyman Jr., who carefully read the manuscript and offered valuable suggestions for improvement. A special thanks to Kay also for her thoughtful inclusion of the gluten-free information.

Sincere thanks to Laura Pici of Infinity Publishing for her gentle spirit and patient guidance throughout the book production process.

Thank you to my dear sister, Linda Toomey - a magician in the kitchen - who gave of her time testing many of the recipes and providing insightful input.

To my dearest husband, Michael Yang, an excellent cook, thank you for your patience and for your help adding *zip* to many of the recipes I have enjoyed for a long time. Your honest, constructive suggestions for my cooking, your love and unwavering support throughout the preparation of this book have made all the difference!

For my in-laws, Xi-Rang and Yu-Ying, thank you for your affection and encouragement and for opening my eyes to the wonders of Beijing and the amazing cuisine of China!

Thank you to my parents, Richard and Rose, for communicating the value of public heath and service; and for instilling in me an appreciation for the enormous importance of sound nutrition. My deepest gratitude for your unconditional love and an unforgettable childhood filled with joy.

When in the kitchen, I'm so inspired by fond childhood memories of my grandmothers from Lithuania and Italy. These amazing women spent literally decades preparing wonderful food for their large families while imparting their love and wisdom. This book is dedicated to them, Louise (Makauskas) Lacey and Agatha (Fisichelli) Tuso.

INTRODUCTION

Many alternatives to home cooking are just not that acceptable. Sure, we could rather be doing many other things. Yes, we are often tired after long days. But the rewards of home cooking, some short-term and others more long-term, are just too beneficial to ignore anymore. With proper planning, as well as efficient shopping and practice, we can successfully move home cooking back to its well-deserved, top position on the priority list. Home cooking not only saves money and improves health but also provides critical family interaction.

Fields of Nourishment is not really a comprehensive primer on cooking or nutrition. It is intended to complement some of the books already on your shelves. I have added topics that might be less often mentioned or less well known. The book begins with an introduction to the major nutrients, followed by a basic overview of food energy. Discussions of cooking methods, key ingredients and general recipe modification principles complete Part 1. In Part 2, recipes are organized into groups of grains, beans, vegetables, sauces and dressings, sea vegetables, soups and desserts; each recipe is followed by a table of specific nutrient information per serving. These values highlight the fact that plants offer a wide variety and rich supply of nutrients. Finally, summary tables give readers a chance to compare different dishes within each group for specific nutrients. In Appendix A, general nutrient requirements are provided. Appendix B includes a shopping list to help streamline your food purchasing.

During one of my earliest visits to the dentist, I remember reading these insightful words on the office wall:

> *"Without teeth, there can be no chewing; without chewing, there can*
> *be no nourishment; without nourishment, there can be no health;*
> *without health, what is life?"*

I sincerely hope this book will contribute to your robust and radiant health.

1. Uneaten Food Has No Nutritional Value

It is often said that we eat food, not nutrients. I have prepared my share of morally superior recipes that failed the taste test, and – uneaten – clearly provided no nutrition. Taste is paramount. Visual appeal is important. To be of any benefit, food must be eaten. Therefore, eating should be pleasurable.

On another level, though, our bodies do recognize and depend upon adequate nutrition, much as a plant relies on sun, water and the compounds in air to allow it to grow and be productive. Concerns about nutrients should not go overboard. Selecting food / eating solely because something is "good for me" or "it is time to eat" cannot be a sound replacement for following one's own rhythms and intuition.

It is amazing how much wonderful nutrition is contained in many plant-based recipes. The aim of this book is to illustrate the abundance of nutrients available on this most-harmonious of dietary approaches. Sometimes health/medical/nutrition books take on a negative spin, referring to „non-meat" diets as if this was an aberration, or "incomplete proteins" as though eating muscle were the norm because it contains the same profile of parts that we possess. It would be like saying we should mainly eat bones so that we can grow better bones. Or drink animal blood to develop rich blood. Our bodies manufacture many important substances provided we give them the raw materials to do so.

The recipes in this book were made without any dairy products, fish, meat or poultry, except for an occasional egg. There is no refined white or brown sugar or honey, and the grains and flours are mainly in their unrefined (whole) forms. All oils were also used in their natural, un-hydrogenated states.

Armed with nutritional information, we can make the most of recipes we enjoy and the diets we choose. We can give our bodies sufficient amounts of the raw materials they need. This gives us freedom. We have ultimate choice in what we eat, so let's know what is in what we eat.

What is nutrient data analysis?
Pulling apart the chemical components of food is the job of food scientists. With sophisticated methods to determine how many calories and how much protein, fiber, iron and other nutrients are in each food, they can assemble this information in data banks. Here others can easily figure out nutrients provided by individual foods, daily menus, or newly designed recipes. Though this can be done by hand (and was done so with excruciating tedium many decades ago), computers have made this process easy and user-friendly.

For one example, if you had a slice of bread, you could find such information as the following, in a textbook (Whitney and Rolfes, 2011):

Whole Wheat Bread, 1 serving (1 slice)
128 calories (kcal)
3.9 g protein
2.8 g fiber
159 mg sodium
1.4 mg iron

The recipes in this book were analyzed using Nutrition Data System for Research, version 2009, developed by the Nutrition Coordinating Center (NCC), University of Minnesota, Minneapolis, MN, and used with permission. This program is a state-of-the-art, comprehensive database that is updated every year with the latest nutrient information. It is amazingly accurate and world-renowned. Each recipe in this book is followed by a listing of key nutrients contained in a single serving. The following sections (2 through 9) describe many of these nutrients and their roles. At the end of the book is a set of tables with selected recipes to illustrate comparatively which recipes have certain noteworthy strengths. Nutrient tables showing the recommended amounts of nutrients for each age and gender group are included in Appendix A (Institute of Medicine, 2006; 2011).

2. The Cost of the Package: PROTEIN

The roles of protein are numerous and well established, ranging from supporting growth and renewal, enzyme production and nutrient transportation, to strengthening our immune system and maintaining the body's water balance. Protein-rich foods, however, can sometimes come in a high-fat/high-cholesterol "package." Smart eating considers this package and the long-term "costs." Cholesterol-free, high-fiber, lower-fat plants can be wonderful sources of protein. With the exception of fruit, crops such as beans, grains and vegetables – as well as recipes made containing mixtures of these – provide reliable amounts of protein.

Because all protein in food is broken down to its component amino acids before being absorbed from the digestive tract, the real benefit in eating foods containing protein is to acquire those individual amino acids to use for creating the body's new protein material. There are 9 essential amino acids, ones that the body cannot typically make in adequate amounts on its own, and these are listed in the nutrient tables for each recipe. Each food group has characteristic strengths – beans are usually high in the amino acid lysine, but not so rich in the amino acids cysteine or methionine. Cereals tend to have the opposite profile - being rich in cysteine & methionine, while being lower in lysine. Eating enough food everyday and a natural variety of plants can give an individual the sufficient amino acids to ensure a balanced availability of all the amino acids needed to make the body's daily proteins. Determinations have been made of the relative amounts of each essential amino acid needed per day; this information is listed in Appendix A.

Digestibility of food is a key to maximizing the breakdown and absorption of amino acids, and therefore, plants need to be prepared in ways that enable the body to utilize the available nutrients. Pre-soaking beans and grains, using a pressure cooker, and checking for done-ness ("Cook by taste, not by time" – Aveline Kushi) are useful factors.

One gram of protein contains approximately 4 calories.[1] According to the Institute of Medicine (2006), a healthy diet can include a wide range of protein intakes, which can represent between 10 to 35% of one's total calories.[2] Because this range is very broad, it is helpful to know the general amount of protein recommended for adults based on their body weight, since a larger person would need more

---

[1] Note: Technically, plant protein calculations are based differently than the standard 4 kcal per gram for energy generation, by the NDSR (NDSR Version 2009, Handbook, Appendix Page A11.1). Characteristics of food take into account the insoluble dietary fiber, nitrogen in the food that is not part of protein molecules, data on foods analyzed in the laboratory, and other established factors. For calculating calories per gram from protein, the following multipliers were used according to food type: Cereals: 3.91; Eggs: 4.36; Fruit: 3.36; Legumes and nuts: 3.47; Vegetables: 2.62.

[2] For example, someone eating 2000 calories a day could safely consume between 10% of 2000 calories (200 calories), which is 50 grams of protein (200/4, since 1 gram of protein has 4 calories), up to 35% of 2000 (700 calories) or about 175 grams of protein (700/4).

protein to support it. The recommendation is currently 0.8 grams per kg (1 kg=2.2 pounds) daily. For a 150-lb person, their weight in kg would be 68 kg (150/2.2). Then the amount of protein recommended would be 68 x 0.8 or about 54 grams per day.

In general, plants can make a substantial contribution to protein intake. The following table illustrates the average amounts of protein per serving from a variety of sources (from Melina & Davis, 2003). On average, one ounce of meat, fish or poultry has approximately 7 grams of protein.

Plant type (cooked)	Protein (g) per serving
Beans (1 cup)	14-18 (28 for soybeans)
Grains (1/2 cup cooked grains)	2-4
Peanuts (1/4 cup)	8.5
Seeds or nuts (2 Tbsp)	2-4
Soymilk (8 oz)	6.4-10
Tofu, firm (refer to package label)	10-20
Tofu, silken firm	8.7
Vegetables (1/2 cup)	2

Besides the nutritional benefits of eating plants, obtaining protein without depending upon animal agriculture can have a positive and widespread environmental impact. Animal protein production involves the often extensive use of fertilizer, pesticides, and antibiotics, and produces a good deal of waste, some of which (in the form of methane gas) contributes to air pollution (Jacobson, 2006). It also requires large amounts of water, compared to growing plants for protein. These are part of the "package costs" of selecting foods for obtaining protein.

3. All CARBOHYDRATES are not sweet!

Carbohydrates abound in plant foods, from the fibrous structures that support their growth, to the varied & delightful sweet tastes they impart. Plants manufacture carbohydrates through a seemingly miraculous chemical process called PHOTOSYNTHESIS, requiring ultraviolet light from the sun. In return, they produce oxygen and deliver sugars to the plants' structures and resulting fruits.

Carbohydrates can be simple or complex, which means that the molecules are either short (simple) or in a long chain (complex). The simplest (monosaccharides) are most rapidly absorbed through the digestive tract. The most complex – and these can be really huge molecules! – are known as either digestible starch or dietary fiber (not-digestible). If digestible, complex carbohydrates may not taste sweet, but if chewed very well, they start to break down in the mouth, releasing more simple sugars. Then the sweetness arrives!

The molecules of complex carbohydrates are broken down more slowly during digestion. The result is that these enter the bloodstream more slowly, delivering a steadier supply of energy over a longer period of time. In between are the carbohydrates with a few molecules (so-called "oligosaccharides") and these can be difficult to digest (names include raffinose and stacchyose). Presoaking beans and discarding the water, as well as cooking well or using a pressure cooking can significantly reduce the presence of these molecules.

Most carbohydrates provide food energy, but the dietary fibers – both soluble and insoluble (referring to whether or not they dissolve in water) – cannot be broken down by our digestive enzymes in the small intestine. They do carry with them distinct health advantages, however, which are widely appreciated by health professionals. Soluble fibers, especially high in beans, oats and barley and fruits, have gel-forming properties in the large intestine. They help dilute the contents of food passage, and also slow the absorption of sugars into the bloodstream. They also can reduce the absorption of fat and cholesterol. Insoluble fibers – most abundant in the outer bran coat of cereals and in many vegetables – bulk up the stool contents and assist with smooth evacuation.

Both types of fiber are important, and a mixture is typically found in most plants. Because of their ability to be broken down (and fermented) by gut-living bacteria, they can cause some gas production, so increasing fiber-rich foods in the diet is best done gradually. Another excellent benefit of plant fiber is its satiating impact, due to water-holding. After a bean burger meal, a person is likely to experience a pleasing fullness that will help to regulate appetite and avoid being hungry a short while after eating. A plus for weight control!

Because sugars are an important fuel for the body – in fact energy is the main role of carbohydrates – they can be delivered at a certain rate to the blood, depending upon what else comes in the mix. For example, a sugary soda, rich with glucose and fructose in the form of sugar and/or high-fructose corn syrup, can readily be absorbed into the bloodstream surrounding the intestine's absorbing cells. The body handles influxes of sugar into the blood by signaling insulin release by the pancreas to keep the blood glucose relatively normal. Large influxes of sugar require higher levels of insulin to maintain balance.

Glycemic index is a measure of how extensively a 50-gram dose of a single (carbohydrate-containing) food contributes to the rise in blood sugar over a 2-hour period when compared to 50 grams of white sugar [some prefer to compare this to white bread, but the theory behind it is the same]. Glycemic load adjusts this index for the actual amount of carbohydrate in a serving. Both of these values are given in the nutrient tables. Over time, eating foods with a high glycemic load can put an increased burden on the pancreas for insulin production/release. Therefore, choosing most foods lower on the scale is recommended for most meals. The contribution of soluble fiber in plant foods helps to slow down sugar absorption. Since many of the recipes in the book contain fair amounts of fiber, many provide low glycemic loads, compared to recipes with refined grains containing little fiber.

Like protein, a gram of carbohydrate contains approximately 4 calories.[3] The Institute of Medicine (2006) recommends that individuals consume at least 130 grams of carbohydrate daily. Approximately 45-65% of calories contributed by carbohydrates are recommended in the daily diet.[4]

Dietary Fiber recommendations (Institute of Medicine, 2006) are 25 g/day for adult females up to age 50 (21 g thereafter) and 38 g/day for adult males (30 g thereafter).

---

[3] Technically, plant carbohydrate calculations are based differently than the standard 4 kcal per gram for energy generation, by the NDSR (NDSR Version 2009, Handbook, Appendix Page A11.1). Characteristics of food take into account the insoluble dietary fiber, data on foods analyzed in the laboratory, and other established factors. For calculating calories-per-gram from carbohydrate, the following multipliers were used according to food type: Cereals: 4.12; Fruits: 3.60; Legumes and nuts: 4.07; Sugars: 3.87; Vegetables: 3.90.

[4] If a person consumes 2000 calories a day, 45% of calories would be 900 calories, which represents (900/4) 225 grams of carbohydrate; 65% of calories would be 1,300 calories, representing (1300/4) 325 grams. Thus, a range of 225 – 325 grams of carbohydrate would be considered a healthy range of intake at this calorie level.

4. Simple Basics: FAT and CHOLESTEROL

Dietary fat adds an important dimension to cooking, by speeding up the cooking process, carrying wonderful flavors and creating a "staying power" from a meal. The good news about plants is they are free of cholesterol – always! Cholesterol from external sources is not essential, as a healthy liver can make all that a body needs every day.

Most vegetable sources of fat/oil (with the exception of tropical oils such as coconut and palm) are relatively low in saturated fat (most fats are a mixture of oil types, so a little saturated fat is usually present, but it is the proportion that counts). If the oils are extracted naturally, they are also free of *trans* fat. Sources of fat in a plant-based diet typically come from nuts, nut butters, seeds and seed butter, as well as oils extracted from these, along with oils from the olive and avocado. Soybeans have a fair amount of oil, so soy products can contribute fat to the diet, again mainly in the unsaturated form.

A **saturated fatty acid** molecule is shown here. Note that there are no double bonds and each carbon (C) atom is filled to capacity with hydrogen (H) atoms for each carbon. This molecule is **stearic acid**.

When a fat is **unsaturated**, spaces still remain on the fat molecule where more hydrogen can be added; this is represented by a double bond in its chain. The more double bonds, the more unsaturated or "polyunsaturated" it is. An unsaturated fatty acid is shown below, in the monounsaturated form, meaning there is only one double bond (highlighted in red) in the chain. This molecule is **oleic acid**.

If the 1st double bond starts on the 3rd carbon atom in the chain, it is labeled an **omega-3** (or "n-3") fatty acid. The example seen here is **alpha-linolenic (α-linolenic) acid**, with three double bonds, a polyunsaturated fatty acid.

On the other hand, if the 1st double bond starts on the 6th carbon atom in the chain, it is labeled an **omega-6** (or "n-6") fatty acid, shown here. This molecule is **linoleic acid,** which has two double bonds.

Omega-3 and omega-6 fatty acids are essential, meaning the body cannot manufacture these from other components. Omega-6 fatty acids are found in animal products, as well as most nuts, seeds and vegetable oils. Good sources of omega-3 fatty acids include flax seeds, soy, walnuts, canola oil, green leafy vegetables, sea vegetables and eggs produced by chickens fed omega-3-rich diets. Fatty fish are also a rich source of omega-3 fat; fish oil can be taken as a supplement. Vegan versions of omega-3 supplements derived from microalgae are now available.

Without awareness and proper planning, it can be challenging to obtain sufficient omega-3 fatty acids, which contribute to reduced inflammation in the body (among many other roles). Generally, the ratio of omega-6 to omega-3 in the modern diet is too high. This can also be a concern for vegetarians.

The recommended range of fat for adults is 20-35% of calories.[5] High-fat diets can provide excessive calories, particularly because fat carries a higher amount of calories per gram - 9 compared to 4 calories for both protein and carbohydrate; so for appropriate weight control, moderation in fat is a key factor.[6] Individuals are advised to get no more than 300 mg a day of cholesterol, which is only found in animal products. There is no adult recommendation for the actual amount of fat in grams, except for two essential fatty acids, alpha-linolenic and linoleic acid, and this information is listed in Appendix A.

Heart healthy diets are also low in saturated fat, since too much of this type tends to raise blood cholesterol levels. Fat is necessary, however, to help the body process and absorb important compounds from food that dissolve in fat – such as fat-soluble vitamins, A, D, E, and K, as well as fat-soluble phytochemicals such as lycopene.

5. Our Cherished FAT SOLUBLE VITAMINS: Vitamin A, D, E and K

Vitamins and minerals are amazing micronutrients. The amounts we need are so small, yet without them, our bodies lose precious functions…vision, blood clotting, bone building.

Vitamin A is critical for vision, reproduction, regulated cell growth, skin health and a sound immune system. Vitamin A is found in animal products as a ready-to-use vitamin, especially in whole and fortified milk, liver, egg yolk. This important vitamin can also be made from precursors, such as beta carotene, abundant in brightly colored vegetables and some fruits. Again, fat is needed to absorb these fat-soluble nutrients.

Vitamin D is a nutrient found naturally in limited numbers of foods, such as fatty fish and fish liver oils, liver, and eggs. A plant-based diet generally does not provide much vitamin D naturally, as you will note on the nutrient tables. However, fortified foods, such as fortified soymilk and breakfast cereals, and newer products coming on the market (such as mushrooms treated with ultraviolet light), do offer substantial amounts. Sunlight is an exceptional source, although northern-living folks will have fewer months in which to obtain (and store) this vitamin in their fat tissue. Individuals who live in cold climates or avoid the sun (either physically or by use of sun block) need to be diligent in

---

[5] For example, someone eating 2000 calories a day could safely consume between 20% of 2000 calories (400 calories), which is ~45 grams of fat (400/9), since 1 gram of fat has 9 calories, up to 35% of 2000 (700 calories) or about ~78 grams of fat (700/9).

[6] Technical calculations for calories from fat by the NDSR (NDSR Version 2009, Handbook, Appendix Page A11.1) take into account data on foods analyzed in the laboratory and other established factors. Calories-per-gram from fat were based on the following multipliers according to food type: Eggs: 9.02; Fats, vegetable: 8.84; Cereals, Fruits, Legumes and nuts, and vegetables: 8.37.

obtaining reliable sources, or turning to a supplement. Vitamin D's roles include helping to absorb calcium, but also may play critical roles throughout the body, from brain health to cancer prevention.

Vitamins E and K are found in HUGE amounts in plants – particularly colorful vegetables and – in the case of vitamin E – in nuts & seeds and plant oils.

Vitamin E is a key fat-soluble antioxidant throughout the body, and may play a role in reducing the risk of oxidized cholesterol particles (particularly LDL) in the blood, which could otherwise lead to plaque accumulation.

Vitamin K is required for blood clotting. This is an interesting nutrient as some is made by our bacteria residing in the large intestine. Another more recently recognized role for vitamin K is in helping to add calcium to bone. Because leafy green vegetables are high in both calcium and vitamin K, these are exquisite foods to eat for a healthy skeleton!

6. Gems in Water: WATER-SOLUBLE VITAMINS

Thiamin (B1), Riboflavin (B2), Niacin, Vitamin B6, Vitamin B12 and Folate; Vitamin C, Pantothenic Acid and Choline

These all-important compounds are essential for reactions ranging from releasing energy from food for fueling all cells (thiamin, riboflavin, niacin and B6), to keeping our red blood cells functioning and maintaining our hearts and nervous system (B12 & folate). Vitamin C – a vital water-soluble antioxidant – is required for the strength of our collagen, the body's "glue" – including healthy gums and other tissues. Choline, one of the most recently recognized essential nutrients, contributes to a healthy liver and to communication between cells, particularly of the nervous system (Institute of Medicine, 2006); it is the starting material for making the neurotransmitter *acetylcholine*.

Although in this country, refined grains and their products are enriched with thiamin, riboflavin, niacin (as well as folate and iron) the bran of whole grains is naturally rich in these vitamins. Vitamin B6, particularly important in chemical reactions involving proteins, is found widely in vegetable foods; good sources include beans, potatoes, bananas, sunflower seeds and peanut butter (Whitney & Rolfes, 2011).

Vitamin B12 is found in animal products, although it is actually bacteria (within the animals) that synthesize this vitamin. Fortified foods (soy products and breakfast cereals among them) can provide vitamin B12, and the requirement is very low.

Folate, named for green leaves or "foliage" is everywhere in a plant-based diet! The recommended intake is 400 mcg a day, and as you can see in the nutrient tables, this is easy to attain. Vitamin C, likewise, is abundant in fruits and vegetables.

Pantothenic acid is important in energy metabolism as part of a larger compound (coenzyme A). Fortunately, it is found in a wide variety of foods and it is unusual to find deficiencies. The adequate intake (AI) set for adults is 5 mg/day.

The AI for choline is 425 mg and 550 mg for females and males, respectively, aged 19 and older. Peanuts and eggs are rich sources of choline (as are milk and liver). There are smaller amounts of choline distributed in a wide variety of foods as well. Whole grains, legumes – including soy products – and vegetables make solid contributions; one cup of Bean Stew, for example provides 50 mg.

7. Selected MAJOR MINERALS

Calcium, Phosphorus, Magnesium

Calcium is an incredibly important nutrient – and not just for maintaining bone health. It is a master "signaler" in cells, regulating activities at many levels. Essential for muscle and nerve function and even blood clotting, calcium in the blood is regulated at a narrow range by an intricate feedback system, involving the digestive system, the bones, and hormones of the thyroid and parathyroid glands. Bones act as a reservoir of calcium, storing 99% of the body's supply. Adequate intake helps to maintain equilibrium without drawing on the bone. Vitamin D is also necessary for effective absorption of dietary calcium. Individuals need to pay particular attention to this nutrient as well.

While calcium is not the only nutrient critical to healthy bones, it is a major component. Throughout the world, individuals enjoy a variety of calcium-rich foods to meet their needs. Vegetables are particularly rich sources of calcium, especially leafy greens and soy products (tofu, fortified soymilk and recipes containing these). With the exception of spinach and Swiss chard which are high in oxalic acid that binds calcium, green leafy vegetables provide calcium that is easily absorbed by the body. In fact, approximately 40-60% of the calcium in leafy greens can be absorbed by the body, compared to about 32% from milk (Weaver et al., 1999).

Adult men and women from ages 19-50, including pregnant and lactating women in these age ranges, should consume 1000 mg a day (Institute of Medicine, 2011). One cup of collard greens contains over 160 mg of calcium (recipe shown is for ½ cup at 83 mg); one tofu burger provides 171 mg. Enjoying a variety of foods from the plant kingdom will enable an individual to "bank" their calcium throughout the day.

Because it is so abundant in our food supply, phosphorus is one nutrient that most people usually consume in sufficient amounts. Rich plant sources include grains, beans, and nuts. It is a component of bones, cell membranes (phospholipids) and makes up the body's energy currency, ATP (adenosine triphosphate). The daily recommendation for adults is 700 mg (Institute of Medicine, 2006).

Magnesium is a key player for hundreds of enzymes in the body. It is essential for the release of energy from food and it helps regulate muscle and nerve function (Gropper et al., 2009). Magnesium is a part of the bone's structure, and is needed to active vitamin D to help absorb calcium. Regulating blood calcium is an example of a hormonal function (in the parathyroid gland) that needs magnesium to take place.

Unrefined plant foods are the best sources of magnesium. Magnesium is at the center of the green chlorophyll molecule, so brightly colored vegetables are a sure contributor of this key nutrient. Other rich sources of magnesium include beans, seeds, nuts and their butters. One serving of black bean soup provides about 100 mg of magnesium; the recommended intake for adults ranges from 310 to 420 mg/day (Institute of Medicine, 2006).

Sodium and Potassium

Both sodium and potassium are considered electrolytes, critically important to muscle movement (including our smooth muscles that are often beyond our awareness) and the transmission of nerve impulses. These two minerals, however, tend to be quite opposite. Sodium is found mostly outside of our cells, potassium is concentrated on the inside. Sodium is found in processed foods and increases as the food industry takes a part; potassium is rich in unprocessed food and declines with industrial alteration. Sodium is easy to consume in excess and contributes to higher risk of hypertension; potassium needs are often unmet and sufficient amounts reduce the risk of hypertension. Excess sodium causes accelerated loss of calcium in the urine; potassium-rich fruits and vegetables contribute to a more alkaline blood condition that reduces the need for calcium "buffering" and thus spares bone mineral.

Sources of sodium are well known – added salt, soy sauce, miso, MSG (monosodium glutamate) and pickles. Lesser appreciated are condiments like ketchup and mustard, store-bought breads and even pastries. Baking soda and baking powder have fair amounts of sodium; salt added to bread acts as both flavor enhancer and preservative. Ideally, adults under 50 should consume no more than 1500 mg a day of sodium, and as one ages, a little less: over 50 and less than 70 years old, up to 1300 mg and for those over 70, 1200 mg.

Many of the recipes in this book have only a modest amount of sodium, from miso, soy sauce or added salt. You can reduce these amounts even further by experimenting with less than the recipe calls for and by using low-sodium baking powder and reduced-sodium salt.

One of the wonderful "perks" of a plant-based diet is the effortless attainment of high levels of potassium on a daily basis. Whereas the recommendations for daily potassium intake seem high at 4,700 mg, the amount of potassium in just a few items indicates the ease of obtaining enough: a serving of roasted potatoes has 656 mg, ½ cup of bok choy 660 mg, 1 cup of vegetable brown rice 718 mg and 1 cup of baked azuki beans provides 927 mg of potassium. See complete tables of recommendations for these nutrients in Appendix A.

8. SELECTED TRACE MINERALS

Iron, Copper, Zinc and Selenium

In general, many people may be aware of iron's role in delivering oxygen around the body; oxygen is a key player in generating energy through metabolism. But iron's importance goes even further. Like magnesium, it is essential for many enzymes to function. It is integral for a sound immune system, and the brain requires it for healthy operations. On a mixed diet, the recommended intake of iron is 8 mg for men and women over age 50, and 18 mg for women in the childbearing years (aged 19-50). The sources of iron matter. Plant-sourced iron is accompanied by fibers and is in a different form compared to animal-sourced iron (the technical terms are "nonheme" compared to "heme" – referring to part of the hemoglobin molecule of blood). Individuals obtaining their iron mostly from plants are therefore recommended to aim for a higher intake: around 14.5 mg for women over 50 and adult males, around 32.5 mg for 19-50 year old women. Heme iron from animal products is absorbed at a higher rate. However, plants are loaded with iron, so typically a relatively high iron intake will result from the enjoyment of plant-based recipes. Beans and greens are especially good sources of iron; one serving of warm bean salad has 3.6 mg of iron, green beans with soy crumbles 3.0 mg. and white bean soup with escarole 2.8 mg; one-half cup of bok choy provides 2.0 mg.

Copper directs iron to be absorbed into the bloodstream and transported around. It has enzyme functions, too: reactions that produce certain nerve chemicals and the myelin sheath of nerve fibers require this important mineral. Like iron, copper is significant in keeping healthy a body's energy producing pathways. In addition, copper is important for keeping collagen strong. Finally, it plays a role as part of an antioxidant system in the body (superoxide dismutase), which – without copper – would be ineffective (Gropper et al., 2009). Plants are the major dietary source of copper; the RDA is 0.9 mg (900 mcg) and most of the recipes have between 0.1 and 0.5 mg.

Zinc is widely available in whole grains and beans. Like iron, the recommended amounts for those on a plant-based diet are higher and – like iron – eating plants provides a good deal of this critical nutrient. Whereas the recommended intake is 8 mg per day for adult women and 11 mg for men, vegetarians are encouraged to consume approximately 50% more, or 12 mg for women and about 16.5 mg for men. A ½-cup serving of azuki beans and squash provides 2.6 mg; a square of banana nut bread has 2.4 mg. Even a slice of tofu cheesecake provides 2 mg! Increased amounts of protein from legumes appear to enhance the amount of zinc absorbed (Sandström et al., 1989), possibly due to an effect of certain amino acids on the process.

Why do we need zinc? If you added up the number of enzymes that require all the other trace minerals combined, zinc would exceed this number. Healthy immunity, appetite, bones, skin, cartilage, metabolism, and overall sound growth and development depend upon zinc adequacy (Gropper et al., 2009).

Selenium is well known for 2 important functions: as an essential ingredient in a powerful antioxidant system (glutathione peroxidase) which protects the membranes of red blood cells and in the transformation of one thyroid hormone (T4) to the more active one (T3) (Gropper et al., 2009). The thyroid hormones are important for metabolism and intricately involved in growth, both physical and mental. Adult men and women are advised to take in 55 mcg a day. A serving of vegetable brown rice medley has 29.3 mcg, and warm bean salad provides 32.7 mcg.

9. Phytonutrients and Other Food Factors:

Phytonutrients: Genistein, Daidzein, Lutein & Zeaxanthin; Lycopene

Genistein and Daidzein are known as isoflavones, a group of molecules that can act as either weak estrogen molecules or mild anti-estrogen factors. Soybeans and their products - tofu, miso, tempeh and others - are rich sources of these compounds, whereas very little is present in other foods. These chemicals have been shown to block the development of cancer cells as well as of blood vessel growth. They may reduce the incidence of some types of cancers, as well as hot flashes in menopausal women. Research is also currently clarifying what possible protector role, if any, isoflavones have on the bones. Lutein & zeaxanthin represent two important plant carotenoids (a family of pigments) in the center of the eye (macula). Foods high in these compounds include green leafy vegetables. One serving (1 cup) of Kale with Sunflower Seeds provides 23,720 mg.

Lycopene, a plant pigment particularly high in tomatoes, is made more available by cooking and it also is increased in the presence of some fat. Recipes including Black Bean Soup, Bean Stew, Vegetarian Bolognese Sauce, Spiral Pasta Salad and Quinoa Stuffed Peppers provide high levels (ranging widely from 539 mg to 21,572 mg!). Although there is no specific, recommended amount, the evidence points to a beneficial effect by consuming this compound, particularly for the prevention of prostate cancer in men.

<u>Other Food Factors:</u> *Phytic Acid and Oxalic Acid*

Phytic acid (also called phytate) is the way plants – especially whole cereal grains and beans - store their supply of phosphorus, typically in the outer layers. Other vegetables contain phytate, but in smaller amounts. The phytate molecule's structure enables it to bind minerals tightly like iron and zinc, making it hard for the body to absorb these minerals. With fermentation, the naturally occurring enzyme – called "phytase" – breaks down the phytate molecule into smaller, related molecules that have a much harder time binding minerals. The result is that the minerals become easier to absorb, reflecting so-called "higher bioavailability" (WHO, 1996). Sprouted grains and beans already have lower phytates because in the process of sprout growth, the phytase [phytate-breaking] enzyme is activated. As phytate is broken down, the stored phosphorus is released and can then be consumed by the growing sprout. Yeast microbes also produce phytase; thus minerals can be better absorbed in yeasted, as well as sprouted, whole grain breads.

In addition, by soaking beans and whole grains, the water-soluble phytic acid can dissolve into the soaking water, which can then be discarded, taking much of the acid with it (Gibson et al., 1998). Presoaking itself helps to activate the dormant phytase enzyme so it can actually begin to break down the phytate (Gibson et al., 1998).

The phytic acid values listed in the nutrient tables for each recipe reflect the amount originally in the product. Food preparation methods can go a long way towards enhancing the nutrients available for the body, particularly important for individuals on a plant-based diet.

Oxalic acid has a similar binding impact on minerals such as calcium and iron. This compound is most prevalent in spinach, rhubarb and Swiss chard. For this reason, spinach is not considered an excellent source of calcium or iron, although this important vegetable has other nutritional strengths such as a high amount of folate, fiber and beta-carotene.

10. Seasonality and Food Energy

Would you send a quiet person out to become a high-powered courtroom attorney? Would you expect a sensitive, quiet musician to be excited about race car driving? Do you crave flavored water-ice on a snowy winter's day? Does thick, hot stew sound good in the midst of a summer heat-wave? For the same reasons we intuitively know the answers to these questions, we can think about the energetic appropriateness of food as another very important consideration.

According to macrobiotic philosophy and traditional Chinese medicine, the key for health and well being is maintaining a sense of balance. We know that mental activity needs to be supplemented with physical activity; one-sidedness or extremes in diet and behavior often cause distress and can result in a radical redirection of behavior. The Golden Mean was a goal in Greek culture, and The Middle Path was advocated by The Buddha. Moderation in all things has become common sense.

Michio Kushi once remarked that "because of our freedom, we are not free." In other words, discipline truly leads to freedom. And having the incredible ability to eat anything, we humans have huge, food-related, decision-making responsibilities. This, according to Michael Pollan in the title of his bestselling book, is *The Omnivore's Dilemma* (2006).

In order to achieve a harmonious balance of food within our environment, eating locally and seasonally is a good place to start. Generally speaking, items that thrive in one's locale present an opportunity to support a wide variety of positive life experiences in that locale. Foods that are in season – typically also implying locally available – are well suited for consumption at that same time of year. Eating out of season – such as ice cream in the middle of winter – can contribute to an internal environment that may feel cold (no pun intended) or "out of balance."

Plants grow in certain ways depending upon their natures. Even within the vegetable kingdom, there are so many varieties: consider a comparison of the carrot versus lettuce. One way to describe these differences is to use the Chinese terms "yin" and "yang," which is a central principle within the macrobiotic approach. The foods which are more broad, juicy and light can be considered more "yin;" others which are drier, heavier and more condensed tend to have more "yang" energy. The more central, so-called balanced, foods are whole grains, beans, vegetables, nuts and seeds and local fruits, prepared with only small amounts of oil and seasoning. Meats and salt are much more "yang," and sugar, alcohol and tropical fruits are much more "yin." Taking in too much of these foods creates a desire for opposite ends of the energy spectrum, making balance somewhat more difficult. For example, eating more meat would create a desire for increased amounts of alcohol or sugary desserts in order to "balance the energies" of each.

Cooking methods can also be similarly categorized, and we often instinctively apply these techniques. We use lighter cooking styles in the summer, while naturally making heartier stews in the cold of winter. Fresh salads round out a heavier meal, while a meal of only raw food might create a desire for something more warm and savory.

Deep-frying in hot oil is a more "yang" method of cooking, as is dry-roasting for a long period of time. Quick par-boiling and stir-frying are more "yin" (i.e., light & watery) cooking styles. In general, longer cooking, with pressure, less water and more salt tends to create a more yang energy in food, while shorter, lower-heat, more water and less salt provide a more yin energy to the resulting dish.

Within the recipes of this book, adjustments can be made for seasonal change and individual considerations. There are many excellent books on this topic (see References), and I would encourage everyone to incorporate principles of food energetics in their cooking.

11. Illuminating the Ingredients

Unique Ingredients
Some ingredients in this book might be unfamiliar, so below are brief descriptions. Most of these ingredients can be found at natural- or whole-food groceries; Asian markets often carry burdock, daikon and lotus root. Many of these ingredients can also be purchased online (www.Edenfoods.com; www.Kushistore.com).

Barley Malt and Brown Rice Syrups are made using sprouted grains (typically barley) that produce the enzymes to naturally break down the grain starch into sweeter, simpler sugars. During processing, the liquid is strained and concentrated into thick, sweet syrup. Barley malt has a stronger flavor, a bit similar to light molasses; brown rice syrup is sweeter, and lighter in both color and taste. Together these syrups make a nice combination and natural alternative to granulated white sugar.

Burdock is a wild plant with a long, sturdy root which has a deep, unmistakably robust flavor. It is available in natural food groceries and many Asian markets. It makes a unique taste contribution to lighter vegetable dishes and hearty stews.

Daikon is a long white radish that comes in a variety of widths and lengths. Pungent and juicy, this traditional Asian radish can be used in salads, soups and root-vegetable stews. When grated and served raw with a dash of soy sauce, daikon is a pleasant accompaniment to a heavy meal or deep-fried foods. Daikon greens are the slightly-bitter greens growing from the root. Sliced thinly, they highlight other vegetable dishes and soups. Choose organic whenever possible. If daikon greens are unavailable, you can substitute kale, turnip or mustard greens.

Guar and xanthan gums are used in the food industry as binders and thickening agents. Guar gum is a bean-derived soluble fiber extract; xanthan gum is produced by bacterial fermentation of sugars which are then purified in a processing plant (McGee, 2004). For gluten-free flour recipes, either can be used to help the dough retain its shape and hold the gas bubbles formed from leavening agents.

Kuzu (Kudzu) is a starch that comes from the sturdy kuzu root (known as „kudzu' in the deep south) and which acts as a smooth thickening agent for puddings, sauces and soups. It is usually sold in small, solid white chunks. After diluting in cold water, it can be heated until it turns translucent.

Lotus Root grows as a horizontal stem beneath a water lily native to Asia (McGee, 2004). It has large spaces inside, which give it a characteristic pattern when sliced. Lotus has a delightfully crunchy texture and a mild flavor. It is wonderful on its own (thinly sliced) or, in larger pieces, as a component in a root vegetable dish.

Mirin is a sweet, Japanese, rice cooking wine used as a flavor enhancer in a variety of recipes, from hearty stews to dressings. Look for traditionally prepared mirin made without sugar.

Sea Vegetables – such as arame, kombu, nori, and wakame – are loaded with minerals. Purchased dry, they can be reconstituted with a quick soak. Wakame is very versatile, fitting in with many soups, stews, cooked vegetable dishes, and, after briefly boiling, atop raw salads. Kombu works well in soups, stews and with other vegetables or even by itself (sliced thinly, with a little seasoning and chopped herbs/garlic). Arame is best with small amounts of one or two companion vegetables (onions, carrots, and/or lotus root). Sheets of nori make excellent wrappers for rice in sushi; smaller strips of nori add flavor to a clear-broth soup.

Soybean-based Condiments have a long and rich history, dating back to ancient China (McGee, 2004). _Miso_ is a fermented soybean paste which adds richness and taste to soups, sauces and dips. Because of the salt content, a little goes a long way. Traditionally made miso starts with cooked soybeans, grains or beans cultured with the microbe _Aspergillus_ (a type of mold),[7] and salt. This mixture is fermented for an extended period of time (from months to years), resulting in amazing, unique flavor development. Enzyme activity from the fermentation process breaks down the soybeans and grains, into digestible compounds that are easily absorbed.

There are many varieties of miso, depending upon the type of grain or bean used. Newer varieties of miso include chickpea miso, millet miso, and others. Barley miso is a dark brown, rich-tasting miso; brown rice miso is slightly milder (and gluten-free). Lighter miso (such as white miso), is sweeter due to higher carbohydrate content and less salty because of a much shorter fermentation periods (Bellame and Bellame, 2007). This is a good choice for introducing to family and friends. Miso, particularly heartier versions such as barley and brown rice, provides a "meaty" flavor to soups, making it a cholesterol-free, vegetarian alternative to beef or chicken broth.

---

[7] This inoculation produces fermented grains or beans, known as "_koji._"

Soy Sauce and Tamari
Traditionally made soy sauce has a richness of flavor and texture, made from fermented soybeans, salt water and varying proportions of cracked wheat. Tamari is soy sauce typically made without wheat. Both add a savory, deep and flavorful quality to many dishes. Both are rich in sodium but low-sodium versions of traditionally made soy sauce are now available. Avoid inexpensive, industrially made soy sauce, which is not fermented, but made using chemicals (hydrochloric acid and sodium carbonate) (McGee, 2004).

"The great appeal of miso and soy sauce, long-fermented soy products, is their strong, distinctive and delicious flavor. It develops when microbes break down the bean proteins and other components and transform them into savory substances that then react with each other to general additional layers of flavor." (McGee, 2004)[8]

Sweet brown rice is a variety of brown rice that is very high in the branched form of starch, which gives the grains a sticky quality when cooked. It is also known as glutinous rice, although it is actually gluten-free! The distinct texture and stickiness enables it to be used for blends of rice with chestnuts or beans and for special treats, such as pounded sweet rice, or "mochi."

Tempeh is a fermented, whole-soybean product developed in Indonesia. High in protein and made with or without added grains, it is sold in rectangular cakes. The fermentation process makes the soybeans more digestible and their minerals more readily absorbed. Tempeh can be sliced in a variety of ways and boiled, pressure-cooked, sautéed or deep-fried; it has a chewy consistency and makes a great meat-replacer.

Umeboshi plums are dried, pickled Japanese plums that come either whole or puréed as a paste. It goes well in salad dressings or spreads (as well as some cooked vegetable dishes), as it has a "bite" – a somewhat sour/pungent/salt flavor that is difficult to find anywhere else. The liquid remaining after the plums have been pickled is umeboshi vinegar, a tart and tangy, somewhat salty seasoning. It can be used in sauces and dressings, replacing vinegar as well as the salt in the recipe (Bellame and Bellame, 2007).

Shopping List
Most of us probably have ingredients that are purchased regularly, so why not develop a cool shopping list, word processed for easy updating? I keep a blank one in the kitchen drawer, to check off items as needed. For an example, please see Appendix B. Every little bit of timesaving helps!

Preparing Basic Brown Rice
Pressure cooked
Use 2 cups short-grain brown rice to 3 c. water, soak overnight. Drain remaining water into a measuring cup; note the amount and add back the same amount of fresh water. Just prior to cooking, add a pinch of salt. Pressure cook for 50 minutes. This yields ~6 cups of cooked rice.

Boiled
Wash and drain 1 cup short-grain brown rice, add 2¼ cups water and soak overnight (or for 5 hours). Drain the remaining water into a measuring cup, noting the amount; add back an equal amount of fresh

---

[8] For an extensive discussion of the production of miso, soy sauce and tamari, see the following: On Food and Cooking: The Science and Lore of the Kitchen (McGee, 2004), pages 493-501; Japanese Foods that Heal (Bellame and Bellame, 2007), chapter 1, 3, and 4; How to Cook with Miso (Kushi, 1978), chapter 8.

water. Add a pinch of salt and bring to a boil in a medium saucepan. Cover and simmer on low heat for 1 hour. This makes ~3¼ cups of cooked rice.

Keeping fresh herbs fresh

Fresh herbs – as well as their dried counterparts – can add a delightful sparkle of nature to many dishes; it is useful to have them on hand whenever you need them. Parsley (curly or flat), cilantro, basil, oregano, Rosemary and thyme are excellent staples. Buy them at the height of freshness, remove any brown edges, and store in a way that maximizes their "lifespan," in one of the following ways:

a. Fill a glass two-thirds with water and place the bunch of fresh herbs into it. Cover the exposed leaves with plastic wrap and set the glass in your refrigerator. Change the water every day, or as often as possible.

b. Wash herbs in a basin of water, towel dry (or spin-dry in a salad-spinner), divide them into manageable portions and store individual portions in zippered, plastic bags. Inserting a paper towel into each will help reduce any excess moisture. [Another trick is to insert a plastic straw into this bag of herbs, close the bag as far as possible around the straw, and suck as much air out of the bag as you can. The bag will start to shrink in size and the rate of oxidation-spoilage will be greatly reduced.] Keep herbs in the crisper drawer of your refrigerator whenever possible.

c. Purchase one of the new herb-saving kitchen devices on the market that keep herbs fresher for longer periods.

Preparing Beans

After all, the main difference between the food plan of someone who is "vegetarian" and the non-vegetarian is typically in the choices of their protein dishes.

The following is a general approach to "rough-and-ready" beans for use at any meal. I make them on weekends and then have several lunches for the week.

Basic ingredients
1 cup of beans
Veggies
Pasta or barley, or other grains
Herbs
Some type of salt

Wash (pick out any stones) and soak in 4 cups of water overnight. If you are in a hurry, you can pressure cook for 5 minutes, then let sit for one hour and proceed to pressure cook regularly. Drain the beans, add water to cover with a 1-inch layer of water (or follow a specific recipe). Pressure cook for 1 hour after pressure reaches maximum (or put in a crock pot, set on high for 3 hours, using the ratio of 1 cup of beans to 3 cups of water).

Using canned beans: Rinse beans in a bowl & strain. [If time permits, add ¼ - ½ cup of water for each can and cook canned beans for 15-20 minutes to soften a little more.] Add to your favorite dishes. If you are going to make a casserole or chili, aim for salt-free beans so you can add your own seasonings.

In general, most beans require about 1 hour of pressure cooking. Before pressure cooking split peas, it is best to cook them uncovered for a few minutes, skimming off any foam that appears; otherwise this foam could clog the pressure cooker.

Separately cooking the veggies (usually carrots, onions, celery, sometimes shiitake mushrooms-which have been pre-soaked) saves time and retains some of the colors. Adding dried pasta near the end will help maximize its flavor; dried herbs can also be added at this time. Fresh herbs are best added at the end, to maintain their taste.

For a fresh bean salad, simply cool the cooked beans, add your favorite combination of raw, chopped, fresh vegetables and toss with a tasty dressing. Marinate ahead of time for deeper flavor development.

Beans and salt
According to Aveline Kushi, the following are preferred types of salt for use with different beans:
Azuki beans – sea salt
Black beans – salt, miso or soy sauce are all o.k.
Black soybeans – sea salt
Chickpeas - sea salt and tamari; umeboshi (pickled) plum is o.k. in the summer
Kidney beans- miso (soy sauce for soups)
Lentils – soy sauce or miso
Soybeans – miso is best
Split peas – usually soy sauce
Pinto beans -miso (soy sauce for soups)
When do you add salt to beans? Always add salt at the end of cooking. All beans should be soaked, with the exception of azuki beans, lentils, and split peas.

I really do love the way miso adds a richness and creaminess to split peas, kidney beans and lentils. Because beans provide a major amount of protein within a plant-based diet, having wonderfully delicious, digestible ways to prepare and enjoy them becomes paramount.

12. Kitchen tools

If cooking is like art, then a clean and well-organized kitchen is a broad, clear canvas full of potential. Well-chosen equipment – the high-quality paints & brushes of an artist – ensures a lovely finished product. Below is a brief summary of important cooking tools; a more complete discussion can be found in comprehensive cookbooks, such as The Joy of Cooking (Rombauer et al., 2006).

Knives
Since vegetables are often the base of the meal, there will be plenty of cutting to go around! The importance of well-maintained, sharp knives cannot be overstated. Not only the original quality but also the care and keeping of these "tools of the trade" at their highest potential will serve you well. Sharp knives enable more variety in slicing & dicing; they are also less likely to pose a problem with slippage. Finally (and, maybe most importantly), the amount of energy to slide a sharp knife through vegetables is so much less than for dull knives, that it makes cooking more fun, and less of a drain! To sharpen dull knives, use a standard sharpening stone on a regular basis. Professional knife sharpening is also available at many hardware stores.

Cutting Boards
Wooden cutting boards provide a natural surface - softer and quieter than plastic. If animal foods are prepared, it is a good idea to dedicate a separate cutting board for these, in order to avoid cross-contamination. Then after each use, wash the board in hot, soapy water and rinse thoroughly. On a regular basis, clean boards with a solution of bleach and water (1-2 tsp. bleach to ~4 cups of water), rinse very well, then rub with lemon juice to refresh.

Pots and Pans
Stainless steel, cast iron, ceramic and glass are wonderful, natural products to use for preparing food. Glass covers provide the added benefit of preventing heat loss when checking the cooking progress. To reduce the amount of oil used, and for ease of clean-up, non-stick cookware is another option, though less natural. Discard any nonstick cookware that has become scratched; layering a towel in between pans during storage can minimize surface damage.

An excellent addition to any kitchen is a stainless steel steamer with two layers for placing food items. This is an excellent investment, as the base can serve as a soup pot when the steamer is not in use and the two layers makes it easy to cook items requiring different cooking times. Bamboo also works well, but keep enough water in the bottom or it can burn easily.

Pressure Cooker
One of the mainstays in my kitchen is the pressure cooker. The weighted cover causes water to boil at a higher temperature, thereby enabling the ingredients inside to cook faster. When preparing beans or whole grains, this can save a significant amount of time, as well as result in a more digestible and creamy product. As an added benefit, food cooks without any need to stand by in vigilance; you can set your timer and go on to other things. Select stainless steel, and invest in a good quality pressure cooker. It will last for many years and the energy-savings alone will pay for this tool in no time!

Slow-cooker
This electronic tool enables you to let food simmer all day while at work or overnight. It is a practical tool that is especially helpful for foods requiring a long cooking period, such as whole oats and baked beans. Avoid lifting the lid throughout, as this can cause substantial heat losses that will increase the required cooking time.

Flame protector
This simple device is a double "plate" of metal with a handle that can be placed over a burner and beneath your pot or pressure cooker. It prevents the food in the bottom of the pan from burning, particularly with extended cooking times and recipes that have less water in them. Flame protectors ("flame-tamers") can be used with both gas and electric stoves.

Suribachi (and pestle)
The Japanese suribachi is similar in use to a mortar-and-pestle, but it has grooves throughout the bowl to facilitate grinding with a wooden pestle. This is particularly useful for diluting miso, for crushing seeds and nuts and for making creamy dressings. The suribachi and pestle can be purchased at natural food grocers and Asian markets.

Sushi mat
Sushi mats consist of small, square rows of thin bamboo tied with string, arranged loosely together to roll easily. This helps form appropriately-shaped rice rolls, traditionally covered in nori seaweed, to

make sushi. Once made, the rolled sushi can be kept inside the mat, held together with a rubber band until it ready to be sliced, helping to maintain the shape.

13. Cooking Veggies – Infinite Variety

Cooking as an Art
"Cooking is the finest and most important art, more challenging than music, painting, poetry and the like"-Michio Kushi (*Macrobiotic Home Remedies*. Tokyo: Japan Publications, 1993, p 45).

<u>The Cooking of Vegetables as Seen by Michio and Aveline Kushi</u>
Michio and Aveline Kushi have been pioneers in the Natural Foods movement in North America and throughout the world. Prolific authors and renowned educators of the macrobiotic approach,[9] they have promoted organic farming, whole foods cooking, health lifestyle practices and an understanding of complementary/alternative medical practices.

Thoughts on cooking from Michio Kushi
In class, Michio often addressed questions of food preparation. In an interesting dialogue about vegetables, the students asked Michio "How can Americans get all their requirements within a macrobiotic diet if they cannot consume as much miso, tamari, salt, etc., as an average Japanese person?" He responded: "with vegetables….really Americans must learn how to cook vegetables very well, creatively, etc.; like the French, Americans must develop a cuisine with many different ways to prepare and enjoy vegetables."

The importance of vegetables cannot be overemphasized. To replace canned, frozen vegetables, bottled salad dressings, and freeze-dried soups, delicious, fresh vegetable cooking is truly the answer.

Vegetable cooking with Aveline
Aveline Kushi, in one of her very illuminating cooking classes, focused upon cooking vegetables:

To begin with, there are three important things to remember:
1. Always wash vegetables well. For root vegetables, scrub with a brush firmly but not too vigorously as in the case of burdock where much goodness remains in the rough dark covering. For leafy vegetables, fill the sink, remove any ties holding the stems together and cut the bottom of the stems so the leaves will separate for easy cleaning. Allow sand and other things to settle to the bottom (but do not soak). Rinse briefly, drain in a colander or large strainer. In this way, many invisible tiny particles, etc. will be rinsed away.

---

[9] The macrobiotic approach is a highly individualized dietary design, according to one's current health condition, activity, seasonality and availability, as well as family tradition for the benefit of mind, body and spirit. In that sense, no food is really proscribed; the selection and preparation of foods varies with the changing seasons, preferences and circumstances of each individual, i.e., that "everything changes." The standard macrobiotic diet includes whole cereal grains, vegetables, beans and seaweed, soup, small amounts of white meat fish (optional), fruit, seeds and nuts, with minimal (if any) intake of other animal protein, dairy products, eggs, refined sugar or sugar-sweetened desserts. Organic foods are encouraged whenever possible. Along with dietary guidelines, macrobiotics encompasses philosophical and spiritual dimensions for optimum health. This includes a sense of gratitude, giving (plant one grain and 10,000 will grow; good work spirals out in ever-widening circles), and minimizing waste. It is a practical approach to everyday life, decision-making and ultimately an orderly, harmonious life. Please see *Reference* section for recommended books on this subject.

2. Do not throw anything away. We live on vegetables and every part is vital for our growth. The top part of a carrot is the connection between the root below the ground and the green leaves rising up to heaven. If we carelessly chop a large chunk to remove the brown part, we are throwing away the richest combination meeting place of heaven and earth, with corresponding effects on our health and mentality as well as spirituality.
3. Treat the vegetables with love, for they are living too. They are our brothers and sisters, with life, potential and feelings. They are graciously giving up their lives for us and we should approach them with utmost gratitude and tenderness.

There is a wide variety of methods for cooking vegetables:
1. Fresh vegetables – without heat
     a.   Salad: raw
     b.   Pickled vegetables
             i.   Long-time pickling, e.g., with rice bran
             ii.   Pressed salad
             iii.   Brine pickles

2. Boiling – cooking with filtered or spring water. With boiled vegetables, save the water. It is full of goodness; use for soup, soft rice, etc.
     a. Quick, one-minute immersion and then vegetables removed
     b. Long-time boiling:
             i.   Juicy vegetables – like daikon – cooked in a pot
             ii.   Pressure cooking – boiling with pressure

3. Steaming

4. Quick sauté - Chinese-style-vegetable cooking wherein vegetables are left crispy, with an optional thickened sauce

5. Sauté- sometimes adding water, but at the end all the juice goes in to the vegetables – it is the opposite of soup; cut vegetables finely

6. Root vegetables cut in big chunks; start with water to almost cover, then cook until all water boils away (oil is not needed)

7. Soup or stew for vegetables – cook from cold water to make nice soft vegetables allowing all juice to go into broth

8. Baking: Baked squash, beans, whole carrots, etc. This involves longer cooking times. In a casserole, some items can be precooked, then put together into the oven for maybe a short time.

9. Broiling

10. Tempura style – deep fried.

Cutting vegetables in different styles makes cooking so exciting! For example, big chunk-style carrots take a long time, with slow flame; thin long strips are just the opposite.

The Layering Method – according to Yin and Yang, by Aveline Kushi (thanks to Mr. Ogawa of Japan)

Aveline said she imagined "the cook as a conductor of an orchestra. The cook must be thoroughly aware of each food and ingredient, but must never lose sight of the whole. And, as a conductor, the cook does not play any one instrument (i.e., does not interfere), but simply guides and directs the individual parts to a comprehensive and orderly whole. The layering method is a most peaceful way to cook, the best way to avoid carelessness. We must listen to the sounds very well and pay attention to the smell, especially since you do not stir. Layering uses nature's forces. The food „cooks itself.' Order to cooking brings order to life."

Secrets of layering method
    A. Make very nice, flat layers;
    B. Do not add water into the center, but very gently from the sides and just enough water to <u>almost</u> cover.
        1. Layer vegetables according to yin and yang, <u>most yin on the bottom</u>.[10] More yin vegetables will have a tendency to go up and the more yang ones to come down, so naturally mixing occurs.
        2. Check water occasionally to see that it is sufficient to prevent burning, adding more water as needed.
        3. Even salt - or miso - does not need to be stirred in, since their natural very strong tendencies are to go down.
        4. The layering principle works in a pressure cooker, but if making rice and beans, it is better to mix the ingredients so that - in case the bottom burns slightly, you will not have lost all the beans.
        5. "After a while, the layering method becomes second nature, and you don't even have to think which is more yin or yang. It is so wonderful."

Other vegetable practices I've found helpful:

1) Keep stems and leaves separate - stems take longer to cook; chop stems rather small, or else they will take a long time to sauté (this doesn't apply to pressure cooking or even boiling as much as stir frying);
2) Start with stems, cook until almost tender, and then add leaves (chopped);
2) For cooking greens, use garlic and a generous amount of (olive) oil;
3) A pinch of salt and a dash of soy sauce complement this dish nicely;
4) Never overcook vegetables or you will lose the green color and no one will eat them.

Variations on a sauté:

1) Use a pressure cooker - just 2 minutes and it's done (or even less!);
2) Add sesame seeds;
3) Steam (or parboil) briefly, then sauté – it's quick and the vegetables stay very bright;
4) Use kale or other dark, leafy greens, in soups, such as bean soups - add just before serving and simmer until tender (a few minutes at the most);
5) Add a little protein (tofu, tempeh, seitan [wheat gluten]), as this can be very enjoyable. Cooking with mushrooms is another great idea;
6) Finally, you can simply boil them and then smother them in a dressing, such as a tofu dressing.

---

[10] See Ch 10, Seasonality and Food Energy, for these distinctions.

14. General Principles of Recipe Modification

Besides the well known ways of reducing trans fat and cholesterol (oil for shortening, egg whites for whole eggs, etc.) the following suggestions can help to change up your recipes very simply, preserving the flavor and memories you have come to enjoy.

<u>Grains and Flours – from white to whole</u>
A great way to introduce whole grains (or cracked grains) into a meal is with lots of vegetables so the familiar is combined with the new. Select grain salads, pasta salads, grain soups and stews, and whole grain desserts.

For whole wheat pastry flour, you can generally use the same amount as white flour. If you are using whole wheat flour instead, you may need a bit less (about 2 tablespoons less for each cup of white flour); otherwise your recipe will tend to be too dry. Alternatively, if you would like to keep the same amount of flour, add a bit more liquid to your recipe, about 2-4 Tbsp liquid per 1 cup of whole wheat flour when substituting a cup of white flour (Stepaniak & Melina, 2002). Experiment with some of the newer flours available, such as spelt, for a tender texture from a whole grain. Sometimes a 50/50 blend makes an interesting transition dish.

<u>How to adapt recipes to be gluten free</u>
Someone who eats a gluten-free diet avoids wheat, barley, rye and often oats. Gluten-free grains include rice, corn, buckwheat, millet, quinoa, amaranth, teff and their products. If soy sauce is an ingredient, be sure to use "wheat free" soy sauce or Tamari. Choose soymilk without malted barley or wheat extract.

For recipes that call for wheat flour or pastry flour, substitute the following rice flour mix, thoughtfully created by Kathleen Dunn, Ed.D. Try making up 6 cups or more of this mix and storing it in the refrigerator so that you have this mix ready whenever you need it. Use the same amount of this mix as called for by the recipe. Measure the flours by spooning in the ingredient into a measuring cup and smoothing the top with a straight edge. Then follow the guidelines for adding xanthan or guar gum.

    A. Rice Flour Mix

Gluten-Free Rice Flour Mix			
Ingredient	Proportions		
Brown rice flour (finely ground)	*2 parts*	2 cups	6 cups
Potato starch (not potato flour)	*2/3 part*	2/3 cup	2 cups
Tapioca flour or tapioca starch	*1/3 part*	1/3 cup	1 cup

    B. Xanthan and Guar Gum

    Xanthan gum and guar gum help dough to be elastic, retain moisture, and feel similar to a product using wheat flour. Teri Lee Gruss, M.S., gives us the following recommended amounts (About.com Guide to Gluten-Free Cooking).

General Tips for Using Xanthan Gum and Guar Gum in Gluten-Free Cooking

- Bread and pizza dough recipes: Add 1 teaspoon xanthan gum or guar gum per cup of gluten-free flour used in bread and pizza dough recipes

- Cake, muffin and quick bread recipes: Add ½ teaspoon xanthan gum or guar gum per one cup of gluten-free flour used

- Cookie and bar recipes: Add ½ teaspoon (or less) xanthan gum or guar gum per one cup gluten-free flour used.

Eggs: from egg to none, especially for vegan practice
Stepaniak and Melina (2002) have several excellent suggestions for replacing eggs in recipes, as follows. In place of one egg, use any of these substitutes:

- 1 Tbsp ground flaxseeds mixed with 3 T water (this will thicken up as it sits for 10 minutes; stir well before using);
- 2-4 Tbsp soft tofu;
- ¼ cup mashed, very ripe banana;
- 1 tsp. powdered (starch-based) egg substitute (depending upon the package directions).

In baked products, adding a little more baking powder (1/8 tsp. baking powder per egg) can provide a lighter product when an egg is removed.

Making a recipe more "meatless"
As you transition to using more plant sources of protein, it is often interesting simply to reduce the amount of meat or poultry and insert small amounts of beans or tofu into the same dish. Then gradually withdraw those ingredients which you would like to replace (meat, extra fat, etc.).

Tempeh makes a good meat substitute. Textured vegetable protein (TVP) protein can also be used; it can easily be reconstituted by mixing 1 part TVP with an equal amount of boiling water and letting it stand for about 10 to 15 minutes. Another interesting substitution is soy "crumbles," available in the frozen food sections of many grocery stores. Sauté chopped tempeh or soy crumbles first in onions and garlic, for a surprisingly-crowd-pleasing substitute for seasoned, chopped/ground meat!

Tofu picks up the flavors of all the other ingredients; to add color, you can add turmeric. This book has some delightful and easy recipes for scrambled tofu, as well as tofu dressing, using tofu, tahini and umeboshi – plus scallions – dressing to replace cream cheese. Placing fresh tofu into the freezer will generate an entirely new texture in your product; defrost, squeeze out the water, chop into bite-sized pieces and add to any sauce or stew. The spongy tofu will easily soak up the delicious flavors of your dish and provide a unique texture.

Vegetarian Soup Stocks: For soup stocks, you can take advantage of store-bought vegetable stock (opt for low sodium when possible) or make your own from flavorful vegetable remnants on hand. Dried vegetable stock can also be found in powdered or bouillon cube form, especially at gourmet shops or natural food stores. Miso dissolved in hot liquid can lend a flavorful, savory quality to broths and vegetable dishes.

<u>Changing the Quantity and/or Quality of the Fat:</u> Fat substitutions can be made in either the amount or type used. One-third to one-half of the fat in a baking recipe can easily be substituted with fruit purees, such as prunes and apricots, as well as applesauce. In a successful recipe makeover, 50% of the recipe's shortening was substituted with pureed cannellini beans, and consumers rated the new version highly (Szafranski et al., 2005). Sauté with olive oil instead of butter or margarine; try ground and pressed granola in place of flaky pie crusts (see Blueberry Tofu Cheesecake recipe). Use nuts and nut butters in place of cheese and solid fats, thereby increasing the fiber and phytochemicals in your favorite dishes.

<u>Dairy-free Recipes:</u> Cow's milk or cream can be replaced with soy, grain or almond milk; a wider variety of fortified types is now available. Starch thickeners (organic cornstarch, arrowroot, or kuzu), vegetable purees such as winter squash, and pureed beans can all create a thick, satisfying texture. Mashed tofu with a little added lemon juice and salt can be used in place of ricotta or cottage cheese (Stepaniak & Melina, 2002). Blended, sweetened tofu can be used for nice desserts and toppings (see Blueberry Tarts and Tofu Topping recipes in this book). In addition, there are many rice- and soy-based frozen desserts that can be used in place of regular ice cream, and as a base for smoothies.

<u>Sweeteners:</u> For adding sweetness to a product, my first choice is typically dried fruit, such as raisins. Chopped fresh fruit, such as apples, can be used as well. Ripe bananas are very versatile for adding flavor, especially to smoothies. For replacing refined white or brown sugar, a substitution of barley malt, brown rice syrup and/or maple syrup can be used (reduce the liquid in your recipe somewhat to account for the added liquid from the syrup). A combination of barley malt with brown rice syrup can reduce the strong flavor of the malt. A little maple syrup goes a long way, while barley malt and brown rice syrup tend to be less sweet. Start with a one-for-one portion substitution [1 cup syrup(s) for one cup of sugar], but be ready to use more to attain a sweeter product. Approximately ¼ cup of liquid in a recipe should be eliminated for each cup of syrup used (Stepaniak & Melina, 2002).

<u>Salt:</u> Replace some of the salt and other salty condiments in your recipes with fresh or dried herbs, and other aromatic vegetables. Ginger, garlic, onions, basil, cilantro and parsley add so much wonderful flavor that the salt will hardly be missed! Experiment with reduced-sodium salt and reduced- or sodium-free baking powder. Overall, one of the biggest benefits of whole-food, home cooking is the ability to measure and control the amount of salt in your daily meals.

*****

The next section includes recipes and nutritional profiles, which I hope will add interest and delight to your healthy cooking. Notations are added to indicate whenever all of the ingredients are vegan (Vegan) and/or gluten-free (GF). If simple modifications can be used to make a recipe gluten-free, the following symbol will be shown (GF w/Mod) and the changes will be listed.

Symbols used for Recipes		
Vegan	Gluten-free	Gluten-free with modifications
(Vegan)	(GF)	(GF w/Mod)

GRAINS AND GRAIN PRODUCTS
~ WHOLE, CRACKED AND GROUND ~

Banana Nut Bread (Vegan)

Make ahead, change the shape, vary the nuts, but you can always rely on this delightful, anytime-bread. The answer to bananas past-the-due-date!

Ingredients

2 cups whole wheat pastry flour

1 tsp baking soda

1 tsp low-sodium baking powder

Pinch salt

2 very ripe bananas (1¼ cups mashed)

½ cup unsweetened applesauce

½ cup maple syrup

2 Tbsp safflower oil

1 tsp vanilla

1 cup coarsely chopped walnuts

Line an 8 x 8 inch glass baking pan with parchment paper on the bottom. Brush the sides well with safflower oil. Preheat oven to 350°F.

In a medium mixing bowl, combine flour, baking soda, baking powder and salt; set aside. In a food processor, combine the mashed bananas, applesauce, maple syrup, oil and vanilla. Blend until smooth. Transfer this mixture to a large mixing bowl, and add the flour mixture slowly, in two batches - do not over mix - and as soon as flour is mixed in, add walnuts. Batter should be thick but still somewhat pour-able. Spoon into the glass baking pan and bake for 25-35 minutes, until a cake tester (or toothpick) comes out clean. The top will be deep, golden brown.

Let cool before cutting into squares. Serve with your favorite spread.

Yield: 9 squares

Inspired by Marilyn Moser-Waxman, *The Nourishing Well*, Havertown, PA, thenourishingwell.com

Banana Nut Bread: 1 serving = 1 square

All nutrients listed are per serving

Energy (kcal) per serving	325		
Total Fat (g)	12.4	Calcium (mg)	64
Total Carbohydrate (g)	50.7	Phosphorus (mg)	228
Total Protein (g)	7.8	Magnesium (mg)	86
% Calories from Fat	32	Iron (mg)	2.3
% Calories from Carbohydrate	59	Zinc (mg)	2.4
% Calories from Protein	9	Copper (mg)	0.4
Cholesterol (g)	0	Selenium (mcg)	29.3
Total Saturated Fatty Acids (g) (SFA)	1.2	Sodium (mg)	161
Total Monounsaturated Fatty Acids (g) (MUFA)	1.7	Potassium (mg)	417
Total Polyunsaturated Fatty Acids (g) (PUFA)	8.7		
Omega-3 Fatty Acids (g)	1.2		
% Calories from SFA	3.0	Linoleic Acid - PUFA (18:2) (g)	7.5
% Calories from MUFA	4.5	Linolenic Acid – PUFA (18:3) (g)	1.2
% Calories from PUFA	22.8		
Polyunsaturated to Saturated Fat (P:S) Ratio	7.6	Tryptophan (mg)	11
		Threonine (mg)	22
Total Dietary Fiber (g)	6.6	Isoleucine (mg)	29
Soluble Dietary Fiber (g)	1.2	Leucine (mg)	54
Insoluble Dietary Fiber (g)	5.4	Lysine (mg)	22
		Methionine (mg)	12
Total Vitamin A (mcg) (Retinol Activity Equivalents)	1	Phenylalanine (mg)	36
Vitamin D (calciferol) (mcg)	0.0	Valine (mg)	36
Vitamin E (mg) (Total Alpha-Tocopherol)	1.5	Histidine (mg)	20
Vitamin K (mg) (phylloquinone)	1.5		
Vitamin C (mg) (ascorbic acid)	2.6	Daidzein (mg)	0.0
Thiamin (mg) (vitamin B1)	0.2	Genistein (mg)	0.0
Riboflavin (mg) (vitamin B2)	0.1		
Niacin (mg) (vitamin B3)	2.9	Caffeine (mg)	0
Pantothenic Acid (mg)	0.6	Phytic Acid (mg)	392.4
Vitamin B6 (mg)	0.3	Oxalic Acid (mg)	38.7
Total Folate (mcg)	36	Choline (mg)	20.7
Vitamin B12 (mcg) (cobalamin)	0.0		
		Glycemic Index (glucose reference)	49
Beta-Carotene (mcg) (provitamin A carotenoid)	12	Glycemic Load (glucose reference)	22
Lutein + Zeaxanthin (mcg)	97		
Lycopene (mcg)	0		

Blueberry Pancakes

Short stack or tall, these blueberry gems are worth waking up for. Light, tasty and nourishing, why go out for breakfast?

Ingredients

¾ cup whole wheat pastry flour

¾ tsp baking powder

¼ tsp salt

1 egg

½ cup vanilla soymilk

5 tsp canola oil, divided

½ cup blueberries (frozen or fresh)

3 tsp blueberry fruit jam (sugar-free)

3 Tbsp maple syrup

In a medium mixing bowl, blend flour, baking powder and salt. In a small bowl, beat egg, add soymilk and 4 tsp of canola oil and whip again until frothy. Add this mix to the bowl of flour and blend well. Heat a medium skillet and brush with about 1 tsp oil. Spoon the batter into the pan with a ¼-cup measuring cup for each pancake. Add a few blueberries on top of each pancake at the start of cooking. When the edges start to brown and bubbles form, flip over and cook until other side is golden brown. Serve with blueberry all-fruit jam and maple syrup.

Yield: 6 pancakes (3 ½-inch diameter)

Blueberry Pancakes: 1 serving = 1 pancake

Energy (kcal)	180		
Total Fat (g)	5.6	Calcium (mg)	80
Total Carbohydrate (g)	29.5	Phosphorus (mg)	123
Total Protein (g)	5.0	Magnesium (mg)	40
% Calories from Fat	27.3	Iron (mg)	1.4
% Calories from Carbohydrate	62.3	Zinc (mg)	1.2
% Calories from Protein	10.4	Copper (mg)	0.1
Cholesterol (g)	35	Selenium (mcg)	19.1
Total Saturated Fatty Acids (g) (SFA)	0.7	Sodium (mg)	184
Total Monounsaturated Fatty Acids (g) (MUFA)	2.9	Potassium (mg)	173
Total Polyunsaturated Fatty Acids (g) (PUFA)	1.6		
Omega-3 Fatty Acids (g)	0.4		
% Calories from SFA	3.4	Linoleic Acid - PUFA (18:2) (g)	1.2
% Calories from MUFA	14.2	Linolenic Acid – PUFA (18:3) (g)	0.4
% Calories from PUFA	7.8		
Polyunsaturated to Saturated Fat (P:S) Ratio	2.3	Tryptophan (mg)	7
		Threonine (mg)	17
Total Dietary Fiber (g)	3.7	Isoleucine (mg)	21
Soluble Dietary Fiber (g)	0.6	Leucine (mg)	36
Insoluble Dietary Fiber (g)	3.1	Lysine (mg)	21
		Methionine (mg)	9
Total Vitamin A (mcg) (Retinol Activity Equivalents)	27	Phenylalanine (mg)	24
Vitamin D (calciferol) (mcg)	0.3	Valine (mg)	25
Vitamin E (mg) (Total Alpha-Tocopherol)	1.3	Histidine (mg)	12
Vitamin K (mg) (phylloquinone)	7.3		
Vitamin C (mg) (ascorbic acid)	0.8	Daidzein (mg)	1.0
Thiamin (mg) (vitamin B1)	0.1	Genistein (mg)	1.0
Riboflavin (mg) (vitamin B2)	0.1		
Niacin (mg) (vitamin B3)	1.7	Caffeine (mg)	0
Pantothenic Acid (mg)	0.4	Phytic Acid (mg)	183.3
Vitamin B6 (mg)	0.1	Oxalic Acid (mg)	18.0
Total Folate (mcg)	18	Choline (mg)	29.2
Vitamin B12 (mcg) (cobalamin)	0.3		
		Glycemic Index (glucose reference)	51
Beta-Carotene (mcg) (provitamin A carotenoid)	9	Glycemic Load (glucose reference)	13
Lutein + Zeaxanthin (mcg)	97		
Lycopene (mcg)	0		

Brown Rice Pilaf (Vegan; GF)

Pilaf showcases the flavorful brown rice and gives it an interesting personality. The vegetables provide a variety of textures that make this a perfect side dish. A good way to introduce brown rice to friends and family.

Ingredients

1 salt-free, vegetable bouillon cube

2 cups boiling water

1 Tbsp sesame oil

1 clove garlic, chopped

1 small onion, chopped (4 oz, 1 cup chopped)

¼ cup chopped celery (1 oz)

4 medium portabella mushrooms (3 oz), sliced thinly

1 cup long-grain brown rice, washed and drained

¼ tsp sea salt

1/8 cup chopped cilantro (or parsley)

In a small bowl, combine bouillon cube and hot water to make a stock. Stir to dissolve. In a medium soup pot, heat oil and sauté garlic and onions until onions are translucent. Add celery, then mushrooms and cook 2 minutes. Add rice and stir well to blend thoroughly. Add stock and salt; bring to a boil and cover. Put a stainless steel flame protector under the pot (this can be used for both gas and electric stoves). Simmer on low for 50 minutes, then remove from heat and keep lid on for 10 more minutes. Remove from heat, add in cilantro, cover for another 5 minutes, then serve.

Note: Jasmine and Basmati brown rice are delicious in this dish.

Yield: 4 cups (8, 1/2-cup servings)

Brown Rice Pilaf: 1 serving = ½ cup

Energy (kcal)	110		
Total Fat (g)	2.5	Calcium (mg)	14
Total Carbohydrate (g)	19.8	Phosphorus (mg)	84
Total Protein (g)	2.5	Magnesium (mg)	36
% Calories from Fat	19.3	Iron (mg)	0.4
% Calories from Carbohydrate	73.3	Zinc (mg)	0.6
% Calories from Protein	7.4	Copper (mg)	0.1
Cholesterol (g)	0	Selenium (mcg)	8.9
Total Saturated Fatty Acids (g) (SFA)	0.4	Sodium (mg)	82
Total Monounsaturated Fatty Acids (g) (MUFA)	0.9	Potassium (mg)	117
Total Polyunsaturated Fatty Acids (g) (PUFA)	1.0		
Omega-3 Fatty Acids (g)	0.0		
% Calories from SFA	3.1	Linoleic Acid - PUFA (18:2) (g)	1.0
% Calories from MUFA	7.4	Linolenic Acid – PUFA (18:3) (g)	0.0
% Calories from PUFA	7.7		
Polyunsaturated to Saturated Fat (P:S) Ratio	2.5	Tryptophan (mg)	3
		Threonine (mg)	9
Total Dietary Fiber (g)	3.0	Isoleucine (mg)	10
Soluble Dietary Fiber (g)	0.4	Leucine (mg)	18
Insoluble Dietary Fiber (g)	2.6	Lysine (mg)	9
		Methionine (mg)	5
Total Vitamin A (mcg) (Retinol Activity Equivalents)	2	Phenylalanine (mg)	12
Vitamin D (calciferol) (mcg)	0.0	Valine (mg)	14
Vitamin E (mg) (Total Alpha-Tocopherol)	0.1	Histidine (mg)	6
Vitamin K (mg) (phylloquinone)	2.8		
Vitamin C (mg) (ascorbic acid)	1.0	Daidzein (mg)	0.0
Thiamin (mg) (vitamin B1)	0.1	Genistein (mg)	0.0
Riboflavin (mg) (vitamin B2)	0.1		
Niacin (mg) (vitamin B3)	1.7	Caffeine (mg)	0
Pantothenic Acid (mg)	0.4	Phytic Acid (mg)	129.2
Vitamin B6 (mg)	0.1	Oxalic Acid (mg)	7.5
Total Folate (mcg)	8	Choline (mg)	10.6
Vitamin B12 (mcg) (cobalamin)	0.0		
		Glycemic Index (glucose reference)	51
Beta-Carotene (mcg) (provitamin A carotenoid)	20	Glycemic Load (glucose reference)	9
Lutein + Zeaxanthin (mcg)	13		
Lycopene (mcg)	0		

Brown Rice Sushi (Vegan; GF)

Pretty, hand-held gems of whole grain goodness…the possibilities are endless. This recipe lends itself to sushi-making parties – add other flavored cooked vegetables, fried tofu and mushrooms. The only limitation (besides the number of sushi mats) is your imagination!

Ingredients for each sushi roll

1/3 of a medium raw carrot, sliced thin, blanched

¼ cup blanched watercress

1¼ cups cooked brown rice

1½ tsp rice vinegar

¼ tsp brown rice syrup

½ pinch salt

1 sheet toasted nori seaweed

½ umeboshi plum, pitted (optional) [umeboshi paste can also be used]

¼ of a medium avocado [Cucumber slices could be used instead of avocado]

½ a medium scallion

Prepare pressure-cooked brown rice, using recipe in Ingredients section (section 11). When it is almost done, prepare other ingredients. Place 1 cup of water in a small saucepan and bring to a boil. Blanch carrots until just tender, and remove. Blanch a half-bunch of watercress for 30 seconds and drain. In a small bowl, whisk together vinegar, brown rice syrup, and salt. Using freshly cooked, hot brown rice, add the flavored vinegar and mix well. Using a fan or rolled newspaper, cool down the rice completely, to avoid a mushy consistency.

To form the sushi:
Place a sushi mat open and face down on a table. Lay a sheet of nori on it, shiny side down. Moisten both hands, spread ½-inch layer of cooled rice evenly over the seaweed, leaving ½ to 1 inch free at the top and 1/4 inch free at the bottom. About 2 inches from the bottom edge, form a thin line of umeboshi, lay over this strips of carrot, scallion, watercress, then avocado.

Using both hands and the mat to help, and starting from the bottom edge nearest you, bring the lower edge of the roll up and over to meet the rice and vegetables laying flat. Keep rolling, while releasing the mat, so you can continue to use it as an aid.

At the end of the mat, moisten the remaining nori slightly to help seal, and press the end over the roll to close tightly. To slice, place sushi roll on a cutting board, wet a sharp knife and slice roll in half, then each half in two even halves again, and repeat a third time, moistening the knife often. This will make 8, ½-inch thick slices.

Yield: 1 roll of sushi, 8 slices (2 servings of 4 slices)

Brown Rice Sushi: 1 serving = 4 slices

Energy (kcal)	170		
Total Fat (g)	3.5	Calcium (mg)	32
Total Carbohydrate (g)	31.5	Phosphorus (mg)	121
Total Protein (g)	4.1	Magnesium (mg)	59
% Calories from Fat	17	Iron (mg)	1.0
% Calories from Carbohydrate	75	Zinc (mg)	1.0
% Calories from Protein	8	Copper (mg)	0.2
Cholesterol (g)	0	Selenium (mcg)	12.2
Total Saturated Fatty Acids (g) (SFA)	0.6	Sodium (mg)	180
Total Monounsaturated Fatty Acids (g) (MUFA)	1.9	Potassium (mg)	212
Total Polyunsaturated Fatty Acids (g) (PUFA)	0.7		
Omega-3 Fatty Acids (g)	0.04		
% Calories from SFA	2.7	Linoleic Acid - PUFA (18:2) (g)	0.6
% Calories from MUFA	9.2	Linolenic Acid – PUFA (18:3) (g)	0.04
% Calories from PUFA	3.4		
Polyunsaturated to Saturated Fat (P:S) Ratio	1.2	Tryptophan (mg)	5
		Threonine (mg)	17
Total Dietary Fiber (g)	6.0	Isoleucine (mg)	17
Soluble Dietary Fiber (g)	1.0	Leucine (mg)	33
Insoluble Dietary Fiber (g)	5.0	Lysine (mg)	17
		Methionine (mg)	9
Total Vitamin A (mcg) (Retinol Activity Equivalents)	93	Phenylalanine (mg)	23
Vitamin D (calciferol) (mcg)	0.0	Valine (mg)	25
Vitamin E (mg) (Total Alpha-Tocopherol)	0.6	Histidine (mg)	10
Vitamin K (mg) (phylloquinone)	25.3		
Vitamin C (mg) (ascorbic acid)	4.8	Daidzein (mg)	0.0
Thiamin (mg) (vitamin B1)	0.143	Genistein (mg)	0.0
Riboflavin (mg) (vitamin B2)	0.1		
Niacin (mg) (vitamin B3)	2.3	Caffeine (mg)	0
Pantothenic Acid (mg)	0.6	Phytic Acid (mg)	212.3
Vitamin B6 (mg)	0.2	Oxalic Acid (mg)	11.4
Total Folate (mcg)	22	Choline (mg)	14.7
Vitamin B12 (mcg) (cobalamin)	0.4		
		Glycemic Index (glucose reference)	51
Beta-Carotene (mcg) (provitamin A carotenoid)	981	Glycemic Load (glucose reference)	13
Lutein + Zeaxanthin (mcg)	462		
Lycopene (mcg)	0		

Buckwheat and Sprouts (Vegan; GF)

An interesting way to enjoy soft and stately buckwheat with light and crunchy sprouts. Both bring out the best in each other, like a great friendship.

Ingredients

2 tsp sesame oil

1½ cups fresh mung bean sprouts

1 cup cooked buckwheat (from 1/3 cup
  uncooked, unroasted buckwheat)-see below*

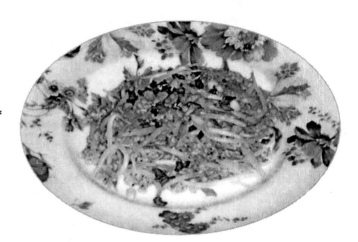

1/8 tsp salt

1/8 tsp black pepper

1 stalk of green onion, sliced thinly

Heat a medium nonstick skillet, add oil and stir-fry sprouts for 2-3 minutes. Add in buckwheat, stirring gently. Cook over medium heat until well heated. Add salt and pepper to taste. Garnish with chopped green onion.

Note: Onions can be used in place of (or in addition to) mung bean sprouts.

Yield: 1¾ cups (1¾, 1-cup servings)

*Basic buckwheat recipe (*makes 3 cups of cooked buckwheat*)

2 c. water

Pinch salt

1 c. white, <u>unroasted</u> buckwheat

Wash and drain buckwheat, using a fine, wire-mesh strainer. In a medium skillet, dry roast over medium heat, stirring often to ensure even roasting. As grains dry out, they will start to turn golden brown and give off a pleasant, nutty aroma.

In the meantime, in a medium saucepan, bring water with pinch of salt to a boil. Add roasted buckwheat, stir and cover. Cook for 20 minutes or longer, until all water is absorbed.

Inspired by Gretchen DeWire

Buckwheat and Sprouts: 1 serving = 1 cup

Energy (kcal)	135		
Total Fat (g)	5.8	Calcium (mg)	21
Total Carbohydrate (g)	19.0	Phosphorus (mg)	89
Total Protein (g)	4.1	Magnesium (mg)	58
% Calories from Fat	38	Iron (mg)	1.2
% Calories from Carbohydrate	53	Zinc (mg)	0.9
% Calories from Protein	9	Copper (mg)	0.2
Cholesterol (g)	0	Selenium (mcg)	2.2
Total Saturated Fatty Acids (g) (SFA)	0.9	Sodium (mg)	187
Total Monounsaturated Fatty Acids (g) (MUFA)	2.3	Potassium (mg)	166
Total Polyunsaturated Fatty Acids (g) (PUFA)	2.4		
Omega-3 Fatty Acids (g)	0.04		
% Calories from SFA	5.8	Linoleic Acid - PUFA (18:2) (g)	2.3
% Calories from MUFA	14.6	Linolenic Acid – PUFA (18:3) (g)	0.04
% Calories from PUFA	15.4		
Polyunsaturated to Saturated Fat (P:S) Ratio	2.7	Tryptophan (mg)	6
		Threonine (mg)	14
Total Dietary Fiber (g)	2.9	Isoleucine (mg)	17
Soluble Dietary Fiber (g)	1.4	Leucine (mg)	26
Insoluble Dietary Fiber (g)	1.5	Lysine (mg)	22
		Methionine (mg)	5
Total Vitamin A (mcg) (Retinol Activity Equivalents)	5	Phenylalanine (mg)	16
Vitamin D (calciferol) (mcg)	0.0	Valine (mg)	20
Vitamin E (mg) (Total Alpha-Tocopherol)	0.2	Histidine (mg)	10
Vitamin K (mg) (phylloquinone)	37.3		
Vitamin C (mg) (ascorbic acid)	10.2	Daidzein (mg)	0.292
Thiamin (mg) (vitamin B1)	0.1	Genistein (mg)	0.322
Riboflavin (mg) (vitamin B2)	0.1		
Niacin (mg) (vitamin B3)	1.7	Caffeine (mg)	0
Pantothenic Acid (mg)	0.4	Phytic Acid (mg)	222.7
Vitamin B6 (mg)	0.1	Oxalic Acid (mg)	36.5
Total Folate (mcg)	36	Choline (mg)	18.9
Vitamin B12 (mcg) (cobalamin)	0.0		
		Glycemic Index (glucose reference)	46
Beta-Carotene (mcg) (provitamin A carotenoid)	55	Glycemic Load (glucose reference)	7
Lutein + Zeaxanthin (mcg)	142		
Lycopene (mcg)	0		

Chestnut Sweet Rice with Hazelnuts (Vegan; GF)

A heartwarming, nourishing dish ~ a unique blend of chewy, crunchy and soft. With a little advanced planning for overnight soaking, the recipe itself is a snap to prepare! Place in a mold for a festive presentation.

Ingredients

2 cups sweet brown rice

¾ cup dried chestnuts

3½ cups water

¼ tsp salt

½ cup chopped, roasted hazelnuts (unsalted)

Soak rice and chestnuts in water overnight. Pressure cook for 50 minutes. After pressure comes down, gently remove cover and, while still hot, sprinkle salt throughout and mix well. Add in chopped hazelnuts.

Yield: 5½ cups (11, ½-cup servings)

Variation: For a wonderful breakfast cereal from leftovers, try adding more water and cooking until creamy; serve with raisins, toasted walnuts, a splash of soymilk (without malted wheat or barley if gluten-free) and a hint of maple syrup…delightful!

Note: If you do not have a pressure cooker, you can use the boiling method, as follows. Soak chestnuts and sweet rice separately, using a total of 4 cups of water. Before cooking, slice the chestnut halves into four small pieces, to speed up the cooking. Combine with sweet rice and bring to a boil. Transfer to a burner with a flame protector (which has already been heating up). Simmer covered over medium-low heat for one hour and 15 minutes.

Chestnut Sweet Rice with Hazelnuts: 1 serving = ½ cup

Energy (kcal)	195		
Total Fat (g)	4.7	Calcium (mg)	25
Total Carbohydrate (g)	34.5	Phosphorus (mg)	123
Total Protein (g)	4.2	Magnesium (mg)	65
% Calories from Fat	20	Iron (mg)	0.9
% Calories from Carbohydrate	73	Zinc (mg)	0.9
% Calories from Protein	7	Copper (mg)	0.3
Cholesterol (g)	0	Selenium (mcg)	11.4
Total Saturated Fatty Acids (g) (SFA)	0.5	Sodium (mg)	64
Total Monounsaturated Fatty Acids (g) (MUFA)	2.9	Potassium (mg)	185
Total Polyunsaturated Fatty Acids (g) (PUFA)	1.0		
Omega-3 Fatty Acids (g)	0.04		
% Calories from SFA	2.2	Linoleic Acid - PUFA (18:2) (g)	0.9
% Calories from MUFA	12.6	Linolenic Acid – PUFA (18:3) (g)	0.04
% Calories from PUFA	4.1		
Polyunsaturated to Saturated Fat (P:S) Ratio	1.9	Tryptophan (mg)	5
		Threonine (mg)	15
Total Dietary Fiber (g)	5.4	Isoleucine (mg)	17
Soluble Dietary Fiber (g)	0.6	Leucine (mg)	33
Insoluble Dietary Fiber (g)	4.8	Lysine (mg)	16
		Methionine (mg)	9
Total Vitamin A (mcg) (Retinol Activity Equivalents)	0	Phenylalanine (mg)	21
Vitamin D (calciferol) (mcg)	0.0	Valine (mg)	23
Vitamin E (mg) (Total Alpha-Tocopherol)	0.9	Histidine (mg)	11
Vitamin K (mg) (phylloquinone)	2.7		
Vitamin C (mg) (ascorbic acid)	1.7	Daidzein (mg)	0.0
Thiamin (mg) (vitamin B1)	0.2	Genistein (mg)	0.0
Riboflavin (mg) (vitamin B2)	0.0		
Niacin (mg) (vitamin B3)	1.9	Caffeine (mg)	0
Pantothenic Acid (mg)	0.5	Phytic Acid (mg)	195.4
Vitamin B6 (mg)	0.3	Oxalic Acid (mg)	29.6
Total Folate (mcg)	20	Choline (mg)	17.3
Vitamin B12 (mcg) (cobalamin)	0.0		
		Glycemic Index (glucose reference)	42
Beta-Carotene (mcg) (provitamin A carotenoid)	2	Glycemic Load (glucose reference)	12
Lutein + Zeaxanthin (mcg)	5		
Lycopene (mcg)	0		

Cold Sesame Noodles (Vegan)

Summer heat or winter blues – what better treat than these luscious, light-but-energizing noodles, covered with smooth sesame sauce. Vary the vegetables toppings, such as fresh mung bean sprouts, steamed watercress or sautéed portabello mushrooms. Add some steamed tofu for a complete meal!

Ingredients

¼ cup sesame butter (roasted tahini)

1 Tbsp lime juice

1 tsp brown rice syrup

½ tsp low-sodium soy sauce

½ tsp mirin

½ tsp salt

1/8 tsp red pepper

2 Tbsp hot water

7 cup cooked noodles*

1¾ medium cucumber, thinly sliced

3½ small carrots, grated

*Udon, somen or other type of light pasta works well; choose unsalted noodles if available.

In a small bowl, combine sesame butter, lime juice, brown rice syrup, soy sauce, mirin, salt and red pepper. Add enough hot water to attain desired consistency and smoothness (about ½ cup). Serve 1 Tbsp over about 1 cup cold udon noodles or other pasta of choice, and top with thinly sliced cucumber and grated carrot.

Note: This could be served hot during the winter months.

Yield: 7 servings (1 cup of noodles with 1 Tbsp dressing per serving)

Cold Sesame Noodles: 1 serving = 1 cup noodles + 1 Tbsp Sauce

Energy (kcal)	303		
Total Fat (g)	5.1	Calcium (mg)	67
Total Carbohydrate (g)	55.0	Phosphorus (mg)	130
Total Protein (g)	9.1	Magnesium (mg)	21
% Calories from Fat	14.1	Iron (mg)	1.9
% Calories from Carbohydrate	74.4	Zinc (mg)	0.9
% Calories from Protein	11.4	Copper (mg)	0.2
Cholesterol (g)	0	Selenium (mcg)	21.7
Total Saturated Fatty Acids (g) (SFA)	0.7	Sodium (mg)	132
Total Monounsaturated Fatty Acids (g) (MUFA)	1.8	Potassium (mg)	239
Total Polyunsaturated Fatty Acids (g) (PUFA)	2.2		
Omega-3 Fatty Acids (g)	0.05		
% Calories from SFA	2.0	Linoleic Acid - PUFA (18:2) (g)	2.1
% Calories from MUFA	4.9	Linolenic Acid - PUFA (18:3) (g)	0.05
% Calories from PUFA	6.0		
Polyunsaturated to Saturated Fat (P:S) Ratio	3.1	Tryptophan (mg)	13
		Threonine (mg)	30
Total Dietary Fiber (g)	6.5	Isoleucine (mg)	36
Soluble Dietary Fiber (g)	1.8	Leucine (mg)	63
Insoluble Dietary Fiber (g)	4.7	Lysine (mg)	22
		Methionine (mg)	17
Total Vitamin A (mcg) (Retinol Activity Equivalents)	212	Phenylalanine (mg)	45
Vitamin D (calciferol) (mcg)	0.0	Valine (mg)	41
Vitamin E (mg) (Total Alpha-Tocopherol)	0.3	Histidine (mg)	20
Vitamin K (mg) (phylloquinone)	3.6		
Vitamin C (mg) (ascorbic acid)	3.8	Daidzein (mg)	0.0
Thiamin (mg) (vitamin B1)	0.2	Genistein (mg)	0.0
Riboflavin (mg) (vitamin B2)	0.1		
Niacin (mg) (vitamin B3)	0.9	Caffeine (mg)	0
Pantothenic Acid (mg)	0.6	Phytic Acid (mg)	566.8
Vitamin B6 (mg)	0.1	Oxalic Acid (mg)	71.0
Total Folate (mcg)	24	Choline (mg)	14.2
Vitamin B12 (mcg) (cobalamin)	0.0		
		Glycemic Index (glucose reference)	48
Beta-Carotene (mcg) (provitamin A carotenoid)	2,098	Glycemic Load (glucose reference)	23
Lutein + Zeaxanthin (mcg)	87		
Lycopene (mcg)	0		

Cornbread with Raisins (GF w/Mod)

A dressed-up version of a traditional favorite. Enjoy as a snack or meal accompaniment. Fiber never tasted so good!

Ingredients

6 Tbsp canola oil, separated

1 cup whole wheat pastry flour

1 cup cornmeal (stone ground)

2 tsp baking powder

½ tsp salt

2 eggs

¾ cup vanilla soymilk

3 Tbsp brown rice syrup

2 Tbsp maple syrup

1 tsp vanilla

1 cup fresh shucked or canned (unsalted) corn (frozen can also be used)

½ cup raisins

Preheat oven to 400°F. Brush 8-inch square glass baking pan with some of the canola oil. In a large mixing bowl, mix together flour, cornmeal, baking powder and salt. In a separate medium mixing bowl, whisk eggs, add soymilk, remaining oil, brown rice syrup, maple syrup and vanilla. Mix well. Gently fold in wet ingredients with dry. Add corn and raisins. Pour batter into baking pan and bake for about 25 minutes, until golden brown.

Yield: 16 squares (2x2x2 inches)

~For gluten-free, substitute 1 cup of gluten-free flour mix for whole wheat pastry flour; add ½ tsp xanthan gum to recipe and be sure soymilk contains no malted barley or wheat~

Adapted from Basic Cornbread recipe: Madison D: *Vegetarian Cooking for Everyone*, New York: Broadway Books, 1997, p 646

Cornbread with Raisins: 1 serving = 1 square (2 x 2 inches)

Energy (kcal)	173		
Total Fat (g)	6.6	Calcium (mg)	60
Total Carbohydrate (g)	26.5	Phosphorus (mg)	101
Total Protein (g)	3.8	Magnesium (mg)	33
% Calories from Fat	34	Iron (mg)	1.1
% Calories from Carbohydrate	58	Zinc (mg)	0.7
% Calories from Protein	8	Copper (mg)	0.1
Cholesterol (g)	27	Selenium (mcg)	11.4
Total Saturated Fatty Acids (g) (SFA)	0.7	Sodium (mg)	159
Total Monounsaturated Fatty Acids (g) (MUFA)	3.7	Potassium (mg)	153
Total Polyunsaturated Fatty Acids (g) (PUFA)	1.9		
Omega-3 Fatty Acids (g)	0.5		
% Calories from SFA	3.6	Linoleic Acid - PUFA (18:2) (g)	1.4
% Calories from MUFA	18.7	Linolenic Acid – PUFA (18:3) (g)	0.5
% Calories from PUFA	10.9		
Polyunsaturated to Saturated Fat (P:S) Ratio	2.7	Tryptophan (mg)	5
		Threonine (mg)	14
Total Dietary Fiber (g)	2.7	Isoleucine (mg)	16
Soluble Dietary Fiber (g)	0.4	Leucine (mg)	32
Insoluble Dietary Fiber (g)	2.3	Lysine (mg)	16
		Methionine (mg)	8
Total Vitamin A (mcg) (Retinol Activity Equivalents)	20	Phenylalanine (mg)	19
Vitamin D (calciferol) (mcg)	0.2	Valine (mg)	19
Vitamin E (mg) (Total Alpha-Tocopherol)	1.3	Histidine (mg)	10
Vitamin K (mg) (phylloquinone)	4.5		
Vitamin C (mg) (ascorbic acid)	0.8	Daidzein (mg)	0.6
Thiamin (mg) (vitamin B1)	0.1	Genistein (mg)	0.6
Riboflavin (mg) (vitamin B2)	0.1		
Niacin (mg) (vitamin B3)	1.3	Caffeine (mg)	0
Pantothenic Acid (mg)	0.3	Phytic Acid (mg)	169.1
Vitamin B6 (mg)	0.1	Oxalic Acid (mg)	13.0
Total Folate (mcg)	16	Choline (mg)	23.8
Vitamin B12 (mcg) (cobalamin)	0.2		
		Glycemic Index (glucose reference)	62
Beta-Carotene (mcg) (provitamin A carotenoid)	16	Glycemic Load (glucose reference)	15
Lutein + Zeaxanthin (mcg)	243		
Lycopene (mcg)	0		

Fried Brown Rice (GF w/Mod)

There are as many ways to make fried rice as there are individuals! Here is a simple one-pot dish with items typically on hand. A great way to use up leftover rice, and an easy way to create an eye-appealing, tasty main course. To make this dish vegan, omit the eggs or replace with your favorite beans, green peas, tofu or tempeh.

Ingredients

3 Tbsp of olive oil, divided

2 medium eggs

¼ cup of egg substitute

1/8 tsp fresh ground pepper, divided

Pinch salt

1 large onion, chopped (about 2 cups)

4 cups of cooked brown rice

1 Tbsp low-sodium soy sauce

¼ cup chopped scallions

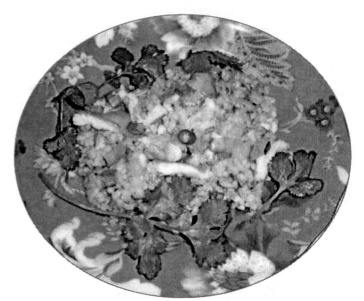

Prepare pressure-cooked brown rice, using recipe in Ingredients section (section 11).

Whisk together eggs and egg substitute with the pepper and a pinch of salt. Place 1 Tbsp of oil in a heated frying pan, and when it gets hot, add eggs and fry on one side, then flip over (as a large-size omelet would look). When cooked well on both sides, remove from pan. After this cools, slice cooked egg into strips. Set aside.

Over medium-high heat, place 2 Tbsp oil, then sauté diced onions until they brown (this makes them very sweet). Add in the cooked rice. Keep turning gently until well mixed. (If rice is leftover and rather dry, you can add a bit of water and place a cover over it to steam a little bit.) Cook over medium-high heat until rice is thoroughly heated throughout. Add back eggs, season with soy sauce; add chopped scallions and remaining pepper (1/8 tsp minus pinch) {and/or cilantro or other aromatics as desired}; cook 2-3 minutes more, garnish and serve.

Note: Other delicious vegetables for this dish include Chinese cabbage or regular cabbage, red pepper, celery, and/or corn. You can also add cooked chickpeas, tofu, tempeh or other protein items. Yield: 5 cups (5, 1-cup servings)

~For gluten free, use tamari in place of soy sauce~

Fried Brown Rice: 1 serving = 1 cup

Energy (kcal)	290		
Total Fat (g)	11.7	Calcium (mg)	36
Total Carbohydrate (g)	39.3	Phosphorus (mg)	178
Total Protein (g)	7.2	Magnesium (mg)	74
% Calories from Fat	35.5	Iron (mg)	1.2
% Calories from Carbohydrate	55.4	Zinc (mg)	1.3
% Calories from Protein	9.1	Copper (mg)	0.2
Cholesterol (g)	85	Selenium (mcg)	21.7
Total Saturated Fatty Acids (g) (SFA)	2.1	Sodium (mg)	169
Total Monounsaturated Fatty Acids (g) (MUFA)	7.2	Potassium (mg)	155
Total Polyunsaturated Fatty Acids (g) (PUFA)	1.7		
Omega-3 Fatty Acids (g)	0.1		
% Calories from SFA	6.3	Linoleic Acid - PUFA (18:2) (g)	1.5
% Calories from MUFA	22.0	Linolenic Acid – PUFA (18:3) (g)	0.1
% Calories from PUFA	5.0		
Polyunsaturated to Saturated Fat (P:S) Ratio	0.8	Tryptophan (mg)	9
		Threonine (mg)	29
Total Dietary Fiber (g)	5.7	Isoleucine (mg)	33
Soluble Dietary Fiber (g)	0.7	Leucine (mg)	58
Insoluble Dietary Fiber (g)	5.0	Lysine (mg)	37
		Methionine (mg)	18
Total Vitamin A (mcg) (Retinol Activity Equivalents)	36	Phenylalanine (mg)	36
Vitamin D (calciferol) (mcg)	0.3	Valine (mg)	41
Vitamin E (mg) (Total Alpha-Tocopherol)	1.4	Histidine (mg)	17
Vitamin K (mg) (phylloquinone)	16.4		
Vitamin C (mg) (ascorbic acid)	2.3	Daidzein (mg)	0.0
Thiamin (mg) (vitamin B1)	0.2	Genistein (mg)	0.0
Riboflavin (mg) (vitamin B2)	0.2		
Niacin (mg) (vitamin B3)	2.6	Caffeine (mg)	0
Pantothenic Acid (mg)	0.8	Phytic Acid (mg)	246.0
Vitamin B6 (mg)	0.3	Oxalic Acid (mg)	15.7
Total Folate (mcg)	23	Choline (mg)	62.5
Vitamin B12 (mcg) (cobalamin)	0.2		
		Glycemic Index (glucose reference)	51
Beta-Carotene (mcg) (provitamin A carotenoid)	32	Glycemic Load (glucose reference)	17
Lutein + Zeaxanthin (mcg)	129		
Lycopene (mcg)	0		

Fried Noodles (Vegan)

This is a basic recipe for sprucing up leftover (or freshly made) noodles of any type. Try adding different vegetables, fresh herbs and varying the ratio of noodles to veggies. A guaranteed crowd-pleaser!

Ingredients

3 cups cooked soba noodles *

1 Tbsp sesame oil

½ medium onion, sliced

½ cup carrots, cut in matchsticks (about ½ a medium carrot)

1 cup Chinese cabbage slices

2 cups fresh mung bean sprouts (washed and drained well)**

1½ Tbsp low-sodium soy sauce

*Cook soba noodles, *al dente*, rinse in cold water and drain well. Other noodles, such as whole wheat or udon, work well in this recipe too.

In a medium, nonstick skillet, sauté onions in sesame oil, then add carrots and Chinese cabbage. When these become softened, add the cooked soba, sauté until well mixed and heated. At the end, add sprouts, then soy sauce to taste. Make sure all are well mixed, but turn gently to keep the noodles intact.

**Draining the sprouts is important; if you have a salad spinner, this is an ideal way to dry them off before adding them to the noodle dish.

Yield: 5 cups (3 1/3, 1½ -cup servings)

Fried Noodles: 1 serving = 1½ cup

Energy (kcal)	168		
Total Fat (g)	4.3	Calcium (mg)	27
Total Carbohydrate (g)	28.2	Phosphorus (mg)	67
Total Protein (g)	7.3	Magnesium (mg)	25
% Calories from Fat	23	Iron (mg)	1.1
% Calories from Carbohydrate	63	Zinc (mg)	0.5
% Calories from Protein	14	Copper (mg)	0.1
Cholesterol (g)	0	Selenium (mcg)	4.2
Total Saturated Fatty Acids (g) (SFA)	0.7	Sodium (mg)	318
Total Monounsaturated Fatty Acids (g) (MUFA)	1.7	Potassium (mg)	216
Total Polyunsaturated Fatty Acids (g) (PUFA)	1.8		
Omega-3 Fatty Acids (g)	0.03		
% Calories from SFA	3.5	Linoleic Acid - PUFA (18:2) (g)	1.8
% Calories from MUFA	8.8	Linolenic Acid – PUFA (18:3) (g)	0.03
% Calories from PUFA	9.4		
Polyunsaturated to Saturated Fat (P:S) Ratio	2.7	Tryptophan (mg)	10
		Threonine (mg)	27
Total Dietary Fiber (g)	5.4	Isoleucine (mg)	31
Soluble Dietary Fiber (g)	1.8	Leucine (mg)	48
Insoluble Dietary Fiber (g)	3.6	Lysine (mg)	35
		Methionine (mg)	10
Total Vitamin A (mcg) (Retinol Activity Equivalents)	147	Phenylalanine (mg)	31
Vitamin D (calciferol) (mcg)	0.0	Valine (mg)	35
Vitamin E (mg) (Total Alpha-Tocopherol)	0.4	Histidine (mg)	17
Vitamin K (mg) (phylloquinone)	26.3		
Vitamin C (mg) (ascorbic acid)	10.9	Daidzein (mg)	0.3
Thiamin (mg) (vitamin B1)	0.2	Genistein (mg)	0.3
Riboflavin (mg) (vitamin B2)	0.1		
Niacin (mg) (vitamin B3)	1.4	Caffeine (mg)	0
Pantothenic Acid (mg)	0.5	Phytic Acid (mg)	78.4
Vitamin B6 (mg)	0.2	Oxalic Acid (mg)	76.6
Total Folate (mcg)	40	Choline (mg)	28.6
Vitamin B12 (mcg) (cobalamin)	0.0		
		Glycemic Index (glucose reference)	48
Beta-Carotene (mcg) (provitamin A carotenoid)	1,444	Glycemic Load (glucose reference)	11
Lutein + Zeaxanthin (mcg)	181		
Lycopene (mcg)	0		

Granola (Vegan)

It is immensely satisfying to make granola at home, particularly to experience the aroma while it's baking. This is a calorie-dense recipe, great for fruit crisp toppings and adding to other cold cereals. It can also be ground and pressed into a spring-form pan for a wonderful pie crust.

Ingredients

3½ cups rolled oats

1½ cups walnuts, chopped very coarsely*

1 cup whole wheat pastry flour

1/3 cup raisins

½ tsp salt

½ tsp cinnamon

½ cup + 1 Tbsp safflower (or canola) oil

½ cup maple syrup

¼ cup apple juice (for moisture)

3/4 tsp vanilla

  *Another kind of nut can also be substituted

Preheat oven to 350°F.

In a large mixing bowl, mix rolled oats, walnuts, flour, raisins, salt and cinnamon. Set aside. In a medium bowl, whisk together the oil, maple syrup, apple juice and vanilla.

Add wet ingredients to dry and mix together. Place on cookie sheet. Bake 45-60 minutes, with frequent turning (at least every 15 minutes) until a nice brown color develops.

This topping can be saved for up to a couple of weeks if covered tightly.

Yield: 6 3/4 cups; (27, ¼-cup servings)

Thanks to Hiroshi Hayashi, The Monadnock School of Natural Cooking and Philosophy (Peterborough, NH)

Granola: 1 serving = ¼ cup

Energy (kcal)	167		
Total Fat (g)	9.6	Calcium (mg)	20
Total Carbohydrate (g)	18.6	Phosphorus (mg)	91
Total Protein (g)	3.3	Magnesium (mg)	36
% Calories from Fat	49	Iron (mg)	1.0
% Calories from Carbohydrate	44	Zinc (mg)	1.0
% Calories from Protein	7	Copper (mg)	0.2
Cholesterol (g)	0	Selenium (mcg)	8.1
Total Saturated Fatty Acids (g) (SFA)	0.8	Sodium (mg)	46
Total Monounsaturated Fatty Acids (g) (MUFA)	1.5	Potassium (mg)	122
Total Polyunsaturated Fatty Acids (g) (PUFA)	6.8		
Omega-3 Fatty Acids (g)	0.6		
% Calories from SFA	4.2	Linoleic Acid - PUFA (18:2) (g)	6.2
% Calories from MUFA	7.5	Linolenic Acid – PUFA (18:3) (g)	0.6
% Calories from PUFA	34.7		
Polyunsaturated to Saturated Fat (P:S) Ratio	8.2	Tryptophan (mg)	5
		Threonine (mg)	11
Total Dietary Fiber (g)	2.4	Isoleucine (mg)	13
Soluble Dietary Fiber (g)	0.8	Leucine (mg)	24
Insoluble Dietary Fiber (g)	1.6	Lysine (mg)	12
		Methionine (mg)	5
Total Vitamin A (mcg) (Retinol Activity Equivalents)	0	Phenylalanine (mg)	16
Vitamin D (calciferol) (mcg)	0.0	Valine (mg)	16
Vitamin E (mg) (Total Alpha-Tocopherol)	1.7	Histidine (mg)	8
Vitamin K (mg) (phylloquinone)	0.9		
Vitamin C (mg) (ascorbic acid)	0.1	Daidzein (mg)	0.0
Thiamin (mg) (vitamin B1)	0.1	Genistein (mg)	0.0
Riboflavin (mg) (vitamin B2)	0.0		
Niacin (mg) (vitamin B3)	0.6	Caffeine (mg)	0
Pantothenic Acid (mg)	0.2	Phytic Acid (mg)	164.8
Vitamin B6 (mg)	0.1	Oxalic Acid (mg)	11.5
Total Folate (mcg)	13	Choline (mg)	9.2
Vitamin B12 (mcg) (cobalamin)	0.0		
		Glycemic Index (glucose reference)	49
Beta-Carotene (mcg) (provitamin A carotenoid)	1	Glycemic Load (glucose reference)	8
Lutein + Zeaxanthin (mcg)	35		
Lycopene (mcg)	0		

Millet soup (or stew) (Vegan; GF w/Mod)

This is a nice starting base of hot whole grain cereal. It is mild and can be spiced up any way you like (or made thinner to be more of a soup). You can add leftovers, and other herbs. Here is the basic recipe. The rest is up to your imagination!

Ingredients

½ tsp sesame oil

1 medium onion cut in large pieces (about 1¼ cups)

1 carrot, sliced (about ½ cup)

1 cup millet, washed and checked for any small stones

7 cups water

1 cup bok choy cut in large pieces (about 160 grams raw); keeping stems separate from leaves

½ tsp salt (alternatively, you could add approx. 1 Tbsp white miso (or any other type), diluted in hot water)

Wash, peel (if non-organic) and dice carrots and onion. In a medium soup pot, sauté onions in sesame oil, cooking until semi-soft, then add carrots. Add water and bring to a boil. Add millet and boil over medium heat, stirring occasionally, for 20 minutes. Add salt, then bok choy stems and simmer for 5 minutes. Add leaves and simmer for 3 minutes more. Serve.

Yield: 6½ cups (6½, 1-cup servings)

~For gluten-free, use brown rice miso in place of barley miso~

Inspired by Gretchen DeWire

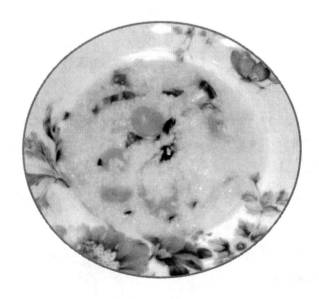

Millet Stew: 1 serving = 1 cup

Energy (kcal)	138		
Total Fat (g)	1.8	Calcium (mg)	41
Total Carbohydrate (g)	26.4	Phosphorus (mg)	107
Total Protein (g)	4.2	Magnesium (mg)	44
% Calories from Fat	11	Iron (mg)	1.3
% Calories from Carbohydrate	78	Zinc (mg)	0.7
% Calories from Protein	11	Copper (mg)	0.3
Cholesterol (g)	0	Selenium (mcg)	1.2
Total Saturated Fatty Acids (g) (SFA)	0.3	Sodium (mg)	207
Total Monounsaturated Fatty Acids (g) (MUFA)	0.4	Potassium (mg)	214
Total Polyunsaturated Fatty Acids (g) (PUFA)	0.9		
Omega-3 Fatty Acids (g)	0.05		
% Calories from SFA	1.8	Linoleic Acid - PUFA (18:2) (g)	0.8
% Calories from MUFA	2.4	Linolenic Acid – PUFA (18:3) (g)	0.05
% Calories from PUFA	5.2		
Polyunsaturated to Saturated Fat (P:S) Ratio	2.9	Tryptophan (mg)	5
		Threonine (mg)	14
Total Dietary Fiber (g)	3.5	Isoleucine (mg)	18
Soluble Dietary Fiber (g)	0.4	Leucine (mg)	48
Insoluble Dietary Fiber (g)	3.1	Lysine (mg)	11
		Methionine (mg)	8
Total Vitamin A (mcg) (Retinol Activity Equivalents)	126	Phenylalanine (mg)	20
Vitamin D (calciferol) (mcg)	0.0	Valine (mg)	21
Vitamin E (mg) (Total Alpha-Tocopherol)	0.1	Histidine (mg)	9
Vitamin K (mg) (phylloquinone)	9.8		
Vitamin C (mg) (ascorbic acid)	7.9	Daidzein (mg)	0.0
Thiamin (mg) (vitamin B1)	0.2	Genistein (mg)	0.0
Riboflavin (mg) (vitamin B2)	0.1		
Niacin (mg) (vitamin B3)	1.7	Caffeine (mg)	0
Pantothenic Acid (mg)	0.3	Phytic Acid (mg)	163.6
Vitamin B6 (mg)	0.2	Oxalic Acid (mg)	20.2
Total Folate (mcg)	41	Choline (mg)	9.0
Vitamin B12 (mcg) (cobalamin)	0.0		
		Glycemic Index (glucose reference)	70
Beta-Carotene (mcg) (provitamin A carotenoid)	1,343	Glycemic Load (glucose reference)	16
Lutein + Zeaxanthin (mcg)	138		
Lycopene (mcg)	0		

Pasta Fagiole (Vegan; GF w/Mod)

A natural pairing of beans and pasta, with an authentic Italian flavor. Nourishing and memorable, this is a classic version of a recipe with many variations. Canned beans work fine, making this a menu item always at-the-ready!

Ingredients

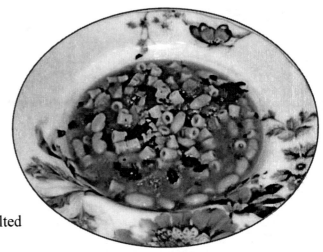

1 cup ditalini pasta (uncooked)

4 cups water to cook pasta

2 Tbsp olive oil

2 cloves of garlic, minced

½ medium onion, chopped

14.5-oz can crushed tomatoes (1½ cups), unsalted

2 Tbsp red wine (optional)

½ tsp salt

½ tsp black pepper

¼ tsp garlic powder

15-oz can of cannellini beans (1½ cups), drained

2 Tbsp fresh, chopped basil

2 Tbsp fresh, chopped Italian parsley

Boil water and cook noodles *al dente*. Reserve the cooking water.

Heat a large soup pot, add olive oil. Sauté garlic briefly, then add onions and cook until just translucent. Mix in crush tomatoes, red wine, salt, pepper and garlic powder and simmer on low heat for 20 minutes. Add in beans and 1 cup of pasta cooking water; simmer for another 10 minutes. Mix in pasta, and add basil, parsley (and any other herbs you wish). Cook 2 minutes more, adjusting seasonings and adding more liquid to make desired consistency. Serve immediately.

Yield: 6 cups (6, 1-cup servings)

~For gluten-free, use rice pasta in place of wheat pasta~

Based on a recipe from Maryanne Zingali

Pasta Fagiole: 1 serving = 1 cup

Energy (kcal)	231*		
Total Fat (g)	5.4	Calcium (mg)	73
Total Carbohydrate (g)	36.3	Phosphorus (mg)	109
Total Protein (g)	9.0	Magnesium (mg)	51
% Calories from Fat	21	Iron (mg)	3.3
% Calories from Carbohydrate	64	Zinc (mg)	1.1
% Calories from Protein	14	Copper (mg)	0.3
Cholesterol (g)	0	Selenium (mcg)	19.0
Total Saturated Fatty Acids (g) (SFA)	0.8	Sodium (mg)	94
Total Monounsaturated Fatty Acids (g) (MUFA)	3.4	Potassium (mg)	536
Total Polyunsaturated Fatty Acids (g) (PUFA)	0.8		
Omega-3 Fatty Acids (g)	0.1		
% Calories from SFA	3.0	Linoleic Acid - PUFA (18:2) (g)	0.7
% Calories from MUFA	13.0	Linolenic Acid – PUFA (18:3) (g)	0.1
% Calories from PUFA	3.0		
Polyunsaturated to Saturated Fat (P:S) Ratio	1.0	Tryptophan (mg)	12
		Threonine (mg)	36
Total Dietary Fiber (g)	4.0	Isoleucine (mg)	37
Soluble Dietary Fiber (g)	0.7	Leucine (mg)	68
Insoluble Dietary Fiber (g)	4.1	Lysine (mg)	42
		Methionine (mg)	12
Total Vitamin A (mcg) (Retinol Activity Equivalents)	11	Phenylalanine (mg)	46
Vitamin D (calciferol) (mcg)	0.0	Valine (mg)	43
Vitamin E (mg) (Total Alpha-Tocopherol)	1.5	Histidine (mg)	23
Vitamin K (mg) (phylloquinone)	30.5		
Vitamin C (mg) (ascorbic acid)	8.2	Daidzein (mg)	0.0
Thiamin (mg) (vitamin B1)	0.3	Genistein (mg)	0.0
Riboflavin (mg) (vitamin B2)	0.2		
Niacin (mg) (vitamin B3)	1.7	Caffeine (mg)	0
Pantothenic Acid (mg)	0.3	Phytic Acid (mg)	209.4
Vitamin B6 (mg)	0.2	Oxalic Acid (mg)	53.4
Total Folate (mcg)	95	Choline (mg)	25.5
Vitamin B12 (mcg) (cobalamin)	0.0		
		Glycemic Index (glucose reference)	43
Beta-Carotene (mcg) (provitamin A carotenoid)	133	Glycemic Load (glucose reference)	13
Lutein + Zeaxanthin (mcg)	177		
Lycopene (mcg)	1,660		

*Calories from alcohol in red wine, so % calories do not add to 100% from CHO, FAT and PRO.

Penne with avocado & tomato (Vegan; GF w/Mod)

Heavenly pasta salad – textural and taste sensation. Avocado and whole wheat pasta make a perfect pair!

Ingredients

1 cup (3 oz) uncooked whole grain penne pasta (or spaghetti) (*makes 1¾ cups cooked pasta*]

4 cups water

1 Tbsp of dressing (see below)

½ medium tomato, chopped

½ medium avocado, cut in cubes

2 Tbsp fresh basil, chopped

Boil water and add pasta. Cook for about 10 minutes, until pasta is done. Drain, but do not rinse. When pasta has cooled, add tomato, avocado and basil. Finally, add 1 Tbsp of dressing and mix well. Serve at room temperature or chill for 1 hour or more (or *overnight*).

Dressing (*makes 4 Tbsp of dressing*)

4 Tbsp olive oil

2 cloves garlic, minced

1½ tsp rice vinegar

1½ tsp balsamic vinegar

¼ tsp Kosher salt

1/8 tsp fresh ground black pepper

In a mixing bowl, combine oil, garlic, vinegars, salt and pepper. Blend with hand blender or in a food processor until smooth.

Yield: 2½ cups (2½, 1-cup servings)

~For gluten-free, use rice penne pasta in place of whole grain penne~

Penne with Avocado and Tomato: 1 serving = 1 cup

Energy (kcal)	212		
Total Fat (g)	10.1	Calcium (mg)	23
Total Carbohydrate (g)	27.8	Phosphorus (mg)	101
Total Protein (g)	5.7	Magnesium (mg)	38
% Calories from Fat	41.1	Iron (mg)	1.3
% Calories from Carbohydrate	49.4	Zinc (mg)	1.0
% Calories from Protein	9.5	Copper (mg)	0.2
Cholesterol (g)	0	Selenium (mcg)	24.4
Total Saturated Fatty Acids (g) (SFA)	1.4	Sodium (mg)	62
Total Monounsaturated Fatty Acids (g) (MUFA)	6.7	Potassium (mg)	199
Total Polyunsaturated Fatty Acids (g) (PUFA)	1.3		
Omega-3 Fatty Acids (g)	0.1		
% Calories from SFA	5.8	Linoleic Acid - PUFA (18:2) (g)	1.2
% Calories from MUFA	27.2	Linolenic Acid – PUFA (18:3) (g)	0.1
% Calories from PUFA	5.2		
Polyunsaturated to Saturated Fat (P:S) Ratio	0.9	Tryptophan (mg)	7
		Threonine (mg)	16
Total Dietary Fiber (g)	4.6	Isoleucine (mg)	22
Soluble Dietary Fiber (g)	1.3	Leucine (mg)	39
Insoluble Dietary Fiber (g)	3.3	Lysine (mg)	15
		Methionine (mg)	9
Total Vitamin A (mcg) (Retinol Activity Equivalents)	9	Phenylalanine (mg)	32
Vitamin D (calciferol) (mcg)	0.0	Valine (mg)	25
Vitamin E (mg) (Total Alpha-Tocopherol)	1.6	Histidine (mg)	13
Vitamin K (mg) (phylloquinone)	18.8		
Vitamin C (mg) (ascorbic acid)	3.5	Daidzein (mg)	0.0
Thiamin (mg) (vitamin B1)	0.1	Genistein (mg)	0.0
Riboflavin (mg) (vitamin B2)	0.1		
Niacin (mg) (vitamin B3)	1.2	Caffeine (mg)	0
Pantothenic Acid (mg)	0.8	Phytic Acid (mg)	314.8
Vitamin B6 (mg)	0.2	Oxalic Acid (mg)	27.7
Total Folate (mcg)	31	Choline (mg)	14.6
Vitamin B12 (mcg) (cobalamin)	0.0		
		Glycemic Index (glucose reference)	42
Beta-Carotene (mcg) (provitamin A carotenoid)	104	Glycemic Load (glucose reference)	10
Lutein + Zeaxanthin (mcg)	274		
Lycopene (mcg)	103		

Polenta pan fry (Vegan; GF w/Mod)

Polenta is like a golden palette on which to develop any number of terrific dishes. This recipe showcases polenta all by itself, crispy on the outside, moist within. Add a side dish of beans and sautéed vegetables for a heart-healthy meal.

Ingredients

4 cups water

¼ tsp salt

1 cup of corn grits

Cooking spray (~13 sprays)

2½ tsp low-sodium soy sauce

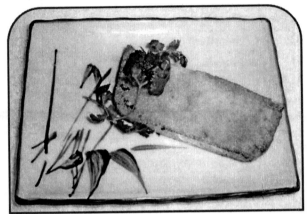

In a medium saucepan, boil water, add salt, slowly stir in grits to blend completely. Turn heat to medium, continue stirring until all water is absorbed and mixture becomes thickened. Let this continue to cook for at least 30 minutes over very low heat (just enough to keep a light simmer), stirring occasionally. [This can be also served as a soft polenta (*recipe makes 4 cups of soft polenta*).]

Spray an 8-inch glass loaf pan with cooking oil spray, then spoon in the polenta and let it set (15-30 minutes). [This can also be refrigerated for later use.] Cut into 3/4-inch thick slices.

Slices of polenta can be served with a sauce, such as mushroom gravy, or fried to give a crispy outer texture, as follows.

Spray a nonstick skillet with cooking spray and heat up. Add slices of firm polenta and pan fry for 2 minutes on each side. Before turning the first time, add a splash of soy sauce, then turn. Add a bit more to the other side, cook briefly, then turn one more time to seal in the wonderful flavor.

Yield: 10, ~3/4-inch thick slices

~For gluten free, use tamari in place of soy sauce~

Polenta Pan Fry: 1 serving = Slice (4 x 2 x 3/4 inches)

Energy (kcal)	62		
Total Fat (g)	0.5	Calcium (mg)	3
Total Carbohydrate (g)	12.6	Phosphorus (mg)	13
Total Protein (g)	1.4	Magnesium (mg)	5
% Calories from Fat	7	Iron (mg)	0.6
% Calories from Carbohydrate	85	Zinc (mg)	0.1
% Calories from Protein	8	Copper (mg)	0.0
Cholesterol (g)	0	Selenium (mcg)	2.7
Total Saturated Fatty Acids (g) (SFA)	0.05	Sodium (mg)	107
Total Monounsaturated Fatty Acids (g) (MUFA)	0.3	Potassium (mg)	24
Total Polyunsaturated Fatty Acids (g) (PUFA)	0.2		
Omega-3 Fatty Acids (g)	0.03		
% Calories from SFA	0.7	Linoleic Acid - PUFA (18:2) (g)	0.1
% Calories from MUFA	3.6	Linolenic Acid – PUFA (18:3) (g)	0.0
% Calories from PUFA	2.4		
Polyunsaturated to Saturated Fat (P:S) Ratio	3.6	Tryptophan (mg)	1
		Threonine (mg)	5
Total Dietary Fiber (g)	0.3	Isoleucine (mg)	5
Soluble Dietary Fiber (g)	0.1	Leucine (mg)	17
Insoluble Dietary Fiber (g)	0.2	Lysine (mg)	4
		Methionine (mg)	3
Total Vitamin A (mcg) (Retinol Activity Equivalents)	0	Phenylalanine (mg)	7
Vitamin D (calciferol) (mcg)	0.0	Valine (mg)	7
Vitamin E (mg) (Total Alpha-Tocopherol)	0.1	Histidine (mg)	4
Vitamin K (mg) (phylloquinone)	0.3		
Vitamin C (mg) (ascorbic acid)	0.0	Daidzein (mg)	0.0
Thiamin (mg) (vitamin B1)	0.1	Genistein (mg)	0.0
Riboflavin (mg) (vitamin B2)	0.1		
Niacin (mg) (vitamin B3)	0.8	Caffeine (mg)	0
Pantothenic Acid (mg)	0.1	Phytic Acid (mg)	20.8
Vitamin B6 (mg)	0.0	Oxalic Acid (mg)	4.1
Total Folate (mcg)	23	Choline (mg)	2.7
Vitamin B12 (mcg) (cobalamin)	0.0		
		Glycemic Index (glucose reference)	68
Beta-Carotene (mcg) (provitamin A carotenoid)	0	Glycemic Load (glucose reference)	8
Lutein + Zeaxanthin (mcg)	1		
Lycopene (mcg)	0		

Polenta with mushroom gravy (Vegan; GF w/Mod)

Ingredients

4 cups water

¼ tsp salt

1 cup of corn grits

Cooking spray (~9 sprays)

10 Tbsp mushroom gravy (see recipe below)*

In a small saucepan, boil water, add salt, and slowly stir in grits to blend completely. Turn heat to medium, continue stirring until all water is absorbed and mixture becomes thickened. Let this continue to cook for at least 30 minutes over very low heat (just enough to keep a light simmer), stirring occasionally.

This can be served as a soft polenta (*recipe makes 4 cups of soft polenta*). To serve in slices, spray an 8-inch glass loaf pan with cooking oil spray, then spoon in the polenta and let it set (15-30 minutes). [This can also be refrigerated for later use.] Cut into 3/4-inch thick slices.

[Pan fry or broil to reheat.]

Yield: 10, ~3/4-inch thick slices each with 2 Tbsp mushroom gravy

*Mushroom – onion gravy (*Makes 1¼ cups gravy*)

2 tsp. sesame oil

1 small yellow onion, minced (about ¾ cup)

10 mushrooms (baby bella) sliced thinly (~2 cups)

2 tsp low-sodium soy sauce

1 Tbsp kuzu (or cornstarch)

½ cup plus 2 Tbsp hot water

2 Tbsp fresh basil, chopped

Heat the sesame oil in a skillet. Sauté onions in oil briefly, then add mushrooms. Cook on medium heat until tender. When vegetables are completely cooked, add soy sauce; dilute kuzu in hot water and add to the pan, stirring constantly. Right before serving, add fresh basil, stir.

Serve over polenta.

~For gluten free, use tamari in place of soy sauce~

Polenta with Mushroom Gravy: 1 serving polenta = Slice (4 x 2 x 3/4 inches) with 2 Tbsp gravy

Energy (kcal)	80		
Total Fat (g)	1.4	Calcium (mg)	10
Total Carbohydrate (g)	14.9	Phosphorus (mg)	34
Total Protein (g)	2.0	Magnesium (mg)	8
% Calories from Fat	15	Iron (mg)	0.7
% Calories from Carbohydrate	77	Zinc (mg)	0.3
% Calories from Protein	8	Copper (mg)	0.1
Cholesterol (g)	0	Selenium (mcg)	6.5
Total Saturated Fatty Acids (g) (SFA)	0.2	Sodium (mg)	99
Total Monounsaturated Fatty Acids (g) (MUFA)	0.6	Potassium (mg)	106
Total Polyunsaturated Fatty Acids (g) (PUFA)	0.5		
Omega-3 Fatty Acids (g)	0.03		
% Calories from SFA	1.9	Linoleic Acid - PUFA (18:2) (g)	0.5
% Calories from MUFA	6.1	Linolenic Acid – PUFA (18:3) (g)	0.03
% Calories from PUFA	5.9		
Polyunsaturated to Saturated Fat (P:S) Ratio	3.0	Tryptophan (mg)	0.02
		Threonine (mg)	0.07
Total Dietary Fiber (g)	0.5	Isoleucine (mg)	0.07
Soluble Dietary Fiber (g)	0.1	Leucine (mg)	0.20
Insoluble Dietary Fiber (g)	0.4	Lysine (mg)	0.09
		Methionine (mg)	0.04
Total Vitamin A (mcg) (Retinol Activity Equivalents)	1	Phenylalanine (mg)	0.09
Vitamin D (calciferol) (mcg)	0.1	Valine (mg)	0.09
Vitamin E (mg) (Total Alpha-Tocopherol)	0.1	Histidine (mg)	0.06
Vitamin K (mg) (phylloquinone)	2.6		
Vitamin C (mg) (ascorbic acid)	0.6	Daidzein (mg)	0.0
Thiamin (mg) (vitamin B1)	0.1	Genistein (mg)	0.0
Riboflavin (mg) (vitamin B2)	0.1		
Niacin (mg) (vitamin B3)	1.4	Caffeine (mg)	0
Pantothenic Acid (mg)	0.3	Phytic Acid (mg)	32.3
Vitamin B6 (mg)	0.1	Oxalic Acid (mg)	5.5
Total Folate (mcg)	27	Choline (mg)	6.5
Vitamin B12 (mcg) (cobalamin)	0.0		
		Glycemic Index (glucose reference)	69
Beta-Carotene (mcg) (provitamin A carotenoid)	17	Glycemic Load (glucose reference)	10
Lutein + Zeaxanthin (mcg)	31		
Lycopene (mcg)	0		

Pumpkin-Carrot-Walnut Muffins

Bet you can't eat just one! Mouth-watering muffins –light, sweet, nutty, flavorful. Not to mention all the beta-carotene…

Ingredients

1½ cups whole wheat pastry flour

1½ tsp pumpkin pie spice (or ¾ tsp cinnamon, ½ tsp nutmeg,
    and ¼ tsp ground ginger)

1 tsp baking soda

½ tsp baking powder

Pinch salt

¼ cup egg substitute or 1 large egg

1 cup canned pumpkin

½ cup barley malt

½ cup brown rice syrup

2 Tbsp unsweetened applesauce

1 Tbsp canola (or safflower) oil

¼ tsp vanilla

1 cup shredded carrots (about 1½ medium carrots)

½ cup raisins

½ cup chopped walnuts

Spray oil (for muffin tin)

Preheat oven to 350°F. Mix flour, pumpkin spice, baking soda, baking powder and salt in a large mixing bowl. In a separate bowl, whisk the egg substitute (or egg), mix together with the pumpkin, barley malt, brown rice syrup, applesauce, canola oil and vanilla.

Add the moist ingredients to the bowl of flour mixture, fold in gently. Add carrots, raisins and walnuts and mix together gently. Do not over mix. Spray a muffin (1-dozen) pan with nonstick cooking spray (or use cupcake liners). Spoon muffin mixture into cups and bake until done, 25-30 minutes, until a toothpick in the center comes out clean. Remove from pan to a cooling rack.

Yield: 12 (1 dozen) muffins

Pumpkin-Carrot-Walnut Muffins: 1 serving = 1 muffin

Energy (kcal)	239		
Total Fat (g)	5.0	Calcium (mg)	47
Total Carbohydrate (g)	45.9	Phosphorus (mg)	147
Total Protein (g)	5.6	Magnesium (mg)	57
% Calories from Fat	18	Iron (mg)	1.8
% Calories from Carbohydrate	74	Zinc (mg)	0.9
% Calories from Protein	8	Copper (mg)	0.2
Cholesterol (g)	0	Selenium (mcg)	19.0
Total Saturated Fatty Acids (g) (SFA)	0.5	Sodium (mg)	181
Total Monounsaturated Fatty Acids (g) (MUFA)	1.3	Potassium (mg)	275
Total Polyunsaturated Fatty Acids (g) (PUFA)	2.8		
Omega-3 Fatty Acids (g)	0.6		
% Calories from SFA	1.8	Linoleic Acid - PUFA (18:2) (g)	2.3
% Calories from MUFA	4.7	Linolenic Acid – PUFA (18:3) (g)	0.6
% Calories from PUFA	10.0		
Polyunsaturated to Saturated Fat (P:S) Ratio	5.5	Tryptophan (mg)	8
		Threonine (mg)	19
Total Dietary Fiber (g)	4.2	Isoleucine (mg)	22
Soluble Dietary Fiber (g)	0.7	Leucine (mg)	39
Insoluble Dietary Fiber (g)	3.5	Lysine (mg)	20
		Methionine (mg)	10
Total Vitamin A (mcg) (Retinol Activity Equivalents)	222	Phenylalanine (mg)	27
Vitamin D (calciferol) (mcg)	0.1	Valine (mg)	27
Vitamin E (mg) (Total Alpha-Tocopherol)	0.8	Histidine (mg)	13
Vitamin K (mg) (phylloquinone)	6.0		
Vitamin C (mg) (ascorbic acid)	1.4	Daidzein (mg)	0.0
Thiamin (mg) (vitamin B1)	0.1	Genistein (mg)	0.0
Riboflavin (mg) (vitamin B2)	0.2		
Niacin (mg) (vitamin B3)	2.7	Caffeine (mg)	0
Pantothenic Acid (mg)	0.5	Phytic Acid (mg)	206.7
Vitamin B6 (mg)	0.2	Oxalic Acid (mg)	21.9
Total Folate (mcg)	25	Choline (mg)	12.4
Vitamin B12 (mcg) (cobalamin)	0.1		
		Glycemic Index (glucose reference)	73
Beta-Carotene (mcg) (provitamin A carotenoid)	2,040	Glycemic Load (glucose reference)	30
Lutein + Zeaxanthin (mcg)	99		
Lycopene (mcg)	0		

Quinoa Stuffed Peppers (Vegan)

Stately and substantial, these fun-to-prepare peppers add grace and beauty to any table. Delve into the velvety smooth outside to a tasty, wholesome filling. A wonderful way to serve quinoa!

Ingredients

½ cup quinoa

1 cup water

3 medium peppers (yellow, orange, red, or green or a combination)

1 Tbsp olive oil

1 tsp sesame oil

2 large cloves garlic, minced

1/3 cup soy crumbles (frozen is fine) [optional]

½ medium onion, diced (about ½ cup)

5 medium crimini mushrooms, thinly sliced (~1½ cups)

1 medium tomato, seeded and chopped

1 Tbsp mirin

1/4 tsp Kosher salt

1/8 tsp black pepper

3 Tbsp fresh basil, chopped

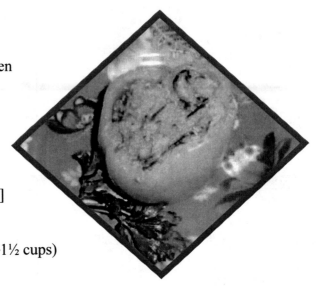

Prepare quinoa, by washing and draining into a fine-mesh strainer to remove saponin coating (foamy). Place in a small saucepan along with water and bring to a boil. Cover and simmer on low heat for 15 minutes, then let rest. Cut the tops off of the pepper and remove seeds and ribs. Steam the peppers for 10 minutes in a steamer.

Preheat oven to 325°F. In a medium skillet, heat oils, sauté garlic over medium-high heat, then add soy crumbles, stirring for about 2 minutes. Add onions, mushrooms, and tomatoes; continue cooking until mushrooms become tender (3-5 minutes). Add mirin, salt, pepper and chopped basil, cooking for another minute. Add cooked quinoa and mix in gently. (This makes about 2¾ cups of stuffing.) Place 1/3 of this mixture into each of the 3 peppers. Arrange stuffed peppers in a baking dish lightly brushed with oil. Bake for 30 minutes.

Yield: 3 stuffed peppers

Adapted from a recipe on box of *Ancient Harvest Quinoa*, Quinoa Corporation (Gardena, CA 90248)

Quinoa Stuffed Peppers: 1 serving = 1 pepper

Energy (kcal)	270		
Total Fat (g)	8.5	Calcium (mg)	69
Total Carbohydrate (g)	34.4	Phosphorus (mg)	302
Total Protein (g)	16.1	Magnesium (mg)	85
% Calories from Fat	28	Iron (mg)	4.1
% Calories from Carbohydrate	49	Zinc (mg)	2.1
% Calories from Protein	23	Copper (mg)	0.7
Cholesterol (g)	0	Selenium (mcg)	15.1
Total Saturated Fatty Acids (g) (SFA)	1.1	Sodium (mg)	256
Total Monounsaturated Fatty Acids (g) (MUFA)	4.4	Potassium (mg)	718
Total Polyunsaturated Fatty Acids (g) (PUFA)	2.3		
Omega-3 Fatty Acids (g)	0.2		
% Calories from SFA	3.6	Linoleic Acid - PUFA (18:2) (g)	2.1
% Calories from MUFA	14.5	Linolenic Acid – PUFA (18:3) (g)	0.1
% Calories from PUFA	7.5		
Polyunsaturated to Saturated Fat (P:S) Ratio	2.1	Tryptophan (mg)	21
		Threonine (mg)	58
Total Dietary Fiber (g)	4.1	Isoleucine (mg)	69
Soluble Dietary Fiber (g)	1.0	Leucine (mg)	114
Insoluble Dietary Fiber (g)	3.1	Lysine (mg)	97
		Methionine (mg)	25
Total Vitamin A (mcg) (Retinol Activity Equivalents)	46	Phenylalanine (mg)	74
Vitamin D (calciferol) (mcg)	0.2	Valine (mg)	74
Vitamin E (mg) (Total Alpha-Tocopherol)	2.0	Histidine (mg)	42
Vitamin K (mg) (phylloquinone)	18.7		
Vitamin C (mg) (ascorbic acid)	185.0	Daidzein (mg)	4.1
Thiamin (mg) (vitamin B1)	0.2	Genistein (mg)	6.7
Riboflavin (mg) (vitamin B2)	0.3		
Niacin (mg) (vitamin B3)	3.2	Caffeine (mg)	0
Pantothenic Acid (mg)	1.1	Phytic Acid (mg)	600.8
Vitamin B6 (mg)	0.5	Oxalic Acid (mg)	97.4
Total Folate (mcg)	118	Choline (mg)	49.2
Vitamin B12 (mcg) (cobalamin)	0.0		
		Glycemic Index (glucose reference)	55
Beta-Carotene (mcg) (provitamin A carotenoid)	550	Glycemic Load (glucose reference)	17
Lutein + Zeaxanthin (mcg)	500		
Lycopene (mcg)	1,125		

Rice Salad (Vegan: GF w/Mod)

This incredibly beautifully dish is a delight to the eye. Then the flavors pop out one by one – pungent, slightly salty, minty, sweet, and savory. Summer never tasted so good.

Ingredients

2 cups short-grain brown rice (boiled)

¼ cup cucumber slices

¼ cup cooked peas (from frozen)

¼ cup chopped red onion

3 medium radishes, sliced

3 Tbsp sliced Kalamata olives

2 Tbsp fresh lemon juice

2 Tbsp chopped basil

1 Tbsp fresh mint, chopped finely

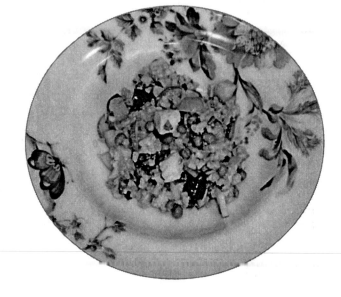

1 Tbsp olive oil

1/8 tsp Kosher salt

1¼ cups Tofu "cheese," cut in ½-inch cubes [starting with 8 oz of tofu & 2 tsp miso] (see directions below)**

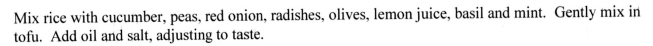

Mix rice with cucumber, peas, red onion, radishes, olives, lemon juice, basil and mint. Gently mix in tofu. Add oil and salt, adjusting to taste.

Prepare brown rice by the boiling method, using recipe in Ingredients section (section 11).

**<u>Tofu Cheese</u> (*makes about 1¼ cups of tofu "cheese" cubes and uses ~2 tsp of miso in all*)

Slice 8 ounces (½ lb) of tofu into layers about ½-inch thick. Spread a thin layer of barley miso (about 2 Tbsp) over the tofu layers and sides (frost almost like a cake). Keep in a covered container in a cool spot for at least 24 hours. Scrape the miso off and rinse. The tofu will have a cheese-like flavor. Chop into 1/2-inch cubes.

Yield: 4 cups (4, 1-cup servings)

~For gluten-free, use brown rice miso in place of barley miso~

Rice Salad: 1 serving = 1 cup

Energy (kcal)	205		
Total Fat (g)	7.6	Calcium (mg)	143
Total Carbohydrate (g)	27.5	Phosphorus (mg)	168
Total Protein (g)	8.3	Magnesium (mg)	71
% Calories from Fat	32	Iron (mg)	2.0
% Calories from Carbohydrate	54	Zinc (mg)	1.3
% Calories from Protein	14	Copper (mg)	0.3
Cholesterol (g)	0	Selenium (mcg)	15.8
Total Saturated Fatty Acids (g) (SFA)	1.3	Sodium (mg)	258
Total Monounsaturated Fatty Acids (g) (MUFA)	4.0	Potassium (mg)	195
Total Polyunsaturated Fatty Acids (g) (PUFA)	1.9		
Omega-3 Fatty Acids (g)	0.2		
% Calories from SFA	5.3	Linoleic Acid - PUFA (18:2) (g)	1.7
% Calories from MUFA	17.0	Linolenic Acid – PUFA (18:3) (g)	0.2
% Calories from PUFA	7.7		
Polyunsaturated to Saturated Fat (P:S) Ratio	1.5	Tryptophan (mg)	12
		Threonine (mg)	32
Total Dietary Fiber (g)	4.8	Isoleucine (mg)	38
Soluble Dietary Fiber (g)	0.8	Leucine (mg)	63
Insoluble Dietary Fiber (g)	4.0	Lysine (mg)	45
		Methionine (mg)	13
Total Vitamin A (mcg) (Retinol Activity Equivalents)	15	Phenylalanine (mg)	40
Vitamin D (calciferol) (mcg)	0.0	Valine (mg)	43
Vitamin E (mg) (Total Alpha-Tocopherol)	0.7	Histidine (mg)	22
Vitamin K (mg) (phylloquinone)	15.7		
Vitamin C (mg) (ascorbic acid)	6.4	Daidzein (mg)	5.8
Thiamin (mg) (vitamin B1)	0.2	Genistein (mg)	8.3
Riboflavin (mg) (vitamin B2)	0.1		
Niacin (mg) (vitamin B3)	1.8	Caffeine (mg)	0
Pantothenic Acid (mg)	0.4	Phytic Acid (mg)	443.2
Vitamin B6 (mg)	0.2	Oxalic Acid (mg)	24.0
Total Folate (mcg)	27	Choline (mg)	31.8
Vitamin B12 (mcg) (cobalamin)	0.0		
		Glycemic Index (glucose reference)	50
Beta-Carotene (mcg) (provitamin A carotenoid)	175	Glycemic Load (glucose reference)	11
Lutein + Zeaxanthin (mcg)	336		
Lycopene (mcg)	0		

Spiral pasta salad (Vegan; GF w/Mod)

All season long, pasta is a grand companion for vegetables – cooked or raw. Hearty and bright, this is a dish that can be made in advance; it marinates and improves with time.

Ingredients

1¼ cups raw broccoli flowerets (3 oz)

Water for boiling

½ cup cooked whole wheat spiral pasta

1 medium tomato, chopped (2/3 cup)

½ cucumber (4 oz), sliced in thick quarter-moons (2/3 cup)

5 Kalamata olives, sliced

3 Tbsp minced red onion (30 g)

2 Tbsp fresh Italian parsley, chopped finely

1 Tbsp fresh basil, chopped finely

1½ Tbsp olive oil

1½ tsp white balsamic vinegar

1 tsp lemon juice

Pinch salt

Pinch black pepper

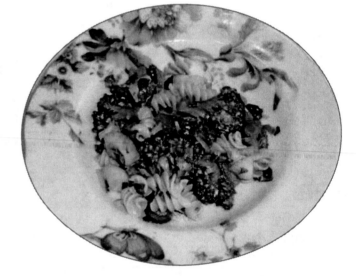

Parboil broccoli flowerets in a small amount of water (about 2 minutes), so they stay fairly crunchy and bright green. Dip in cold water to stop the cooking process. In a medium mixing bowl, combine the broccoli with cooked pasta, chopped tomato, cucumber, olives, red onion, parsley and basil. In a small bowl, whisk together olive oil, vinegar, lemon juice, salt and pepper. Pour onto the salad and mix thoroughly. Serve or chill ahead to give flavors a chance to meld.

Yield: 3½ cups (3½, 1-cup servings)

~For gluten-free, substitute spiral rice pasta for whole wheat pasta~

Spiral Pasta Salad: 1 serving = 1 cup

Energy (kcal)	110		
Total Fat (g)	6.8	Calcium (mg)	36
Total Carbohydrate (g)	11.4	Phosphorus (mg)	58
Total Protein (g)	2.5	Magnesium (mg)	23
% Calories from Fat	54	Iron (mg)	1.0
% Calories from Carbohydrate	39	Zinc (mg)	0.5
% Calories from Protein	7	Copper (mg)	0.1
Cholesterol (g)	0	Selenium (mcg)	5.8
Total Saturated Fatty Acids (g) (SFA)	0.9	Sodium (mg)	108
Total Monounsaturated Fatty Acids (g) (MUFA)	4.7	Potassium (mg)	256
Total Polyunsaturated Fatty Acids (g) (PUFA)	0.8		
Omega-3 Fatty Acids (g)	0.1		
% Calories from SFA	7.5	Linoleic Acid - PUFA (18:2) (g)	0.7
% Calories from MUFA	37.7	Linolenic Acid – PUFA (18:3) (g)	0.1
% Calories from PUFA	6.3		
Polyunsaturated to Saturated Fat (P:S) Ratio	0.8	Tryptophan (mg)	0.03
		Threonine (mg)	0.08
Total Dietary Fiber (g)	2.7	Isoleucine (mg)	0.09
Soluble Dietary Fiber (g)	0.4	Leucine (mg)	0.15
Insoluble Dietary Fiber (g)	2.3	Lysine (mg)	0.10
		Methionine (mg)	0.04
Total Vitamin A (mcg) (Retinol Activity Equivalents)	51	Phenylalanine (mg)	0.13
Vitamin D (calciferol) (mcg)	0.0	Valine (mg)	0.11
Vitamin E (mg) (Total Alpha-Tocopherol)	1.8	Histidine (mg)	0.05
Vitamin K (mg) (phylloquinone)	88.9		
Vitamin C (mg) (ascorbic acid)	29.6	Daidzein (mg)	0.0
Thiamin (mg) (vitamin B1)	0.1	Genistein (mg)	0.0
Riboflavin (mg) (vitamin B2)	0.1		
Niacin (mg) (vitamin B3)	0.6	Caffeine (mg)	0
Pantothenic Acid (mg)	0.4	Phytic Acid (mg)	67.0
Vitamin B6 (mg)	0.1	Oxalic Acid (mg)	15.7
Total Folate (mcg)	49	Choline (mg)	20.2
Vitamin B12 (mcg) (cobalamin)	0.0		
		Glycemic Index (glucose reference)	47
Beta-Carotene (mcg) (provitamin A carotenoid)	596	Glycemic Load (glucose reference)	4
Lutein + Zeaxanthin (mcg)	586		
Lycopene (mcg)	887		

Steamed Onion Strudel (Vegan; GF w/Mod)

Appetizing slices of deeply-sweet onions, paired with Italian flavors that give it a pizza-like quality. Soft and digestible, this is an unforgettable treat for onion lovers everywhere!

Ingredients

1 Tbsp olive oil

1 medium yellow onion (6 oz), sliced – 1¼ cups

½ large red onion (5 ½ oz), sliced - 1½ cups

¼ tsp salt

Cooking spray (about 3 seconds)

1 lb of whole wheat pizza dough

1 medium tomato, sliced in thin rounds

2 Tbsp sliced Kalamata olives

3 Tbsp chopped basil

½ tsp rosemary, chopped finely

½ tsp dried Italian seasoning

In a medium skillet, heat olive oil, then sauté onions over medium heat, adding salt to bring out sweetness. (This amount of onions yields 1½ cups.) Cook until they start to brown (for maximum sweetness). Cool.

Boil water in a large steamer. Spray cooking oil onto the steamer base.

On a lightly-floured surface, roll the dough out. In the middle third of the dough, layer onions, then sliced tomatoes, and finally olives, basil, rosemary and Italian seasoning. Roll carefully from one end, and pinch the edges to seal. Place inside the steamer base, bending strudel into an arc to fit. Make light knife strokes to divide the strudel into slices, but stay close to the surface, to prevent any tears.

Let steam for 30 minutes. Remove and cool before slicing into wedges.

Yield: 10 servings (wedges)

~For gluten-free, use a gluten-free pizza dough in place of whole wheat dough~

Steamed Onion Strudel: 1 serving = 1 wedge

Energy (kcal)	120		
Total Fat (g)	2.9	Calcium (mg)	48
Total Carbohydrate (g)	23.2	Phosphorus (mg)	60
Total Protein (g)	4.7	Magnesium (mg)	23
% Calories from Fat	21	Iron (mg)	1.6
% Calories from Carbohydrate	65	Zinc (mg)	0.6
% Calories from Protein	14	Copper (mg)	0.1
Cholesterol (g)	0	Selenium (mcg)	14.0
Total Saturated Fatty Acids (g) (SFA)	0.4	Sodium (mg)	307
Total Monounsaturated Fatty Acids (g) (MUFA)	1.4	Potassium (mg)	134
Total Polyunsaturated Fatty Acids (g) (PUFA)	0.7		
Omega-3 Fatty Acids (g)	0.1		
% Calories from SFA	2.8	Linoleic Acid - PUFA (18:2) (g)	0.6
% Calories from MUFA	10.1	Linolenic Acid – PUFA (18:3) (g)	0.1
% Calories from PUFA	4.9		
Polyunsaturated to Saturated Fat (P:S) Ratio	1.8	Tryptophan (mg)	0.06
		Threonine (mg)	0.14
Total Dietary Fiber (g)	6.0	Isoleucine (mg)	0.18
Soluble Dietary Fiber (g)	2.4	Leucine (mg)	0.31
Insoluble Dietary Fiber (g)	3.4	Lysine (mg)	0.14
		Methionine (mg)	0.08
Total Vitamin A (mcg) (Retinol Activity Equivalents)	8	Phenylalanine (mg)	0.22
Vitamin D (calciferol) (mcg)	0.0	Valine (mg)	0.19
Vitamin E (mg) (Total Alpha-Tocopherol)	0.5	Histidine (mg)	0.10
Vitamin K (mg) (phylloquinone)	6.1		
Vitamin C (mg) (ascorbic acid)	3.2	Daidzein (mg)	0.3
Thiamin (mg) (vitamin B1)	0.2	Genistein (mg)	0.3
Riboflavin (mg) (vitamin B2)	0.1		
Niacin (mg) (vitamin B3)	1.9	Caffeine (mg)	0
Pantothenic Acid (mg)	0.3	Phytic Acid (mg)	34.5
Vitamin B6 (mg)	0.1	Oxalic Acid (mg)	14.8
Total Folate (mcg)	48	Choline (mg)	11.5
Vitamin B12 (mcg) (cobalamin)	0.0		
		Glycemic Index (glucose reference)	67
Beta-Carotene (mcg) (provitamin A carotenoid)	87	Glycemic Load (glucose reference)	12
Lutein + Zeaxanthin (mcg)	89		
Lycopene (mcg)	317		

Tabouli salad <small>(Vegan)</small>

Homemade tabouli has the advantage of being ready when you are, always fresh and having all your favorite, colorful ingredients. A great picnic item, the raisins and avocados make it distinctive. Make ahead and let the flavors mesmerize.

Ingredients

2½ cups water

Pinch salt

1 cup bulghur, uncooked

½ cucumber, diced (135 g)

4 medium red radishes

1 chopped avocado (about 1 cup, diced)

½ red onion – diced (3/4 cup)

1 chopped plum tomato

¼ cup chopped cilantro

2 Tbsp chopped basil

2 Tbsp chopped fresh mint

¼ cup raisins

Roast bulghur over a medium heat, in a dry skillet, until it starts to smell nutty (being careful not to burn). Bring water to a boil and add salt. Add bulghur, gently, while stirring. Cook, uncovered for 35 minutes, then cover and cook another 10 minutes. Cool.

Prepare cucumbers, radishes, avocado, onion, tomato, cilantro, basil and mint. Mix together and add raisins. Add to the cooled bulghur and mix in the following dressing:

<u>Blend together (hand blender)</u>
½ small onion, grated (60 g / 2 Tbsp)
4 tsp juice of one lime
3 tsp olive oil
2 tsp rice vinegar
2 cloves garlic, minced
1 tsp sesame oil
¼ tsp salt
1/8 tsp black pepper

Yield: 7 cups (7, 1-cup servings)

Tabouli Salad: 1 serving = 1 cup

Energy (kcal)	152		
Total Fat (g)	6.0	Calcium (mg)	29
Total Carbohydrate (g)	23.8	Phosphorus (mg)	90
Total Protein (g)	3.5	Magnesium (mg)	48
% Calories from Fat	34	Iron (mg)	1.1
% Calories from Carbohydrate	58	Zinc (mg)	0.7
% Calories from Protein	8	Copper (mg)	0.2
Cholesterol (g)	0	Selenium (mcg)	1.1
Total Saturated Fatty Acids (g) (SFA)	0.8	Sodium (mg)	115
Total Monounsaturated Fatty Acids (g) (MUFA)	3.6	Potassium (mg)	311
Total Polyunsaturated Fatty Acids (g) (PUFA)	1.0		
Omega-3 Fatty Acids (g)	0.1		
% Calories from SFA	4.7	Linoleic Acid - PUFA (18:2) (g)	0.9
% Calories from MUFA	20.4	Linolenic Acid – PUFA (18:3) (g)	0.1
% Calories from PUFA	5.4		
Polyunsaturated to Saturated Fat (P:S) Ratio	1.1	Tryptophan (mg)	10
		Threonine (mg)	10
Total Dietary Fiber (g)	5.9	Isoleucine (mg)	10
Soluble Dietary Fiber (g)	1.3	Leucine (mg)	20
Insoluble Dietary Fiber (g)	4.6	Lysine (mg)	10
		Methionine (mg)	10
Total Vitamin A (mcg) (Retinol Activity Equivalents)	11	Phenylalanine (mg)	20
Vitamin D (calciferol) (mcg)	0.0	Valine (mg)	20
Vitamin E (mg) (Total Alpha-Tocopherol)	0.8	Histidine (mg)	10
Vitamin K (mg) (phylloquinone)	15.8		
Vitamin C (mg) (ascorbic acid)	6.5	Daidzein (mg)	0.0
Thiamin (mg) (vitamin B1)	0.1	Genistein (mg)	0.0
Riboflavin (mg) (vitamin B2)	0.1		
Niacin (mg) (vitamin B3)	1.6	Caffeine (mg)	0
Pantothenic Acid (mg)	0.6	Phytic Acid (mg)	335.5
Vitamin B6 (mg)	0.2	Oxalic Acid (mg)	26.3
Total Folate (mcg)	33	Choline (mg)	12.3
Vitamin B12 (mcg) (cobalamin)	0.0		
		Glycemic Index (glucose reference)	52
Beta-Carotene (mcg) (provitamin A carotenoid)	118	Glycemic Load (glucose reference)	9
Lutein + Zeaxanthin (mcg)	200		
Lycopene (mcg)	196		

Vegetable-Rice Medley (Vegan; GF w/Mod)

A warming, delectable, winter dish. Accents of distinctive vegetables weave in and out of the taste forefront.

Ingredients

2 cups short grain brown rice, uncooked

3 cups + ¼ cup water

2 medium dried shiitake mushrooms

4 oz firm tofu (1 cup diced)

1 small carrot – 1/3 c diced

1/3 large piece of burdock root, 1/3 c diced

2 tsp sesame oil

5 tsp low-sodium soy sauce, divided

Wash, rinse, and drain brown rice. Add 3 cups water. Soak a few hours or, if possible, overnight. Drain remaining water into a measuring cup, noting the amount; add back an equal amount of fresh water.

Soak shiitake mushrooms in 1 cup of hot water (¼ cup of this will be saved to flavor the rice). While these are soaking, slice tofu into small ½-inch cubes. Wash and chop carrot (peel first if not organic) and burdock root into small cubes. Heat a medium non-stick skillet and add the oil. Heat carrots, then burdock and add in the tofu. Stir over medium-heat until the burdock starts to get soft. Add the soy sauce. Remove mushrooms from water and squeeze out the excess water. Slice thinly. Add to the rice. Measure ¼ cup of the soaking liquid and add this to the rice as well. Finally, mix in the cooked vegetables. Cover the pressure cooker and cook for 50 minutes.

Once the pressure comes down completely, carefully remove the lid and stir the rice/vegetables. Add in the remaining 3 tsp of soy sauce, and mix well. Serve.

Yield: 5 cups (5, 1-cup servings)

~For gluten free, use tamari in place of soy sauce~

Vegetable Brown Rice Medley: 1 serving = 1 cup

Energy (kcal)	329		
Total Fat (g)	5.4	Calcium (mg)	93
Total Carbohydrate (g)	61.3	Phosphorus (mg)	260
Total Protein (g)	9.5	Magnesium (mg)	125
% Calories from Fat	14	Iron (mg)	1.8
% Calories from Carbohydrate	76	Zinc (mg)	2.0
% Calories from Protein	10	Copper (mg)	0.4
Cholesterol (g)	0	Selenium (mcg)	29.3
Total Saturated Fatty Acids (g) (SFA)	1.0	Sodium (mg)	199
Total Monounsaturated Fatty Acids (g) (MUFA)	1.9	Potassium (mg)	217
Total Polyunsaturated Fatty Acids (g) (PUFA)	2.1		
Omega-3 Fatty Acids (g)	0.1		
% Calories from SFA	2.5	Linoleic Acid - PUFA (18:2) (g)	2.0
% Calories from MUFA	5.0	Linolenic Acid – PUFA (18:3) (g)	0.1
% Calories from PUFA	5.5		
Polyunsaturated to Saturated Fat (P:S) Ratio	2.2	Tryptophan (mg)	13
		Threonine (mg)	37
Total Dietary Fiber (g)	9.1	Isoleucine (mg)	42
Soluble Dietary Fiber (g)	1.3	Leucine (mg)	76
Insoluble Dietary Fiber (g)	7.8	Lysine (mg)	44
		Methionine (mg)	18
Total Vitamin A (mcg) (Retinol Activity Equivalents)	66	Phenylalanine (mg)	48
Vitamin D (calciferol) (mcg)	0.5	Valine (mg)	53
Vitamin E (mg) (Total Alpha-Tocopherol)	0.2	Histidine (mg)	25
Vitamin K (mg) (phylloquinone)	3.6		
Vitamin C (mg) (ascorbic acid)	0.6	Daidzein (mg)	2.9
Thiamin (mg) (vitamin B1)	0.3	Genistein (mg)	4.1
Riboflavin (mg) (vitamin B2)	0.1		
Niacin (mg) (vitamin B3)	4.2	Caffeine (mg)	0
Pantothenic Acid (mg)	1.1	Phytic Acid (mg)	546.4
Vitamin B6 (mg)	0.4	Oxalic Acid (mg)	23.7
Total Folate (mcg)	21	Choline (mg)	37.5
Vitamin B12 (mcg) (cobalamin)	0.0		
		Glycemic Index (glucose reference)	50
Beta-Carotene (mcg) (provitamin A carotenoid)	646	Glycemic Load (glucose reference)	26
Lutein + Zeaxanthin (mcg)	53		
Lycopene (mcg)	0		

BEANS AND BEAN PRODUCTS

Azuki Beans and Squash (Vegan; GF)

The combination of rich, sweet squash and nourishing, hearty beans make this a winning winter dish.

Ingredients

½ cup azuki beans

4 cups water, separated

1½ cups buttercup squash*

1/8 tsp salt

*Peel the squash, slice in half and core. Cut into medium-sized pieces and measure out 1½ cups. [Other types of winter squash can be used, such as butternut and acorn.]

Wash and drain beans. If time allows, soak beans for 5 hours or overnight in 1 cup water. Discard soaking water. [These beans can be prepared without pre-soaking, but it will take a few minutes longer for them to soften.] Place squash pieces in the bottom of a medium saucepan, put beans on top. Add enough water just to reach to top of the beans (1 cup). Bring to a boil, uncovered. Simmer for 15 minutes. Add 1 more cup of water, cover and simmer on low for one hour. Midway through the cooking process, add another cup of water and check occasionally to be sure beans do not dry out, adding additional water if needed. (Too much water will dilute the sweet squash taste, so use only the minimum amount needed). When beans start to soften, add salt and cook 5 more minutes. {This dish is more delicious (less bitter) when boiled rather than pressure cooked.} Sweetener and/or raisins can be included for a lighter, sweeter dish.

Yield: 2½ cups (5, ½-cup servings)

From: Kushi M and Jack A: *The Macrobiotic Path to Total Health*, NY: Ballantine Books, 2003, with permission from Alex Jack.

Azuki Beans and Squash: 1 serving = ½ cup

Energy (kcal)	203		
Total Fat (g)	0.4	Calcium (mg)	58
Total Carbohydrate (g)	40.6	Phosphorus (mg)	246
Total Protein (g)	11.0	Magnesium (mg)	82
% Calories from Fat	2	Iron (mg)	3.1
% Calories from Carbohydrate	80	Zinc (mg)	2.6
% Calories from Protein	18	Copper (mg)	0.5
Cholesterol (g)	0	Selenium (mcg)	1.9
Total Saturated Fatty Acids (g) (SFA)	0.1	Sodium (mg)	137
Total Monounsaturated Fatty Acids (g) (MUFA)	0.0	Potassium (mg)	909
Total Polyunsaturated Fatty Acids (g) (PUFA)	0.1		
Omega-3 Fatty Acids (g)	0.1		
% Calories from SFA	0.4	Linoleic Acid - PUFA (18:2) (g)	0.1
% Calories from MUFA	0.1	Linolenic Acid – PUFA (18:3) (g)	0.1
% Calories from PUFA	0.6		
Polyunsaturated to Saturated Fat (P:S) Ratio	1.5	Tryptophan (mg)	11
		Threonine (mg)	37
Total Dietary Fiber (g)	12.1	Isoleucine (mg)	44
Soluble Dietary Fiber (g)	2.8	Leucine (mg)	91
Insoluble Dietary Fiber (g)	9.3	Lysine (mg)	81
		Methionine (mg)	12
Total Vitamin A (mcg) (Retinol Activity Equivalents)	190	Phenylalanine (mg)	58
Vitamin D (calciferol) (mcg)	0	Valine (mg)	56
Vitamin E (mg) (Total Alpha-Tocopherol)	0.1	Histidine (mg)	29
Vitamin K (mg) (phylloquinone)	5.5		
Vitamin C (mg) (ascorbic acid)	7.0	Daidzein (mg)	0.4
Thiamin (mg) (vitamin B1)	0.2	Genistein (mg)	0.6
Riboflavin (mg) (vitamin B2)	0.1		
Niacin (mg) (vitamin B3)	1.3	Caffeine (mg)	0
Pantothenic Acid (mg)	0.8	Phytic Acid (mg)	682.4
Vitamin B6 (mg)	0.2	Oxalic Acid (mg)	35.2
Total Folate (mcg)	181	Choline (mg)	50.3
Vitamin B12 (mcg) (cobalamin)	0		
		Glycemic Index (glucose reference)	35
Beta-Carotene (mcg) (provitamin A carotenoid)	2,032	Glycemic Load (glucose reference)	10
Lutein + Zeaxanthin (mcg)	1,027		
Lycopene (mcg)	0		

Baked Azuki Beans (Vegan)

A variation on traditional baked beans, these cute small beans are light yet hearty. Well worth the effort, baked beans take just twice the time as regular beans and can be left alone in the oven while you bask in the incredible aroma!

Ingredients

1 cup azuki beans (6 ounces, dry)

2½ cups water

1 tsp olive oil

1 medium onion, diced (about 1 cup)

1 stalk celery, sliced (about ½ cup)

1 large apple (9 ounces), diced (~1½ cups)

1 Tbsp apple butter

2 tsp barley malt

¼ tsp salt

Optional: any dried herbs and spices

Wash azuki beans, add water and pressure cook for 1 hour.* When beans are almost ready, preheat oven to 375°F. Heat a small casserole pot with oil, sauté onions until they begin to soften, add celery and apples and stir for about 5 minutes. When beans have finished cooking, and pressure is completely down, remove cover and pour beans and all cooking liquid into casserole pot with the vegetables and apples. Mix well. Add apple butter, barley malt, and salt, along with your favorite herbs and/or spices. Cover and bake at 375 degrees for ½ hour, then reduce to 300 degrees for 30 minutes more. This will give sufficient time to let vegetables flavor the beans as they cook through.

*When the beans are separated from the liquid, it yields 2½ cups of cooked beans and ¾ cup water.

Yield: 4 cups (4, 1-cup servings)

Variation: Kidney or pinto beans may be used – either alone or in combination – in place of azuki beans for scrumptious baked beans.

Inspired by Marilyn Moser-Waxman, *The Nourishing Well*, Havertown, PA, www.thenourishingwell.com

Baked Azuki Beans: 1 serving = 1 cup

Energy (kcal)	256		
Total Fat (g)	1.4	Calcium (mg)	62
Total Carbohydrate (g)	51.0	Phosphorus (mg)	271
Total Protein (g)	11.8	Magnesium (mg)	86
% Calories from Fat	5	Iron (mg)	3.1
% Calories from Carbohydrate	79	Zinc (mg)	2.7
% Calories from Protein	16	Copper (mg)	0.5
Cholesterol (g)	0	Selenium (mcg)	2.5
Total Saturated Fatty Acids (g) (SFA)	0.2	Sodium (mg)	176
Total Monounsaturated Fatty Acids (g) (MUFA)	0.9	Potassium (mg)	927
Total Polyunsaturated Fatty Acids (g) (PUFA)	0.2		
Omega-3 Fatty Acids (g)	0.03		
% Calories from SFA	0.8	Linoleic Acid - PUFA (18:2) (g)	0.2
% Calories from MUFA	2.9	Linolenic Acid – PUFA (18:3) (g)	0.03
% Calories from PUFA	0.8		
Polyunsaturated to Saturated Fat (P:S) Ratio	0.9	Tryptophan (mg)	12
		Threonine (mg)	39
Total Dietary Fiber (g)	12.0	Isoleucine (mg)	46
Soluble Dietary Fiber (g)	1.8	Leucine (mg)	95
Insoluble Dietary Fiber (g)	10.2	Lysine (mg)	86
		Methionine (mg)	12
Total Vitamin A (mcg) (Retinol Activity Equivalents)	5	Phenylalanine (mg)	60
Vitamin D (calciferol) (mcg)	0	Valine (mg)	59
Vitamin E (mg) (Total Alpha-Tocopherol)	0.3	Histidine (mg)	30
Vitamin K (mg) (phylloquinone)	8.9		
Vitamin C (mg) (ascorbic acid)	5.0	Daidzein (mg)	0.4
Thiamin (mg) (vitamin B1)	0.2	Genistein (mg)	0.6
Riboflavin (mg) (vitamin B2)	0.1		
Niacin (mg) (vitamin B3)	1.5	Caffeine (mg)	0
Pantothenic Acid (mg)	0.7	Phytic Acid (mg)	736.0
Vitamin B6 (mg)	0.2	Oxalic Acid (mg)	38.8
Total Folate (mcg)	183	Choline (mg)	49.9
Vitamin B12 (mcg) (cobalamin)	0		
		Glycemic Index (glucose reference)	39
Beta-Carotene (mcg) (provitamin A carotenoid)	59	Glycemic Load (glucose reference)	15
Lutein + Zeaxanthin (mcg)	58		
Lycopene (mcg)	0		

Bean Burgers (Vegan)

Yummy burgers reminiscent of a backyard barbeque. Try them with a toasted bun, lettuce, tomato and other fixins for an interesting, satisfying high-fiber lunch. Cooked ahead of time, they make handy leftovers too.

Ingredients

1 large onion, diced (about 1¾ cups diced)

2 Tbsp + 1 tsp olive oil, divided

¼ tsp salt, divided

2 cups black beans, canned (rinsed + drained)

¼ cup boiling water

1/3 cup fresh cilantro, chopped

2 tsp fresh-squeezed lemon juice

½ tsp Dijon mustard

¼ tsp pepper

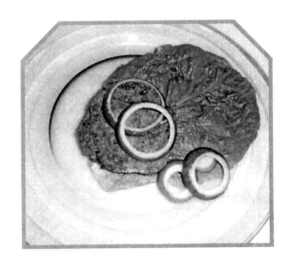

1 cup cooked brown rice (long-grain, esp. Jasmine, is very nice for this dish)

½ cup + 6 Tbsp oatmeal flakes, ground, divided

In a small skillet, sauté onion in 1 tsp olive oil until translucent, adding a pinch of salt near the end. Let cool.

Rinse and drain canned beans, and place in food processor, along with boiling water and process until smooth. Add cilantro, lemon juice, mustard, remaining salt, and pepper and blend. Move to a small bowl; add the cooked brown rice and sautéed onions. Grind oat flakes in a coffee grinder and add ½ cup to this mixture. Mix well and let rest for about 30 minutes, for the oat flour to absorb water and make the patties easy to form.

Prepare a plate with 6 Tbsp of oat flour and another one to make 3" patties. Dredge each patty in the oat flour.

In a large skillet, heat 1 Tbsp of oil and add the burgers. Cook over medium-high heat for at least 3 minutes, until they brown and get crispy on the outside, turn over and add 1 more Tbsp of oil and fry the other side until brown. (The burger will be soft on the inside.)

Remove and serve with red onion, lettuce and ketchup.

Yield: 9 burgers, 3" diameter

Bean Burger: 1 serving = 1 burger (3-inch diameter)

Energy (kcal)	151		
Total Fat (g)	4.5	Calcium (mg)	40
Total Carbohydrate (g)	23.1	Phosphorus (mg)	115
Total Protein (g)	5.1	Magnesium (mg)	44
% Calories from Fat	26	Iron (mg)	1.4
% Calories from Carbohydrate	62	Zinc (mg)	0.9
% Calories from Protein	12	Copper (mg)	0.2
Cholesterol (g)	0	Selenium (mcg)	5.7
Total Saturated Fatty Acids (g) (SFA)	0.7	Sodium (mg)	75
Total Monounsaturated Fatty Acids (g) (MUFA)	2.9	Potassium (mg)	236
Total Polyunsaturated Fatty Acids (g) (PUFA)	0.8		
Omega-3 Fatty Acids (g)	0.1		
% Calories from SFA	3.8	Linoleic Acid - PUFA (18:2) (g)	0.7
% Calories from MUFA	16.6	Linolenic Acid – PUFA (18:3) (g)	0.1
% Calories from PUFA	4.7		
Polyunsaturated to Saturated Fat (P:S) Ratio	1.3	Tryptophan (mg)	7
		Threonine (mg)	17
Total Dietary Fiber (g)	5.9	Isoleucine (mg)	22
Soluble Dietary Fiber (g)	0.8	Leucine (mg)	41
Insoluble Dietary Fiber (g)	5.1	Lysine (mg)	29
		Methionine (mg)	7
Total Vitamin A (mcg) (Retinol Activity Equivalents)	2	Phenylalanine (mg)	27
Vitamin D (calciferol) (mcg)	0	Valine (mg)	29
Vitamin E (mg) (Total Alpha-Tocopherol)	0.6	Histidine (mg)	12
Vitamin K (mg) (phylloquinone)	4.7		
Vitamin C (mg) (ascorbic acid)	2.4	Daidzein (mg)	0.0
Thiamin (mg) (vitamin B1)	0.2	Genistein (mg)	0.0
Riboflavin (mg) (vitamin B2)	0.1		
Niacin (mg) (vitamin B3)	0.7	Caffeine (mg)	0
Pantothenic Acid (mg)	0.3	Phytic Acid (mg)	169.7
Vitamin B6 (mg)	0.1	Oxalic Acid (mg)	26.1
Total Folate (mcg)	61	Choline (mg)	24.3
Vitamin B12 (mcg) (cobalamin)	0		
		Glycemic Index (glucose reference)	44
Beta-Carotene (mcg) (provitamin A carotenoid)	25	Glycemic Load (glucose reference)	8
Lutein + Zeaxanthin (mcg)	21		
Lycopene (mcg)	0		

Bean Stew (Vegan)

This colorful, one-pot meal lends itself to creative variations, from the type of beans to your favorite vegetables and seasonings. A crowd-pleaser: rich and satisfying - packed with nutrition.

Ingredients

1 cup dry pinto beans
1 cup dry kidney beans
5 cups water
2 tsp olive oil, divided
1 medium onion, diced (~1¼ cups)
2 medium carrots, diced (~1 cup)
5 medium button mushrooms, sliced (~1½ cups)
2 plum tomatoes, chopped tomatoes (~1¼ cups)
5 cloves of garlic, minced
1 cup soy crumbles
1¼ cups salt-free, canned (or fresh) corn kernels
1 Tbsp low-sodium soy sauce
½ tsp salt
1 tsp black pepper
¼ tsp red pepper
1/8 tsp cinnamon (optional)
¼ cup cilantro
¼ cup parsley
¼ cup fresh basil

Wash beans and drain, picking out any stones and soak in 4 cups of water for 5 to 6 hours before cooking (or overnight). [If you are in a hurry, you can pressure cook 5 minutes, then let sit for one hour and proceed to cook them as follows.] Drain beans of the soaking water, then add fresh water to cover with a 1-inch layer of water (this is about 5 cups of water). Pressure cook for 1 hour. Set aside.

Heat medium skillet and add 1 tsp olive oil. When the oil it hot, sauté the onions, carrots, mushrooms and tomatoes until softened (about 5 minutes). In a small skillet, heat the other 1 tsp of oil and sauté the garlic, then add the soy crumbles and pan fry, stirring often, for about 2 minutes. Add all the cooked vegetable and soy ingredients to the beans. Mix in corn kernels; simmer over medium heat for 20 minutes or more. Add soy sauce, salt, black pepper, red pepper and cinnamon and simmer briefly. Just before serving, adjust spices; add fresh herbs: cilantro, parsley and basil.

Yield: 10 cups: (10, 1-cup servings)

Bean Stew: 1 serving = 1 cup

Energy (kcal)	205		
Total Fat (g)	2.1	Calcium (mg)	69
Total Carbohydrate (g)	31.2	Phosphorus (mg)	237
Total Protein (g)	17.7	Magnesium (mg)	57
% Calories from Fat	9	Iron (mg)	4.0
% Calories from Carbohydrate	60	Zinc (mg)	1.6
% Calories from Protein	31	Copper (mg)	0.4
Cholesterol (g)	0	Selenium (mcg)	6.7
Total Saturated Fatty Acids (g) (SFA)	0.3	Sodium (mg)	185
Total Monounsaturated Fatty Acids (g) (MUFA)	0.9	Potassium (mg)	555
Total Polyunsaturated Fatty Acids (g) (PUFA)	0.7		
Omega-3 Fatty Acids (g)	0.2		
% Calories from SFA	1.4	Linoleic Acid - PUFA (18:2) (g)	0.5
% Calories from MUFA	3.8	Linolenic Acid – PUFA (18:3) (g)	0.2
% Calories from PUFA	2.8		
Polyunsaturated to Saturated Fat (P:S) Ratio	2.1	Tryptophan (mg)	22
		Threonine (mg)	67
Total Dietary Fiber (g)	8.9	Isoleucine (mg)	84
Soluble Dietary Fiber (g)	2.9	Leucine (mg)	147
Insoluble Dietary Fiber (g)	6.0	Lysine (mg)	115
		Methionine (mg)	24
Total Vitamin A (mcg) (Retinol Activity Equivalents)	114	Phenylalanine (mg)	96
Vitamin D (calciferol) (mcg)	0.0	Valine (mg)	95
Vitamin E (mg) (Total Alpha-Tocopherol)	0.9	Histidine (mg)	47
Vitamin K (mg) (phylloquinone)	39.2		
Vitamin C (mg) (ascorbic acid)	10.2	Daidzein (mg)	3.8
Thiamin (mg) (vitamin B1)	0.2	Genistein (mg)	6.1
Riboflavin (mg) (vitamin B2)	0.1		
Niacin (mg) (vitamin B3)	1.4	Caffeine (mg)	0
Pantothenic Acid (mg)	0.6	Phytic Acid (mg)	386.0
Vitamin B6 (mg)	0.3	Oxalic Acid (mg)	48.4
Total Folate (mcg)	172	Choline (mg)	49.6
Vitamin B12 (mcg) (cobalamin)	0		
		Glycemic Index (glucose reference)	39
Beta-Carotene (mcg) (provitamin A carotenoid)	1,134	Glycemic Load (glucose reference)	9
Lutein + Zeaxanthin (mcg)	433		
Lycopene (mcg)	538		

Black Bean Soup (Vegan; GF)

A delicate, velvety bowl of goodness. The potatoes add an interesting texture contrast. A tribute to the versatile black bean!

Ingredients

1 cup dried black beans

6 cups water, divided

2 bay leaves

1 Tbsp olive oil

2 cloves garlic, minced (about 1 Tbsp)

1 medium onion, diced finely (1 cup)

1 stalk celery (20 g), diced finely (½ cup)

1 medium carrot, diced finely (½ cup)

1 fresh plum tomato, chopped

1 Tbsp mirin (cooking wine)

½ tsp black pepper

¼ tsp Italian seasoning

½ tsp Kosher salt

½ cup chopped cilantro

1 medium potato (about 7 oz), cut in cubes (about 1½ cups of cubes)

Wash and soak 1 cup black beans in 2½ cups water. Soak 5-6 hours or overnight. (This yields 2¼ cups of beans). Drain and rinse the beans; place in pressure cooker, along with 2½ cups water and the bay leaves. Pressure cook beans for 1 hour.

Heat a medium, nonstick skillet, add olive oil, and sauté garlic, onions, celery, and carrots until onions start to soften. When beans are finished and pressure is down fully, remove lid and take out bay leaves. Add in the sautéed vegetables, tomatoes, water, mirin, pepper, Italian seasoning and salt. Simmer over medium heat for about 20 minutes more.

Add cilantro and mix well. Puree using a hand blender (or place in a blender or food processor and return to pot). Add potatoes and cook soup over medium heat until potatoes are tender (about 10 minutes).

Note: Other seasonings can be used: chili powder, cumin, crushed red pepper; 1/3 cup canned, chopped tomatoes (salt-free) can be used instead of fresh.

Yield: 6 cups (4, 1½-cup servings)

Black Bean Soup: 1 serving = 1½ cups

Energy (kcal)	251		
Total Fat (g)	4.2	Calcium (mg)	62
Total Carbohydrate (g)	43.5	Phosphorus (mg)	206
Total Protein (g)	11.9	Magnesium (mg)	99
% Calories from Fat	15	Iron (mg)	3.1
% Calories from Carbohydrate	69	Zinc (mg)	1.6
% Calories from Protein	16	Copper (mg)	0.4
Cholesterol (g)	0	Selenium (mcg)	2.3
Total Saturated Fatty Acids (g) (SFA)	0.7	Sodium (mg)	356
Total Monounsaturated Fatty Acids (g) (MUFA)	2.5	Potassium (mg)	740
Total Polyunsaturated Fatty Acids (g) (PUFA)	0.7		
Omega-3 Fatty Acids (g)	0.2		
% Calories from SFA	2.3	Linoleic Acid - PUFA (18:2) (g)	0.5
% Calories from MUFA	8.9	Linolenic Acid – PUFA (18:3) (g)	0.2
% Calories from PUFA	2.4		
Polyunsaturated to Saturated Fat (P:S) Ratio	1.1	Tryptophan (mg)	0.14
		Threonine (mg)	0.50
Total Dietary Fiber (g)	12.2	Isoleucine (mg)	0.51
Soluble Dietary Fiber (g)	1.1	Leucine (mg)	0.90
Insoluble Dietary Fiber (g)	11.1	Lysine (mg)	0.79
		Methionine (mg)	0.17
Total Vitamin A (mcg) (Retinol Activity Equivalents)	142	Phenylalanine (mg)	0.61
Vitamin D (calciferol) (mcg)	0	Valine (mg)	0.61
Vitamin E (mg) (Total Alpha-Tocopherol)	1.0	Histidine (mg)	0.32
Vitamin K (mg) (phylloquinone)	21.1		
Vitamin C (mg) (ascorbic acid)	13.1	Daidzein (mg)	0
Thiamin (mg) (vitamin B1)	0.4	Genistein (mg)	.005
Riboflavin (mg) (vitamin B2)	0.1		
Niacin (mg) (vitamin B3)	1.5	Caffeine (mg)	0
Pantothenic Acid (mg)	0.6	Phytic Acid (mg)	492.5
Vitamin B6 (mg)	0.3	Oxalic Acid (mg)	104.6
Total Folate (mcg)	189	Choline (mg)	47.7
Vitamin B12 (mcg) (cobalamin)	0		
		Glycemic Index (glucose reference)	38
Beta-Carotene (mcg) (provitamin A carotenoid)	1430	Glycemic Load (glucose reference)	12
Lutein + Zeaxanthin (mcg)	195		
Lycopene (mcg)	844		

Chickpea Salad (Vegan; GF w/Mod)

This is a joyful picnic salad. Colorful, protein-rich and tasting better with time, it is an ideal summer dish. While canned chickpeas can be used for this recipe, chickpeas prepared from scratch lend a more delicious taste and an appealing consistency.

Ingredients

1 cup dried chickpeas

6 cups water, divided

½ cup daikon radish, cubed

½ cup carrots, cubed

½ cup cauliflower cut into small flowerets

½ cup chopped Italian parsley

2 red radishes, sliced paper thin

3 Tbsp grated onion (2 oz)

5 tsp umeboshi plum vinegar*

2 tsp low-sodium soy sauce

1 tsp balsamic vinegar

¼ tsp sesame oil

* Or substitute with 2 tsp red wine vinegar plus ¼ tsp salt.

Wash chickpeas and soak overnight in 3 cups of water. Drain water and add 2 cups more water. Pressure cook for 1 hour (this makes 2½ cups of cooked chickpeas). Cool and drain, but save cooking liquid. In a small saucepan, boil the daikon, carrot and cauliflower for 3 minutes. Put chopped parsley at the bottom of a strainer and when vegetables are done, drain them through this strainer, blanching the parsley. Drain well and add all the cooked vegetables along with radishes to the chickpeas in a large bowl. In a small mixing bowl, combine 1 cup water, ¼ cup of the reserved cooking liquid (if canned chickpeas are used, simply use plain water instead). Add the grated onion, plum vinegar, soy sauce, balsamic vinegar and sesame oil. (Add more grated onion, soy sauce or vinegar to adjust taste.) Mix into the salad and refrigerate for a couple of hours or more to marinate.

Yield: 4½ cups (4½ servings of 1 cup)

Note: if you are using canned chickpeas, use 2½ cups of canned, drained and rinsed. In place of reserved cooking liquid, simply use plain water for marinade. However, cooking chickpeas from dried is <u>highly recommended,</u> for better flavor and softer texture.

~For gluten free, use tamari in place of soy sauce~

Inspired by Gretchen DeWire

Chickpea Salad: 1 serving = 1 cup

Energy (kcal)	172		
Total Fat (g)	2.74	Calcium (mg)	69
Total Carbohydrate (g)	29.3	Phosphorus (mg)	176
Total Protein (g)	9.0	Magnesium (mg)	55
% Calories from Fat	13	Iron (mg)	3.3
% Calories from Carbohydrate	69	Zinc (mg)	1.6
% Calories from Protein	18	Copper (mg)	0.4
Cholesterol (g)	0	Selenium (mcg)	3.7
Total Saturated Fatty Acids (g) (SFA)	0.3	Sodium (mg)	237
Total Monounsaturated Fatty Acids (g) (MUFA)	0.7	Potassium (mg)	419
Total Polyunsaturated Fatty Acids (g) (PUFA)	1.2		
Omega-3 Fatty Acids (g)	0.05		
% Calories from SFA	1.5	Linoleic Acid - PUFA (18:2) (g)	1.2
% Calories from MUFA	3.2	Linolenic Acid - PUFA (18:3) (g)	0.05
% Calories from PUFA	5.9		
Polyunsaturated to Saturated Fat (P:S) Ratio	3.9	Tryptophan (mg)	9
		Threonine (mg)	35
Total Dietary Fiber (g)	8.3	Isoleucine (mg)	38
Soluble Dietary Fiber (g)	2.9	Leucine (mg)	63
Insoluble Dietary Fiber (g)	5.4	Lysine (mg)	60
		Methionine (mg)	12
Total Vitamin A (mcg) (Retinol Activity Equivalents)	141	Phenylalanine (mg)	47
Vitamin D (calciferol) (mcg)	0	Valine (mg)	38
Vitamin E (mg) (Total Alpha-Tocopherol)	0.5	Histidine (mg)	24
Vitamin K (mg) (phylloquinone)	116.7		
Vitamin C (mg) (ascorbic acid)	19.1	Daidzein (mg)	0.0
Thiamin (mg) (vitamin B1)	0.1	Genistein (mg)	0.1
Riboflavin (mg) (vitamin B2)	0.1		
Niacin (mg) (vitamin B3)	0.8	Caffeine (mg)	0
Pantothenic Acid (mg)	0.4	Phytic Acid (mg)	129.0
Vitamin B6 (mg)	0.2	Oxalic Acid (mg)	21.1
Total Folate (mcg)	182	Choline (mg)	48.8
Vitamin B12 (mcg) (cobalamin)	0		
		Glycemic Index (glucose reference)	39
Beta-Carotene (mcg) (provitamin A carotenoid)	1,440	Glycemic Load (glucose reference)	8
Lutein + Zeaxanthin (mcg)	465		
Lycopene (mcg)	0		

Curry Chickpeas (Vegan; GF)

Colorful and juicy, chickpeas are highlighted with an interesting, full-bodied flavor here. It's a fine complement to your favorite bread or grain dish.

Ingredients

1 Tbsp olive oil

3 cloves garlic, sliced

Medium onion, chopped

2 Tbsp curry powder

1 potato, peeled & diced (Yukon gold, 1½ cups diced)

1¾ cup chickpeas, canned (preferably salt-free) or
   cooked from dried (if canned, rinsed & drained)

1 small carrot, diced (½ cup diced)

3 cups + 2 Tbsp water

3 Tbsp raisins

¼ tsp salt

2 Tbsp organic corn starch

1 Tbsp fresh basil, sliced thinly

¼ cup chopped fresh cilantro (or parsley)

1 tsp lemon juice

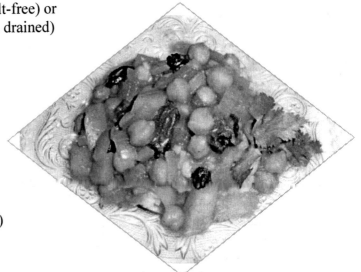

In a large skillet or medium pot, heat oil, and sauté garlic and onions for a few minutes – until onions get very soft. Add curry and sauté for a couple of minutes. Add diced potatoes, chickpeas and diced carrot, sauté briefly then add 3 cups of water and the raisins. Simmer, covered, until the potatoes become tender. Add salt (adjust amount if canned chickpeas had added salt). In a small bowl, dilute the corn starch with 2 Tbsp of water, then mix in, simmering for 1 minute until the mixture becomes thickened. Add in fresh basil and cilantro (and any additional fresh herbs desired), along with the lemon juice; stir. Serve over brown rice* (or with bread).

Yield: 5 cups (5, 1-cup servings)

*Prepare rice separately. Jasmine rice is very nice for this dish.

Curry Chickpeas: 1 serving = 1 cup

Energy (kcal)	208		
Total Fat (g)	4.7	Calcium (mg)	64
Total Carbohydrate (g)	36.9	Phosphorus (mg)	143
Total Protein (g)	6.8	Magnesium (mg)	50
% Calories from Fat	19	Iron (mg)	2.8
% Calories from Carbohydrate	70	Zinc (mg)	1.2
% Calories from Protein	11	Copper (mg)	0.4
Cholesterol (g)	0	Selenium (mcg)	3.3
Total Saturated Fatty Acids (g) (SFA)	0.6	Sodium (mg)	84
Total Monounsaturated Fatty Acids (g) (MUFA)	2.5	Potassium (mg)	466
Total Polyunsaturated Fatty Acids (g) (PUFA)	1.1		
Omega-3 Fatty Acids (g)	0.1		
% Calories from SFA	2.5	Linoleic Acid - PUFA (18:2) (g)	1.0
% Calories from MUFA	10.3	Linolenic Acid – PUFA (18:3) (g)	0.1
% Calories from PUFA	4.3		
Polyunsaturated to Saturated Fat (P:S) Ratio	1.7	Tryptophan (mg)	7
		Threonine (mg)	25
Total Dietary Fiber (g)	6.2	Isoleucine (mg)	27
Soluble Dietary Fiber (g)	0.9	Leucine (mg)	44
Insoluble Dietary Fiber (g)	4.5	Lysine (mg)	42
		Methionine (mg)	9
Total Vitamin A (mcg) (Retinol Activity Equivalents)	106	Phenylalanine (mg)	33
Vitamin D (calciferol) (mcg)	0	Valine (mg)	28
Vitamin E (mg) (Total Alpha-Tocopherol)	1.3	Histidine (mg)	17
Vitamin K (mg) (phylloquinone)	14.0		
Vitamin C (mg) (ascorbic acid)	7.2	Daidzein (mg)	0.0
Thiamin (mg) (vitamin B1)	0.1	Genistein (mg)	0.3
Riboflavin (mg) (vitamin B2)	0.1		
Niacin (mg) (vitamin B3)	1.1	Caffeine (mg)	0
Pantothenic Acid (mg)	0.5	Phytic Acid (mg)	117.5
Vitamin B6 (mg)	0.3	Oxalic Acid (mg)	41.7
Total Folate (mcg)	112	Choline (mg)	35.6
Vitamin B12 (mcg) (cobalamin)	0		
		Glycemic Index (glucose reference)	57
Beta-Carotene (mcg) (provitamin A carotenoid)	1,052	Glycemic Load (glucose reference)	17
Lutein + Zeaxanthin (mcg)	123		
Lycopene (mcg)	0		

Lentil Pasta Soup (Vegan; GF w/Mod)

Pressure-cooking lentils gives an amazing consistency: smooth, digestible and creamy. This recipe for a hearty, one-pot-meal is just waiting for your creative spin!

Ingredients

1 cup dried lentils (green or red)

3 cups water + 1½ cups

2 tsp olive oil

1 small onion, diced (3/4 cup)

1 large carrot, sliced (3/4 cup)

1 large stalk celery, sliced (½ cup)

½ cup pasta (elbow)

¼ cup chopped fresh Italian parsley

1 Tbsp fresh basil

1 tsp dried Italian seasoning

½ tsp oregano

⅛ tsp salt

¼ tsp black pepper

Wash lentils (checking for and discarding any stones) and put in a pressure cooker. Cover and bring up to pressure, cooking on low for 30 minutes over medium heat. In a medium soup pot, heat oil, add chopped onions and cook 1-2 minutes, then add in carrots and celery. Add 1½ cups water and simmer over medium heat for about 5 minutes or until vegetables are tender.

When pressure comes down on lentils, remove lid, add to soup pot with vegetables and simmer. Add pasta and cook until it is just tender, then add fresh basil, dried Italian seasoning, oregano, salt and pepper; simmer for another 2 minutes, and serve.

Yield: 6 cups (6, 1-cup servings)

~Gluten-free if rice pasta is used instead of wheat macaroni~

Lentil Soup: 1 serving = 1 cup

Energy (kcal)	179		
Total Fat (g)	2.2	Calcium (mg)	42
Total Carbohydrate (g)	30.6	Phosphorus (mg)	191
Total Protein (g)	10.2	Magnesium (mg)	45
% Calories from Fat	11	Iron (mg)	3.9
% Calories from Carbohydrate	69	Zinc (mg)	1.4
% Calories from Protein	20	Copper (mg)	0.3
Cholesterol (g)	0	Selenium (mcg)	10.6
Total Saturated Fatty Acids (g) (SFA)	0.3	Sodium (mg)	219
Total Monounsaturated Fatty Acids (g) (MUFA)	1.2	Potassium (mg)	447
Total Polyunsaturated Fatty Acids (g) (PUFA)	0.5		
Omega-3 Fatty Acids (g)	0.1		
% Calories from SFA	1.6	Linoleic Acid - PUFA (18:2) (g)	0.4
% Calories from MUFA	6.0	Linolenic Acid – PUFA (18:3) (g)	0.1
% Calories from PUFA	2.2		
Polyunsaturated to Saturated Fat (P:S) Ratio	1.4	Tryptophan (mg)	10
		Threonine (mg)	38
Total Dietary Fiber (g)	6.7	Isoleucine (mg)	43
Soluble Dietary Fiber (g)	0.7	Leucine (mg)	74
Insoluble Dietary Fiber (g)	5.9	Lysine (mg)	63
		Methionine (mg)	9
Total Vitamin A (mcg) (Retinol Activity Equivalents)	135	Phenylalanine (mg)	50
Vitamin D (calciferol) (mcg)	0	Valine (mg)	49
Vitamin E (mg) (Total Alpha-Tocopherol)	0.6	Histidine (mg)	28
Vitamin K (mg) (phylloquinone)	53.9		
Vitamin C (mg) (ascorbic acid)	6.9	Daidzein (mg)	0.0
Thiamin (mg) (vitamin B1)	0.3	Genistein (mg)	0.0
Riboflavin (mg) (vitamin B2)	0.1		
Niacin (mg) (vitamin B3)	1.6	Caffeine (mg)	0
Pantothenic Acid (mg)	0.7	Phytic Acid (mg)	172.2
Vitamin B6 (mg)	0.2	Oxalic Acid (mg)	18.4
Total Folate (mcg)	193	Choline (mg)	34.3
Vitamin B12 (mcg) (cobalamin)	0		
		Glycemic Index (glucose reference)	33
Beta-Carotene (mcg) (provitamin A carotenoid)	1,356	Glycemic Load (glucose reference)	8
Lutein + Zeaxanthin (mcg)	296		
Lycopene (mcg)	0		

Quick Red Lentil Spread (Vegan; GF)

This tasty, full-bodied spread can be used as an accompaniment for chips and crackers or as a spread for bread or toast. Chock full of nutrition, it can be made well in advance of company.

Ingredients

½ cup dry red lentils*

1 cup water*

½ cup walnuts, chopped

½ tsp olive oil

¾ cup onion, chopped

3 Tbsp fresh basil chopped

½ tsp sea salt

½ tsp balsamic vinegar

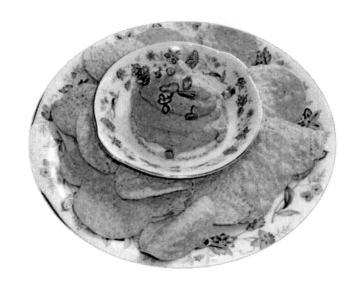

*It is easier to pressure cook a larger amount of lentils, so start with 1 cup of lentils and 2 cups of water. This makes about 2½ cups of cooked lentils, so you can use one-half of that (1¼ cups cooked) for this recipe.

Pressure-cook the lentils for 30 minutes. Toast walnuts carefully in a skillet over medium-low heat, stirring frequently. In a small skillet, heat olive oil and sauté onion over medium heat until translucent. In a food processor, blend the walnuts to a crumbly texture. Add 1¼ cups cooked lentils, onion, basil, salt and vinegar; blend until smooth and creamy.

Yield: 2¼ cups (9, ¼-cup servings)

Note: This is a basic recipe, which is mild and can easily be "spiced up" as desired, with extra herbs, garlic, more vinegar, red pepper, green onion, etc.

From Verne Varona's *Exceptional Health* seminars

Quick Red Lentil Spread: 1 serving = ¼ cup

Energy (kcal)	82		
Total Fat (g)	4.6	Calcium (mg)	16
Total Carbohydrate (g)	7.7	Phosphorus (mg)	77
Total Protein (g)	3.7	Magnesium (mg)	22
% Calories from Fat	47	Iron (mg)	1.2
% Calories from Carbohydrate	38	Zinc (mg)	0.6
% Calories from Protein	15	Copper (mg)	0.2
Cholesterol (g)	0	Selenium (mcg)	1.2
Total Saturated Fatty Acids (g) (SFA)	0.5	Sodium (mg)	131
Total Monounsaturated Fatty Acids (g) (MUFA)	0.8	Potassium (mg)	152
Total Polyunsaturated Fatty Acids (g) (PUFA)	3.2		
Omega-3 Fatty Acids (g)	0.6		
% Calories from SFA	4.6	Linoleic Acid - PUFA (18:2) (g)	2.5
% Calories from MUFA	8.1	Linolenic Acid – PUFA (18:3) (g)	0.6
% Calories from PUFA	32.2		
Polyunsaturated to Saturated Fat (P:S) Ratio	7.0	Tryptophan (mg)	4
		Threonine (mg)	13
Total Dietary Fiber (g)	2.2	Isoleucine (mg)	16
Soluble Dietary Fiber (g)	0.2	Leucine (mg)	26
Insoluble Dietary Fiber (g)	2.0	Lysine (mg)	21
		Methionine (mg)	4
Total Vitamin A (mcg) (Retinol Activity Equivalents)	3	Phenylalanine (mg)	17
Vitamin D (calciferol) (mcg)	0	Valine (mg)	18
Vitamin E (mg) (Total Alpha-Tocopherol)	0.1	Histidine (mg)	10
Vitamin K (mg) (phylloquinone)	4.5		
Vitamin C (mg) (ascorbic acid)	1.2	Daidzein (mg)	0.0
Thiamin (mg) (vitamin B1)	0.1	Genistein (mg)	0.0
Riboflavin (mg) (vitamin B2)	0.0		
Niacin (mg) (vitamin B3)	0.4	Caffeine (mg)	0
Pantothenic Acid (mg)	0.2	Phytic Acid (mg)	83.5
Vitamin B6 (mg)	0.1	Oxalic Acid (mg)	8.3
Total Folate (mcg)	58	Choline (mg)	12.4
Vitamin B12 (mcg) (cobalamin)	0.0		
		Glycemic Index (glucose reference)	27
Beta-Carotene (mcg) (provitamin A carotenoid)	30	Glycemic Load (glucose reference)	1
Lutein + Zeaxanthin (mcg)	51		
Lycopene (mcg)	0		

Red Pepper Hummus (Vegan; GF)

Roasted red pepper is a natural complement to chickpeas and really adds a new dimension to ordinary hummus. Great as a vegetable dip, a sandwich spread or butter-substitute.

Ingredients

1¾ cups garbanzo beans (chick peas), drained – salt free

1 roasted red pepper (packed in oil, rinsed + drained)

2 Tbsp olive oil

1 Tbsp tahini (or roasted sesame butter)

5 tsp fresh lemon juice

1 Tbsp water (more or less for desired consistency)

2 cloves garlic, minced

¼ tsp salt

¼ cup of chopped fresh parsley (or fresh cilantro)

In a food processor (or blender), combine beans, red pepper, oil, tahini, lemon juice, water, garlic and salt; blend into a thick paste. Add parsley and blend just briefly (to avoid bitterness). Chill and serve with whole wheat pita triangles.

OPTIONAL
¼ tsp cayenne pepper

¼ tsp cumin

Yield: 1¾ cups (7, ¼-cup servings)

Adapted from recipe of student Brenda Korban

Red Pepper Hummus: 1 serving = ¼ cup

Energy (kcal)	124		
Total Fat (g)	6.5	Calcium (mg)	36
Total Carbohydrate (g)	13.2	Phosphorus (mg)	90
Total Protein (g)	4.2	Magnesium (mg)	25
% Calories from Fat	46	Iron (mg)	1.6
% Calories from Carbohydrate	42	Zinc (mg)	0.8
% Calories from Protein	12	Copper (mg)	0.2
Cholesterol (g)	0	Selenium (mcg)	1.7
Total Saturated Fatty Acids (g) (SFA)	0.9	Sodium (mg)	105
Total Monounsaturated Fatty Acids (g) (MUFA)	3.8	Potassium (mg)	187
Total Polyunsaturated Fatty Acids (g) (PUFA)	1.4		
Omega-3 Fatty Acids (g)	0.6		
% Calories from SFA	6.1	Linoleic Acid - PUFA (18:2) (g)	1.4
% Calories from MUFA	26.8	Linolenic Acid – PUFA (18:3) (g)	0.06
% Calories from PUFA	10.0		
Polyunsaturated to Saturated Fat (P:S) Ratio	1.7	Tryptophan (mg)	5
		Threonine (mg)	16
Total Dietary Fiber (g)	3.0	Isoleucine (mg)	18
Soluble Dietary Fiber (g)	0.4	Leucine (mg)	30
Insoluble Dietary Fiber (g)	2.6	Lysine (mg)	27
		Methionine (mg)	6
Total Vitamin A (mcg) (Retinol Activity Equivalents)	28	Phenylalanine (mg)	22
Vitamin D (calciferol) (mcg)	0	Valine (mg)	18
Vitamin E (mg) (Total Alpha-Tocopherol)	1.0	Histidine (mg)	12
Vitamin K (mg) (phylloquinone)	40.0		
Vitamin C (mg) (ascorbic acid)	26.0	Daidzein (mg)	0
Thiamin (mg) (vitamin B1)	0.1	Genistein (mg)	0.0
Riboflavin (mg) (vitamin B2)	0.0		
Niacin (mg) (vitamin B3)	0.4	Caffeine (mg)	0
Pantothenic Acid (mg)	0.2	Phytic Acid (mg)	98.0
Vitamin B6 (mg)	0.1	Oxalic Acid (mg)	18.9
Total Folate (mcg)	78	Choline (mg)	19.5
Vitamin B12 (mcg) (cobalamin)	0		
		Glycemic Index (glucose reference)	42
Beta-Carotene (mcg) (provitamin A carotenoid)	301	Glycemic Load (glucose reference)	4
Lutein + Zeaxanthin (mcg)	125		
Lycopene (mcg)	0		

Split Pea Soup (Vegan; GF w/Mod)

A creamy, dreamy, comfort-food; this split pea soup has a full-bodied, savory flavor. A satisfying and heart-warming dish!

Ingredients

1 cup dried split peas (yellow or green)

¼ tsp sesame oil

½ large (or 1 small) onion, diced (1 cup)

1 carrot cut in half moons (½ cup)

1 stalk of celery, sliced

4+1½ cups water

2 Tbsp white miso (or to taste)

½ tsp. black pepper

¼ tsp oregano

½ tsp dried Italian seasoning

1 Tbsp fresh basil

2 Tbsp fresh cilantro

Wash split peas and put in a pressure cooker. Add 4 cups of water and boil for about 15 minutes, skimming any foam that surfaces. Cover and bring up to pressure, then cook over low heat (to maintain pressure) for 40 minutes.

In a soup pot, heat oil, sauté onions briefly, then add celery and carrots; cook for a couple minutes. Add water to just cover (about 1½ cups) and simmer over medium heat for ~10 minutes, until vegetables soften.

Pour cooked peas over the vegetables, stir, and then simmer about 10 more minutes. Add pepper, oregano, and dried Italian seasoning. In a small bowl, dilute miso with some hot soup, and add back to the pot. Simmer briefly. Just before serving, mix in fresh basil and cilantro.

Yield: 5 cups (5, 1-cup servings)

~Gluten-free if brown-rice miso is used in place of white miso~

Split Pea Soup: 1 serving = 1 cup

Energy (kcal)	148		
Total Fat (g)	0.9	Calcium (mg)	61
Total Carbohydrate (g)	27.3	Phosphorus (mg)	119
Total Protein (g)	9.1	Magnesium (mg)	49
% Calories from Fat	5	Iron (mg)	1.7
% Calories from Carbohydrate	74	Zinc (mg)	1.2
% Calories from Protein	21	Copper (mg)	0.2
Cholesterol (g)	0	Selenium (mcg)	1.2
Total Saturated Fatty Acids (g) (SFA)	0.1	Sodium (mg)	157
Total Monounsaturated Fatty Acids (g) (MUFA)	0.2	Potassium (mg)	472
Total Polyunsaturated Fatty Acids (g) (PUFA)	0.4		
Omega-3 Fatty Acids (g)	0.1		
% Calories from SFA	0.8	Linoleic Acid - PUFA (18:2) (g)	0.4
% Calories from MUFA	1.3	Linolenic Acid – PUFA (18:3) (g)	0.1
% Calories from PUFA	2.4		
Polyunsaturated to Saturated Fat (P:S) Ratio	2.8	Tryptophan (mg)	10
		Threonine (mg)	34
Total Dietary Fiber (g)	11.6	Isoleucine (mg)	38
Soluble Dietary Fiber (g)	0.2	Leucine (mg)	64
Insoluble Dietary Fiber (g)	11.2	Lysine (mg)	63
		Methionine (mg)	9
Total Vitamin A (mcg) (Retinol Activity Equivalents)	107	Phenylalanine (mg)	41
Vitamin D (calciferol) (mcg)	0	Valine (mg)	0.421
Vitamin E (mg) (Total Alpha-Tocopherol)	0.2	Histidine (mg)	0.217
Vitamin K (mg) (phylloquinone)	17.4		
Vitamin C (mg) (ascorbic acid)	3.2	Daidzein (mg)	1.3
Thiamin (mg) (vitamin B1)	0.2	Genistein (mg)	0.8
Riboflavin (mg) (vitamin B2)	0.1		
Niacin (mg) (vitamin B3)	1.1	Caffeine (mg)	0
Pantothenic Acid (mg)	0.7	Phytic Acid (mg)	109.7
Vitamin B6 (mg)	0.1	Oxalic Acid (mg)	13.0
Total Folate (mcg)	73	Choline (mg)	38.3
Vitamin B12 (mcg) (cobalamin)	0		
		Glycemic Index (glucose reference)	42
Beta-Carotene (mcg) (provitamin A carotenoid)	1,059	Glycemic Load (glucose reference)	7
Lutein + Zeaxanthin (mcg)	153		
Lycopene (mcg)	0		

Warm Bean Salad (Vegan; GF w/Mod)

This is a great, portable lunch meal all by itself. The flavor of cooked celery blends beautifully with kidney beans. A peaceful, comfort food!

Ingredients

4 cups water, divided

1 cup uncooked elbow macaroni

½ cup celery, sliced in large chunks

2 tsp olive oil

2 cloves garlic, minced

½ large onion, diced

1¼ cups canned, drained kidney beans – unsalted

½ tsp salt (use less if beans have salt added)

½ tsp dried parsley

½ tsp dried oregano

½ tsp black pepper

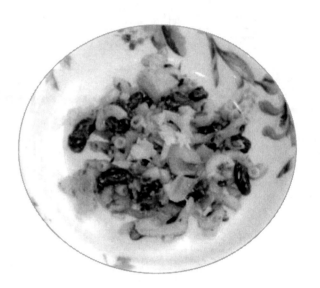

Boil 4 cups of water, add macaroni and cook *al dente*. Remove pasta using a strainer but save the cooking water. Bring water back to a boil, add celery and simmer lightly for ~2 minutes. Remove.

Heat a medium saucepan, add olive oil. Sauté garlic until it lightly browns. Add onions and cook until soft. Add beans and mix gently. Mix in cooked pasta and celery. Finally, add salt, parsley, oregano and black pepper. Serve.

Note: If unsalted beans are not available, use less salt at the end.

Yield: 3 cups (3, 1-cup servings)

~Gluten-free if rice pasta used in place of elbow macaroni~

Warm Bean Salad: serving = 1 cup

Energy (kcal)	325		
Total Fat (g)	4.6	Calcium (mg)	56
Total Carbohydrate (g)	57.3	Phosphorus (mg)	187
Total Protein (g)	13.9	Magnesium (mg)	59
% Calories from Fat	12	Iron (mg)	3.6
% Calories from Carbohydrate	72	Zinc (mg)	1.5
% Calories from Protein	16	Copper (mg)	0.3
Cholesterol (g)	0	Selenium (mcg)	32.8
Total Saturated Fatty Acids (g) (SFA)	0.7	Sodium (mg)	215
Total Monounsaturated Fatty Acids (g) (MUFA)	2.4	Potassium (mg)	457
Total Polyunsaturated Fatty Acids (g) (PUFA)	0.9		
Omega-3 Fatty Acids (g)	0.2		
% Calories from SFA	1.9	Linoleic Acid - PUFA (18:2) (g)	0.8
% Calories from MUFA	6.5	Linolenic Acid – PUFA (18:3) (g)	0.2
% Calories from PUFA	2.5		
Polyunsaturated to Saturated Fat (P:S) Ratio	1.4	Tryptophan (mg)	18
		Threonine (mg)	50
Total Dietary Fiber (g)	7.6	Isoleucine (mg)	59
Soluble Dietary Fiber (g)	1.8	Leucine (mg)	109
Insoluble Dietary Fiber (g)	5.8	Lysine (mg)	63
		Methionine (mg)	17
Total Vitamin A (mcg) (Retinol Activity Equivalents)	6	Phenylalanine (mg)	75
Vitamin D (calciferol) (mcg)	0	Valine (mg)	70
Vitamin E (mg) (Total Alpha-Tocopherol)	0.6	Histidine (mg)	34
Vitamin K (mg) (phylloquinone)	17.9		
Vitamin C (mg) (ascorbic acid)	4.0	Daidzein (mg)	0.0
Thiamin (mg) (vitamin B1)	0.5	Genistein (mg)	0.0
Riboflavin (mg) (vitamin B2)	0.2		
Niacin (mg) (vitamin B3)	2.6	Caffeine (mg)	0
Pantothenic Acid (mg)	0.4	Phytic Acid (mg)	331.1
Vitamin B6 (mg)	0.2	Oxalic Acid (mg)	31.5
Total Folate (mcg)	192	Choline (mg)	33.6
Vitamin B12 (mcg) (cobalamin)	0		
		Glycemic Index (glucose reference)	43
Beta-Carotene (mcg) (provitamin A carotenoid)	70	Glycemic Load (glucose reference)	22
Lutein + Zeaxanthin (mcg)	77		
Lycopene (mcg)	0		

SOY PRODUCTS: TOFU AND TEMPEH

Deep-Fried tempeh (Vegan; GF w/Mod)

Tempeh cooked in this way is delicious with crispy-boiled cabbage, a simple arame-seaweed sauté, in a pasta salad, or with fried rice. Use as a way to boost protein content of vegetable dishes. A little goes a long way, and – due to its higher-fat content – this tempeh is best used as an accompaniment, rather than a main bean course.

Ingredients

¾ cup canola oil*

8 oz tempeh

1½ Tbsp low-sodium soy sauce

1 tsp fresh grated ginger

1 tsp mirin

2 Tbsp water as needed

Cut tempeh in half, lengthwise, then into half-inch-wide (bite-size) pieces. Heat ¾ cup of canola oil in a medium cast-iron frying pan. When oil becomes hot, add tempeh and turn once, until the pieces become deeply golden brown on all sides. Drain on paper towels. In a small bowl, mix soy sauce, ginger, mirin and water; heat in a medium saucepan until it starts to simmer. Add drained tempeh pieces, and heat over low until the sauce is absorbed.

*Approximately 2 tablespoons of canola oil are absorbed in the frying process.

Yield: 2 cups (8, ¼-cup servings)

~For gluten free, use plain (grain-free) tempeh and tamari in place of soy sauce~

Deep Fried Tempeh: 1 serving = ¼ cup

Energy (kcal)	88		
Total Fat (g)	6.5	Calcium (mg)	32
Total Carbohydrate (g)	3.3	Phosphorus (mg)	79
Total Protein (g)	5.4	Magnesium (mg)	24
% Calories from Fat	64	Iron (mg)	0.8
% Calories from Carbohydrate	15	Zinc (mg)	0.3
% Calories from Protein	21	Copper (mg)	0.2
Cholesterol (g)	0	Selenium (mcg)	0.0
Total Saturated Fatty Acids (g) (SFA)	0.9	Sodium (mg)	108
Total Monounsaturated Fatty Acids (g) (MUFA)	3.0	Potassium (mg)	123
Total Polyunsaturated Fatty Acids (g) (PUFA)	2.0		
Omega-3 Fatty Acids (g)	0.4		
% Calories from SFA	8.5	Linoleic Acid - PUFA (18:2) (g)	1.7
% Calories from MUFA	29.8	Linolenic Acid – PUFA (18:3) (g)	0.4
% Calories from PUFA	20.1		
Polyunsaturated to Saturated Fat (P:S) Ratio	2.3	Tryptophan (mg)	6
		Threonine (mg)	23
Total Dietary Fiber (g)	0.9	Isoleucine (mg)	26
Soluble Dietary Fiber (g)	0.4	Leucine (mg)	42
Insoluble Dietary Fiber (g)	0.5	Lysine (mg)	27
		Methionine (mg)	5
Total Vitamin A (mcg) (Retinol Activity Equivalents)	0	Phenylalanine (mg)	26
Vitamin D (calciferol) (mcg)	0	Valine (mg)	27
Vitamin E (mg) (Total Alpha-Tocopherol)	0.7	Histidine (mg)	14
Vitamin K (mg) (phylloquinone)	7.9		
Vitamin C (mg) (ascorbic acid)	0.0	Daidzein (mg)	5.0
Thiamin (mg) (vitamin B1)	0.0	Genistein (mg)	7.1
Riboflavin (mg) (vitamin B2)	0.1		
Niacin (mg) (vitamin B3)	0.9	Caffeine (mg)	0
Pantothenic Acid (mg)	0.1	Phytic Acid (mg)	148.9
Vitamin B6 (mg)	0.1	Oxalic Acid (mg)	16.9
Total Folate (mcg)	7	Choline (mg)	9.0
Vitamin B12 (mcg) (cobalamin)	0.0		
		Glycemic Index (glucose reference)	27
Beta-Carotene (mcg) (provitamin A carotenoid)	0	Glycemic Load (glucose reference)	1
Lutein + Zeaxanthin (mcg)	0		
Lycopene (mcg)	0		

Scrambled Tofu with Mushrooms (Vegan [version 1]: GF w/Mod)

This protein-rich dish makes a great breakfast accompaniment, as well as a main dish for lunch or dinner. It's quick and yummy; the texture lends itself to lots of variation with other vegetables, nuts, seeds and herbs.

Ingredients

Version 1 – Without egg substitute

3 large shiitake mushrooms (dried 1 oz), soaked in
~1 cup hot water, then diced (~¾ cup)

14 oz extra-firm tofu

2 tsp sesame oil

6 scallions (~3 oz) – tops and bulbs included

1 oil-roasted red pepper, chopped (¼ cup)

2 tsp low-sodium soy sauce

1/8 tsp fresh-ground black pepper

Soak mushrooms in hot water to cover. When mushrooms are soft, dice and set aside.

Drain tofu, and crumble into large pieces. Heat the oil in medium skillet. Sauté scallions for 1 minute, add shiitake mushrooms, and cook over medium heat until tender. Mix in red pepper; simmer for 1 minute. Add tofu pieces mixture and cook for 8 minutes, stirring occasionally. Then add soy sauce and black pepper; cook 1 minute more and serve.

Yield: 3½ cups (7, ½-cup servings)

Version 2 – With egg substitute

Heat 1 tsp sesame oil and add ½ cup of egg substitute.

Cook briefly on one side, then flip over and cook a minute on the other side. Remove from pan.

Follow above directions, adding cooked egg substitute at the end and mixing in, gently breaking it into bite-sized pieces in the process. Serve.

Yield: 3¾ cup (7½ servings of ½-cup)

~For gluten free, use tamari in place of soy sauce~

Scrambled Tofu with Mushrooms: 1 serving = ½ cup

Energy (kcal)	97		
Total Fat (g)	5.9	Calcium (mg)	142
Total Carbohydrate (g)	5.1	Phosphorus (mg)	114
Total Protein (g)	8.1	Magnesium (mg)	46
% Calories from Fat	52	Iron (mg)	1.7
% Calories from Carbohydrate	20	Zinc (mg)	1.1
% Calories from Protein	28	Copper (mg)	0.3
Cholesterol (g)	0	Selenium (mcg)	13.7
Total Saturated Fatty Acids (g) (SFA)	0.6	Sodium (mg)	73
Total Monounsaturated Fatty Acids (g) (MUFA)	3.9	Potassium (mg)	163
Total Polyunsaturated Fatty Acids (g) (PUFA)	1.0		
Omega-3 Fatty Acids (g)	0.0		
% Calories from SFA	5.6	Linoleic Acid - PUFA (18:2) (g)	0.6
% Calories from MUFA	34.2	Linolenic Acid – PUFA (18:3) (g)	0.0
% Calories from PUFA	8.8		
Polyunsaturated to Saturated Fat (P:S) Ratio	1.6	Tryptophan (mg)	12
		Threonine (mg)	33
Total Dietary Fiber (g)	1.1	Isoleucine (mg)	39
Soluble Dietary Fiber (g)	0.2	Leucine (mg)	60
Insoluble Dietary Fiber (g)	0.9	Lysine (mg)	52
		Methionine (mg)	10
Total Vitamin A (mcg) (Retinol Activity Equivalents)	14	Phenylalanine (mg)	39
Vitamin D (calciferol) (mcg)	1.2	Valine (mg)	40
Vitamin E (mg) (Total Alpha-Tocopherol)	0.2	Histidine (mg)	23
Vitamin K (mg) (phylloquinone)	27.4		
Vitamin C (mg) (ascorbic acid)	8.8	Daidzein (mg)	6.2
Thiamin (mg) (vitamin B1)	0.1	Genistein (mg)	9.4
Riboflavin (mg) (vitamin B2)	0.1		
Niacin (mg) (vitamin B3)	0.6	Caffeine (mg)	0
Pantothenic Acid (mg)	0.9	Phytic Acid (mg)	152.2
Vitamin B6 (mg)	0.1	Oxalic Acid (mg)	8.8
Total Folate (mcg)	24	Choline (mg)	24.4
Vitamin B12 (mcg) (cobalamin)	0.0		
		Glycemic Index (glucose reference)	39
Beta-Carotene (mcg) (provitamin A carotenoid)	152	Glycemic Load (glucose reference)	2
Lutein + Zeaxanthin (mcg)	128		
Lycopene (mcg)	0		

Scrambled Tofu with Eggbeaters and Mushrooms: 1 serving = ½ cup

Energy (kcal)	111		
Total Fat (g)	7.1	Calcium (mg)	138
Total Carbohydrate (g)	5.0	Phosphorus (mg)	109
Total Protein (g)	9.2	Magnesium (mg)	45
% Calories from Fat	55	Iron (mg)	1.9
% Calories from Carbohydrate	16	Zinc (mg)	1.2
% Calories from Protein	29	Copper (mg)	0.3
Cholesterol (g)	0	Selenium (mcg)	15.9
Total Saturated Fatty Acids (g) (SFA)	0.8	Sodium (mg)	99
Total Monounsaturated Fatty Acids (g) (MUFA)	4.3	Potassium (mg)	178
Total Polyunsaturated Fatty Acids (g) (PUFA)	1.6		
Omega-3 Fatty Acids (g)	0.0		
% Calories from SFA	6.3	Linoleic Acid - PUFA (18:2) (g)	1.2
% Calories from MUFA	32.6	Linolenic Acid – PUFA (18:3) (g)	0.0
% Calories from PUFA	12.2		
Polyunsaturated to Saturated Fat (P:S) Ratio	1.9	Tryptophan (mg)	13
		Threonine (mg)	38
Total Dietary Fiber (g)	1.1	Isoleucine (mg)	47
Soluble Dietary Fiber (g)	0.3	Leucine (mg)	72
Insoluble Dietary Fiber (g)	0.8	Lysine (mg)	61
		Methionine (mg)	16
Total Vitamin A (mcg) (Retinol Activity Equivalents)	23	Phenylalanine (mg)	47
Vitamin D (calciferol) (mcg)	1.4	Valine (mg)	50
Vitamin E (mg) (Total Alpha-Tocopherol)	0.4	Histidine (mg)	26
Vitamin K (mg) (phylloquinone)	25.8		
Vitamin C (mg) (ascorbic acid)	8.2	Daidzein (mg)	5.8
Thiamin (mg) (vitamin B1)	0.1	Genistein (mg)	8.8
Riboflavin (mg) (vitamin B2)	0.3		
Niacin (mg) (vitamin B3)	0.6	Caffeine (mg)	0
Pantothenic Acid (mg)	1.1	Phytic Acid (mg)	142.0
Vitamin B6 (mg)	0.1	Oxalic Acid (mg)	8.2
Total Folate (mcg)	39	Choline (mg)	26.7
Vitamin B12 (mcg) (cobalamin)	0.3		
		Glycemic Index (glucose reference)	38
Beta-Carotene (mcg) (provitamin A carotenoid)	262	Glycemic Load (glucose reference)	1
Lutein + Zeaxanthin (mcg)	119		
Lycopene (mcg)	0		

Scrambled Tofu with Onions (Vegan; GF w/Mod)

This is a mild and sweet, satisfying tofu dish. Prepare the vegetables the night before, for a quick pick-up breakfast.

Ingredients

14 oz extra-firm tofu

4 tsp white miso

1 Tbsp sesame oil

1 small onion, diced (2/3 cup)

2 large fresh crimini mushrooms, sliced (½ cup)

1 medium carrot, diced (1/3 cup)

½ medium red pepper, diced (½ cup)

Drain tofu, and crumble into large pieces. Mix in miso, dividing evenly throughout. Mash gently into the tofu and let flavors blend for 20 minutes.

Heat the oil in a medium, nonstick skillet. Sauté onions until they start to become translucent; add mushrooms and cook over medium heat until tender. Mix in carrot and red pepper; simmer for 1 minute. Add tofu/miso mixture and cook for 10 minutes, stirring occasionally.

Yield: 3¼ cup (6½ servings of ½ cup)

~Gluten-free if brown-rice miso is used in place of white miso~

From Sheri DeMaris: Similar recipes to these can be found in Sheri DeMaris's cookbook *Macro Magic for Kids and Parents* found on www.cedartreebooks.com

Scrambled Tofu with Onion: 1 serving = ½ cup

Energy (kcal)	111		
Total Fat (g)	7.0	Calcium (mg)	150
Total Carbohydrate (g)	5.5	Phosphorus (mg)	128
Total Protein (g)	8.7	Magnesium (mg)	47
% Calories from Fat	54	Iron (mg)	1.7
% Calories from Carbohydrate	19	Zinc (mg)	1.1
% Calories from Protein	27	Copper (mg)	0.2
Cholesterol (g)	0	Selenium (mcg)	12.3
Total Saturated Fatty Acids (g) (SFA)	0.8	Sodium (mg)	78
Total Monounsaturated Fatty Acids (g) (MUFA)	4.4	Potassium (mg)	186
Total Polyunsaturated Fatty Acids (g) (PUFA)	1.4		
Omega-3 Fatty Acids (g)	0.0		
% Calories from SFA	6.0	Linoleic Acid - PUFA (18:2) (g)	0.9
% Calories from MUFA	33.5	Linolenic Acid – PUFA (18:3) (g)	0.0
% Calories from PUFA	10.9		
Polyunsaturated to Saturated Fat (P:S) Ratio	1.8	Tryptophan (mg)	14
		Threonine (mg)	36
Total Dietary Fiber (g)	0.9	Isoleucine (mg)	43
Soluble Dietary Fiber (g)	0.3	Leucine (mg)	65
Insoluble Dietary Fiber (g)	0.6	Lysine (mg)	57
		Methionine (mg)	11
Total Vitamin A (mcg) (Retinol Activity Equivalents)	63	Phenylalanine (mg)	42
Vitamin D (calciferol) (mcg)	0.0	Valine (mg)	43
Vitamin E (mg) (Total Alpha-Tocopherol)	0.2	Histidine (mg)	25
Vitamin K (mg) (phylloquinone)	3.7		
Vitamin C (mg) (ascorbic acid)	15.2	Daidzein (mg)	7.0
Thiamin (mg) (vitamin B1)	0.1	Genistein (mg)	10.5
Riboflavin (mg) (vitamin B2)	0.1		
Niacin (mg) (vitamin B3)	0.6	Caffeine (mg)	0
Pantothenic Acid (mg)	0.5	Phytic Acid (mg)	157.1
Vitamin B6 (mg)	0.1	Oxalic Acid (mg)	7.9
Total Folate (mcg)	19	Choline (mg)	27.2
Vitamin B12 (mcg) (cobalamin)	0.0		
		Glycemic Index (glucose reference)	47
Beta-Carotene (mcg) (provitamin A carotenoid)	621	Glycemic Load (glucose reference)	2
Lutein + Zeaxanthin (mcg)	45		
Lycopene (mcg)	0		

Spicy Simmered Tofu (Vegan, GF w/Mod)

Tofu shines in this saucy, spicy, and distinct preparation. Serve over a simple dish of brown rice or polenta. This is a great go-to recipe, with ingredients that are easy to keep on hand.

Ingredients

1 lb firm tofu

2 Tbsp canola oil

3 scallions (1½ ounces), cut into 1-inch pieces

4 cloves garlic, minced

1 Tbsp minced ginger

2 tsp hot chili paste

2 Tbsp low-sodium soy sauce

½ cube (5 g) vegetable bouillon (low-sodium)

½ cup hot water

1 Tbsp cornstarch

2 Tbsp cold water

Cut tofu into ½-inch cubes. Drain any excess water out. In a medium sauté pan or wok, heat oil and stir-fry scallions and garlic for 1 minute. Add ginger, chili paste and soy sauce; cook an additional minute. Add tofu and mix gently. Dissolve bouillon in hot water and add to pan, bringing to a boil. Reduce heat and simmer for 5 minutes. Dilute cornstarch in cold water, add to vegetable dish and stir fry for ½ minute until a thick sauce develops.

Yield: 3½ cups (7, ½-cup servings)

~For gluten free, use tamari in place of soy sauce~

Spicy Simmered Tofu: 1 serving = ½ cup

Energy (kcal)	92		
Total Fat (g)	6.6	Calcium (mg)	139
Total Carbohydrate (g)	3.7	Phosphorus (mg)	89
Total Protein (g)	5.8	Magnesium (mg)	28
% Calories from Fat	62	Iron (mg)	1.3
% Calories from Carbohydrate	16	Zinc (mg)	0.6
% Calories from Protein	22	Copper (mg)	0.2
Cholesterol (g)	0	Selenium (mcg)	6.8
Total Saturated Fatty Acids (g) (SFA)	0.9	Sodium (mg)	171
Total Monounsaturated Fatty Acids (g) (MUFA)	3.3	Potassium (mg)	131
Total Polyunsaturated Fatty Acids (g) (PUFA)	2.3		
Omega-3 Fatty Acids (g)	0.5		
% Calories from SFA	7.9	Linoleic Acid - PUFA (18:2) (g)	1.8
% Calories from MUFA	31.0	Linolenic Acid – PUFA (18:3) (g)	0.5
% Calories from PUFA	21.3		
Polyunsaturated to Saturated Fat (P:S) Ratio	2.7	Tryptophan (mg)	9
		Threonine (mg)	23
Total Dietary Fiber (g)	0.8	Isoleucine (mg)	28
Soluble Dietary Fiber (g)	0.3	Leucine (mg)	44
Insoluble Dietary Fiber (g)	0.5	Lysine (mg)	37
		Methionine (mg)	7
Total Vitamin A (mcg) (Retinol Activity Equivalents)	3	Phenylalanine (mg)	28
Vitamin D (calciferol) (mcg)	0.0	Valine (mg)	29
Vitamin E (mg) (Total Alpha-Tocopherol)	0.7	Histidine (mg)	17
Vitamin K (mg) (phylloquinone)	17.1		
Vitamin C (mg) (ascorbic acid)	1.8	Daidzein (mg)	6.2
Thiamin (mg) (vitamin B1)	0.0	Genistein (mg)	8.7
Riboflavin (mg) (vitamin B2)	0.1		
Niacin (mg) (vitamin B3)	0.3	Caffeine (mg)	0
Pantothenic Acid (mg)	0.1	Phytic Acid (mg)	325.1
Vitamin B6 (mg)	0.1	Oxalic Acid (mg)	14.7
Total Folate (mcg)	16	Choline (mg)	20.7
Vitamin B12 (mcg) (cobalamin)	0.0		
		Glycemic Index (glucose reference)	64
Beta-Carotene (mcg) (provitamin A carotenoid)	34	Glycemic Load (glucose reference)	2
Lutein + Zeaxanthin (mcg)	65		
Lycopene (mcg)	0		

Tempeh Salad

(Vegan [without mayo]; GF w/Mod)

Looking for a protein-rich take-anywhere salad? Look no further...with or without mayonnaise, this is a sure crowd-pleaser! Bursting with flavor and with real staying-power, it has maximum sparkle when made in advance.

Ingredients

1 Tbsp low-sodium soy sauce

1 Tbsp balsamic vinegar

1½ tsp mirin

1¼ cups water

Tempeh, 8 oz, cut in small ¼" cubes

1 tsp sesame oil

1 medium onion (5½ oz), diced (1 1/3 cups)

Pinch Kosher salt

¼ medium carrot (2 oz), diced (about ½ cup)

2 stalks celery (3 oz), diced (2/3 cup)

2 Tbsp chopped fresh basil

¼ tsp black pepper

3 Tbsp mayonnaise (optional)

Vegan Tempeh Salad

In a small saucepan, combine soy sauce, vinegar, mirin and water. Add tempeh cubes (liquid should reach the top of tempeh; if not, add just enough water to do so.) Bring to a boil, cover and turn heat to medium-low. Simmer for 15 minutes, then uncover, stir and continue to cook until all the liquid has cooked away. Transfer to a bowl to cool.

In a small skillet, heat oil, then fry onions with a pinch of salt, until they become translucent. Cool. To the tempeh, add sautéed onion, carrot, celery, basil and black pepper. Mix well. If desired, add mayonnaise.

Yield: Without mayo: 3¾ cups (7½, ½-cup servings); with mayo: 3½ cups (7, ½-cup servings)

~For gluten-free, use plain (grain-free) tempeh and tamari in place of soy sauce~

From Marilyn Moser-Waxman, *The Nourishing Well*, Havertown, PA, www.thenourishingwell.com

118

Tempeh Salad-Vegan: 1 serving = ½ cup

Energy (kcal)	79		
Total Fat (g)	3.9	Calcium (mg)	47
Total Carbohydrate (g)	6.2	Phosphorus (mg)	93
Total Protein (g)	6.1	Magnesium (mg)	30
% Calories from Fat	42	Iron (mg)	1.0
% Calories from Carbohydrate	32	Zinc (mg)	0.4
% Calories from Protein	26	Copper (mg)	0.2
Cholesterol (g)	0	Selenium (mcg)	0.2
Total Saturated Fatty Acids (g) (SFA)	0.8	Sodium (mg)	118
Total Monounsaturated Fatty Acids (g) (MUFA)	1.2	Potassium (mg)	208
Total Polyunsaturated Fatty Acids (g) (PUFA)	1.4		
Omega-3 Fatty Acids (g)	0.1		
% Calories from SFA	8.2	Linoleic Acid - PUFA (18:2) (g)	1.4
% Calories from MUFA	12.4	Linolenic Acid – PUFA (18:3) (g)	0.1
% Calories from PUFA	15.4		
Polyunsaturated to Saturated Fat (P:S) Ratio	1.9	Tryptophan (mg)	7
		Threonine (mg)	27
Total Dietary Fiber (g)	1.6	Isoleucine (mg)	29
Soluble Dietary Fiber (g)	0.5	Leucine (mg)	46
Insoluble Dietary Fiber (g)	1.1	Lysine (mg)	30
		Methionine (mg)	6
Total Vitamin A (mcg) (Retinol Activity Equivalents)	68	Phenylalanine (mg)	29
Vitamin D (calciferol) (mcg)	0	Valine (mg)	30
Vitamin E (mg) (Total Alpha-Tocopherol)	0.2	Histidine (mg)	15
Vitamin K (mg) (phylloquinone)	12.9		
Vitamin C (mg) (ascorbic acid)	1.6	Daidzein (mg)	5.3
Thiamin (mg) (vitamin B1)	0.0	Genistein (mg)	7.5
Riboflavin (mg) (vitamin B2)	0.1		
Niacin (mg) (vitamin B3)	1.0	Caffeine (mg)	0
Pantothenic Acid (mg)	0.2	Phytic Acid (mg)	161.6
Vitamin B6 (mg)	0.1	Oxalic Acid (mg)	26.0
Total Folate (mcg)	15	Choline (mg)	11.6
Vitamin B12 (mcg) (cobalamin)	0.0		
		Glycemic Index (glucose reference)	44
Beta-Carotene (mcg) (provitamin A carotenoid)	679	Glycemic Load (glucose reference)	2
Lutein + Zeaxanthin (mcg)	92		
Lycopene (mcg)	0		

Tempeh Salad + Mayo: 1 serving = ½ cup

Energy (kcal)	127		
Total Fat (g)	8.9	Calcium (mg)	51
Total Carbohydrate (g)	6.9	Phosphorus (mg)	102
Total Protein (g)	6.6	Magnesium (mg)	32
% Calories from Fat	60	Iron (mg)	1.1
% Calories from Carbohydrate	22	Zinc (mg)	0.5
% Calories from Protein	18	Copper (mg)	0.2
Cholesterol (g)	2	Selenium (mcg)	0.3
Total Saturated Fatty Acids (g) (SFA)	1.5	Sodium (mg)	160
Total Monounsaturated Fatty Acids (g) (MUFA)	2.4	Potassium (mg)	224
Total Polyunsaturated Fatty Acids (g) (PUFA)	4.0		
Omega-3 Fatty Acids (g)	0.4		
% Calories from SFA	10.3	Linoleic Acid - PUFA (18:2) (g)	3.7
% Calories from MUFA	16.3	Linolenic Acid – PUFA (18:3) (g)	0.4
% Calories from PUFA	27.6		
Polyunsaturated to Saturated Fat (P:S) Ratio	2.6	Tryptophan (mg)	7
		Threonine (mg)	29
Total Dietary Fiber (g)	1.8	Isoleucine (mg)	31
Soluble Dietary Fiber (g)	0.6	Leucine (mg)	50
Insoluble Dietary Fiber (g)	1.2	Lysine (mg)	33
		Methionine (mg)	7
Total Vitamin A (mcg) (Retinol Activity Equivalents)	77	Phenylalanine (mg)	31
Vitamin D (calciferol) (mcg)	0.0	Valine (mg)	32
Vitamin E (mg) (Total Alpha-Tocopherol)	0.5	Histidine (mg)	16
Vitamin K (mg) (phylloquinone)	16.3		
Vitamin C (mg) (ascorbic acid)	1.7	Daidzein (mg)	5.7
Thiamin (mg) (vitamin B1)	0.0	Genistein (mg)	8.1
Riboflavin (mg) (vitamin B2)	0.1		
Niacin (mg) (vitamin B3)	1.1	Caffeine (mg)	0
Pantothenic Acid (mg)	0.2	Phytic Acid (mg)	173.4
Vitamin B6 (mg)	0.1	Oxalic Acid (mg)	28.6
Total Folate (mcg)	17	Choline (mg)	13.7
Vitamin B12 (mcg) (cobalamin)	0.0		
		Glycemic Index (glucose reference)	45
Beta-Carotene (mcg) (provitamin A carotenoid)	728	Glycemic Load (glucose reference)	2
Lutein + Zeaxanthin (mcg)	110		
Lycopene (mcg)	0		

Tempeh with Orange Glaze (Vegan; GF w/Mod)

What a great way to enjoy tempeh! Cooked thoroughly, the tempeh is very digestible; flavored with delectable ingredients, it is tender and unforgettable. Pairs well with grains or other vegetables. Leftovers make excellent sandwiches.

Ingredients

1 cup freshly squeezed orange juice

1 Tbsp freshly grated ginger

2 tsp low-sodium soy sauce

1½ Tbsp mirin

2 tsp maple syrup

½ tsp ground coriander

2 small garlic cloves, crushed

8-oz package of tempeh

2½ Tbsp olive oil, divided

2 Tbsp lime juice

½ cup chopped cilantro leaves

Put the orange juice in a small bowl. Squeeze the grated ginger over the bowl to extract the juices (about 1 Tbsp of ginger juice), then discard the pulp. Add the soy sauce, mirin, and maple syrup, ground coriander, and garlic. Mix together and set aside. Cut the tempeh into 1-inch blocks, and then split each into thirds (it cooks more thoroughly this way). Put the 1½ Tbsp of the olive oil in a large frying pan over medium-high heat. When the oil is hot but not smoking, add the tempeh and fry for 5 minutes, or until golden underneath. Turn, add the remaining 1 Tbsp of oil and cook the other side for another 5 minutes, or until golden. Pour the orange juice mixture into the pan, cover and simmer on low for 10 minutes, or until the sauce has reduced to a lovely thick glaze. Turn the tempeh once more during this time and spoon the sauce over the tempeh from time to time. Serve the tempeh drizzled with any remaining sauce and a squeeze of lime, with the cilantro sprinkled on top.

Yield: 9 ounces, (4¼, 2-oz portions)

~For gluten-free, use plain (grain-free) tempeh and tamari in place of soy sauce~

From: Jude Blereau, *Coming Home to Eat, Wholefood for the Family*, Australia: Murdoch Books, 2006.

Tempeh with Orange Glaze: 1 serving = 2-ounce portion

Energy (kcal)	229		
Total Fat (g)	13.9	Calcium (mg)	74
Total Carbohydrate (g)	18.331	Phosphorus (mg)	161
Total Protein (g)	10.7	Magnesium (mg)	55
% Calories from Fat	52	Iron (mg)	1.8
% Calories from Carbohydrate	32	Zinc (mg)	0.8
% Calories from Protein	16	Copper (mg)	0.3
Cholesterol (g)	0	Selenium (mcg)	0.4
Total Saturated Fatty Acids (g) (SFA)	2.3	Sodium (mg)	139
Total Monounsaturated Fatty Acids (g) (MUFA)	7.4	Potassium (mg)	399
Total Polyunsaturated Fatty Acids (g) (PUFA)	2.9		
Omega-3 Fatty Acids (g)	0.2		
% Calories from SFA	8.7	Linoleic Acid - PUFA (18:2) (g)	2.7
% Calories from MUFA	28.3	Linolenic Acid – PUFA (18:3) (g)	0.2
% Calories from PUFA	10.8		
Polyunsaturated to Saturated Fat (P:S) Ratio	1.3	Tryptophan (mg)	11
		Threonine (mg)	44
Total Dietary Fiber (g)	2.2	Isoleucine (mg)	49
Soluble Dietary Fiber (g)	1.0	Leucine (mg)	79
Insoluble Dietary Fiber (g)	1.2	Lysine (mg)	51
		Methionine (mg)	10
Total Vitamin A (mcg) (Retinol Activity Equivalents)	12	Phenylalanine (mg)	49
Vitamin D (calciferol) (mcg)	0	Valine (mg)	51
Vitamin E (mg) (Total Alpha-Tocopherol)	1.5	Histidine (mg)	26
Vitamin K (mg) (phylloquinone)	22.0		
Vitamin C (mg) (ascorbic acid)	33.0	Daidzein (mg)	9.4
Thiamin (mg) (vitamin B1)	0.1	Genistein (mg)	13.3
Riboflavin (mg) (vitamin B2)	0.2		
Niacin (mg) (vitamin B3)	1.7	Caffeine (mg)	0
Pantothenic Acid (mg)	0.3	Phytic Acid (mg)	289.9
Vitamin B6 (mg)	0.2	Oxalic Acid (mg)	43.4
Total Folate (mcg)	30	Choline (mg)	22.2
Vitamin B12 (mcg) (cobalamin)	0.0		
		Glycemic Index (glucose reference)	47
Beta-Carotene (mcg) (provitamin A carotenoid)	94	Glycemic Load (glucose reference)	8
Lutein + Zeaxanthin (mcg)	88		
Lycopene (mcg)	0		

Tofu Burgers (Vegan)

A simply splendid burger. There are many ingredients to gather, but well worth the effort. YUM!

Ingredients

1 Tbsp ground flax seed

3 Tbsp water

1 pkg firm tofu, 16 oz (~2¼ cups mashed)

¼ cup ground oatmeal, (about ¼ cup oatmeal
   flakes, ground in coffee grinder)

¼ cup fresh cilantro, chopped

¼ cup onion, chopped

1 jalapeno pepper, seeded and chopped

1 tsp sunflower seeds, roasted and ground*

1 tsp low-sodium soy sauce

½ tsp salt

¼ tsp ground black pepper

½ cup bread crumbs, unseasoned

1½ Tbsp olive oil, divided

* Flax could also be used instead of, or in combination with, sunflower seeds.

Yield: 8 burgers (3 oz each, 2" diameter and about 3/4" high)

In a small bowl, mix flax seed with water and set aside to thicken. Drain tofu well, then crumble. In a separate medium mixing bowl, combine ground oatmeal, cilantro, onion, pepper, ground sunflower seeds, soy sauce, salt, and black pepper. Gently fold in the drained tofu. Add in the flax-meal-water slurry, which helps bind all the ingredients together. Add bread crumbs slowly, until mixture can form burgers, being careful not to over-handle. (You may need less than or more than ½ cup). If time permits, let this mixture rest, covered, in the refrigerator for 30 minutes, to allow the flavors to meld together; the burgers will also be easier to form). To form burgers, take enough mixture to form the size of a billiard ball and then gently flatten into a burger about 2 inches in diameter.

Heat a non-stick skillet with 1 Tbsp olive oil. Place burgers into the hot oil, and cook on medium heat, slowly, until deeply browned. Turn over gently; add the remaining ½ Tbsp oil and brown well on the other side.

Thanks to student Shirley Hedin for sharing this recipe.

Tofu Burgers: 1 serving = 1 burger

Energy (kcal)	121		
Total Fat (g)	6.8	Calcium (mg)	170
Total Carbohydrate (g)	8.8	Phosphorus (mg)	125
Total Protein (g)	7.8	Magnesium (mg)	40
% Calories from Fat	48	Iron (mg)	1.8
% Calories from Carbohydrate	30	Zinc (mg)	0.9
% Calories from Protein	22	Copper (mg)	0.2
Cholesterol (g)	0	Selenium (mcg)	10.4
Total Saturated Fatty Acids (g) (SFA)	1.2	Sodium (mg)	228
Total Monounsaturated Fatty Acids (g) (MUFA)	3.0	Potassium (mg)	159
Total Polyunsaturated Fatty Acids (g) (PUFA)	2.2		
Omega-3 Fatty Acids (g)	0.4		
% Calories from SFA	8.2	Linoleic Acid - PUFA (18:2) (g)	1.8
% Calories from MUFA	21.4	Linolenic Acid – PUFA (18:3) (g)	0.4
% Calories from PUFA	15.3		
Polyunsaturated to Saturated Fat (P:S) Ratio	1.9	Tryptophan (mg)	12
		Threonine (mg)	30
Total Dietary Fiber (g)	1.6	Isoleucine (mg)	37
Soluble Dietary Fiber (g)	0.6	Leucine (mg)	58
Insoluble Dietary Fiber (g)	1.0	Lysine (mg)	47
		Methionine (mg)	11
Total Vitamin A (mcg) (Retinol Activity Equivalents)	2	Phenylalanine (mg)	38
Vitamin D (calciferol) (mcg)	0.0	Valine (mg)	39
Vitamin E (mg) (Total Alpha-Tocopherol)	0.5	Histidine (mg)	22
Vitamin K (mg) (phylloquinone)	5.4		
Vitamin C (mg) (ascorbic acid)	1.2	Daidzein (mg)	7.1
Thiamin (mg) (vitamin B1)	0.1	Genistein (mg)	10.1
Riboflavin (mg) (vitamin B2)	0.1		
Niacin (mg) (vitamin B3)	0.7	Caffeine (mg)	0
Pantothenic Acid (mg)	0.2	Phytic Acid (mg)	411.3
Vitamin B6 (mg)	0.1	Oxalic Acid (mg)	9.4
Total Folate (mcg)	26	Choline (mg)	24.8
Vitamin B12 (mcg) (cobalamin)	0.0		
		Glycemic Index (glucose reference)	62
Beta-Carotene (mcg) (provitamin A carotenoid)	28	Glycemic Load (glucose reference)	4
Lutein + Zeaxanthin (mcg)	23		
Lycopene (mcg)	0		

Tofu Cream Cheese / Dressing (Vegan; GF)

Serve "cream cheese" with crackers or blanched vegetables. As a dressing, it can be drizzled over green salad, pasta salad, or other cooked vegetables (such as steamed kale or broccoli). The secret of this delicious dish is to make sure your tofu is very fresh.

Ingredients

1 cake of tofu (medium, although any consistency will do)
   about 8 oz (230 g), 1¼ cups mashed

1 Tbsp water to obtain desired consistency

2 tsp of tahini (roasted sesame butter can also be used)

½ tsp rice vinegar

¼ tsp salt

¼ cup scallions, sliced very thinly

Place the tofu, water, tahini, vinegar, and salt into the food processor and blend until smooth. {You can also blanch the tofu in advance if you prefer.} For cream cheese use just enough water to make a spread, for dressing add enough to make a thinner, but creamy dressing. At the end, add scallions and pulse only a few times (to avoid a bitter flavor).

Yield: 1 cup cream cheese (8, 2-Tbsp servings)

Variations: 1 pitted, chopped umeboshi plum may be used instead of ¼ tsp of salt plus ½ tsp brown rice vinegar; use almond or peanut butter for the sesame; use ¼ tsp. sesame oil instead of sesame butter

NOTE: This dish can be made with just mashing the tofu, rather than blending, and then stirring in the remaining ingredients.

Tofu Cream Cheese: 1 serving = 2 Tbsp.

Energy (kcal)	26		
Total Fat (g)	1.7	Calcium (mg)	39
Total Carbohydrate (g)	1.0	Phosphorus (mg)	36
Total Protein (g)	2.1	Magnesium (mg)	10
% Calories from Fat	56	Iron (mg)	0.5
% Calories from Carbohydrate	16	Zinc (mg)	0.3
% Calories from Protein	28	Copper (mg)	0.1
Cholesterol (g)	0	Selenium (mcg)	2.6
Total Saturated Fatty Acids (g) (SFA)	0.2	Sodium (mg)	77
Total Monounsaturated Fatty Acids (g) (MUFA)	0.5	Potassium (mg)	48
Total Polyunsaturated Fatty Acids (g) (PUFA)	0.9		
Omega-3 Fatty Acids (g)	0.1		
% Calories from SFA	8.0	Linoleic Acid - PUFA (18:2) (g)	0.8
% Calories from MUFA	15.8	Linolenic Acid – PUFA (18:3) (g)	0.1
% Calories from PUFA	28.8		
Polyunsaturated to Saturated Fat (P:S) Ratio	3.6	Tryptophan (mg)	3
		Threonine (mg)	9
Total Dietary Fiber (g)	0.3	Isoleucine (mg)	10
Soluble Dietary Fiber (g)	0.1	Leucine (mg)	16
Insoluble Dietary Fiber (g)	0.2	Lysine (mg)	13
		Methionine (mg)	3
Total Vitamin A (mcg) (Retinol Activity Equivalents)	2	Phenylalanine (mg)	10
Vitamin D (calciferol) (mcg)	0.0	Valine (mg)	11
Vitamin E (mg) (Total Alpha-Tocopherol)	0.0	Histidine (mg)	6
Vitamin K (mg) (phylloquinone)	7.0		
Vitamin C (mg) (ascorbic acid)	0.6	Daidzein (mg)	3.4
Thiamin (mg) (vitamin B1)	0.0	Genistein (mg)	5.2
Riboflavin (mg) (vitamin B2)	0.0		
Niacin (mg) (vitamin B3)	0.2	Caffeine (mg)	0
Pantothenic Acid (mg)	0.0	Phytic Acid (mg)	85.2
Vitamin B6 (mg)	0.0	Oxalic Acid (mg)	10.1
Total Folate (mcg)	16	Choline (mg)	8.3
Vitamin B12 (mcg) (cobalamin)	0.0		
		Glycemic Index (glucose reference)	22
Beta-Carotene (mcg) (provitamin A carotenoid)	20	Glycemic Load (glucose reference)	0
Lutein + Zeaxanthin (mcg)	36		
Lycopene (mcg)	0		

Tofu "Lunchmeat" (Vegan; GF w/Mod)

A simple, tasty, high-protein —meat" for sandwiches, on salads, or set atop crackers. Enjoy!

Ingredients

½ lb firm tofu, sliced into 4 slabs, each ½-inch thick

Spray oil – 4 sprays

1 tsp low-sodium soy sauce, divided

Slice a square of tofu into ½-inch slices. In a small, nonstick skillet, spray the surface with 4 short spritzes, and let the pan get hot. Place each slice of tofu on pan, and heat over medium for 1 minute. Sprinkle ½ tsp of soy sauce over the slabs and flip over. Cook for 2 minutes. Sprinkle ½ tsp over the slices and flip over once more. Cook for 2 more minutes.

Yield: 4 slices (2 servings of 2 slices each)

~Gluten-free if tamari used instead of soy sauce~

Based on recipe from: Kushi A and Esko W: *The Good Morning Macrobiotic Breakfast Book*, 1991, with permission of Wendy Esko.

Tofu Lunchmeat: 1 serving = 2 slices

Energy (kcal)	87		
Total Fat (g)	5.5	Calcium (mg)	228
Total Carbohydrate (g)	2.1	Phosphorus (mg)	140
Total Protein (g)	9.4	Magnesium (mg)	43
% Calories from Fat	53	Iron (mg)	1.9
% Calories from Carbohydrate	10	Zinc (mg)	1.0
% Calories from Protein	37	Copper (mg)	0.2
Cholesterol (g)	0	Selenium (mcg)	11.2
Total Saturated Fatty Acids (g) (SFA)	1.0	Sodium (mg)	102
Total Monounsaturated Fatty Acids (g) (MUFA)	1.9	Potassium (mg)	173
Total Polyunsaturated Fatty Acids (g) (PUFA)	2.2		
Omega-3 Fatty Acids (g)	0.3		
% Calories from SFA	9.9	Linoleic Acid - PUFA (18:2) (g)	2.0
% Calories from MUFA	18.1	Linolenic Acid – PUFA (18:3) (g)	0.3
% Calories from PUFA	21.6		
Polyunsaturated to Saturated Fat (P:S) Ratio	2.2	Tryptophan (mg)	15
		Threonine (mg)	39
Total Dietary Fiber (g)	1.0	Isoleucine (mg)	47
Soluble Dietary Fiber (g)	0.5	Leucine (mg)	72
Insoluble Dietary Fiber (g)	0.6	Lysine (mg)	62
		Methionine (mg)	12
Total Vitamin A (mcg) (Retinol Activity Equivalents)	0.0	Phenylalanine (mg)	46
Vitamin D (calciferol) (mcg)	0.0	Valine (mg)	48
Vitamin E (mg) (Total Alpha-Tocopherol)	0.1	Histidine (mg)	28
Vitamin K (mg) (phylloquinone)	2.8		
Vitamin C (mg) (ascorbic acid)	0.2	Daidzein (mg)	10.7
Thiamin (mg) (vitamin B1)	0.1	Genistein (mg)	15.2
Riboflavin (mg) (vitamin B2)	0.1		
Niacin (mg) (vitamin B3)	0.2	Caffeine (mg)	0
Pantothenic Acid (mg)	0.1	Phytic Acid (mg)	554.8
Vitamin B6 (mg)	0.1	Oxalic Acid (mg)	10.4
Total Folate (mcg)	22	Choline (mg)	32.7
Vitamin B12 (mcg) (cobalamin)	0.0		
		Glycemic Index (glucose reference)	20
Beta-Carotene (mcg) (provitamin A carotenoid)	0	Glycemic Load (glucose reference)	0
Lutein + Zeaxanthin (mcg)	0		
Lycopene (mcg)	0		

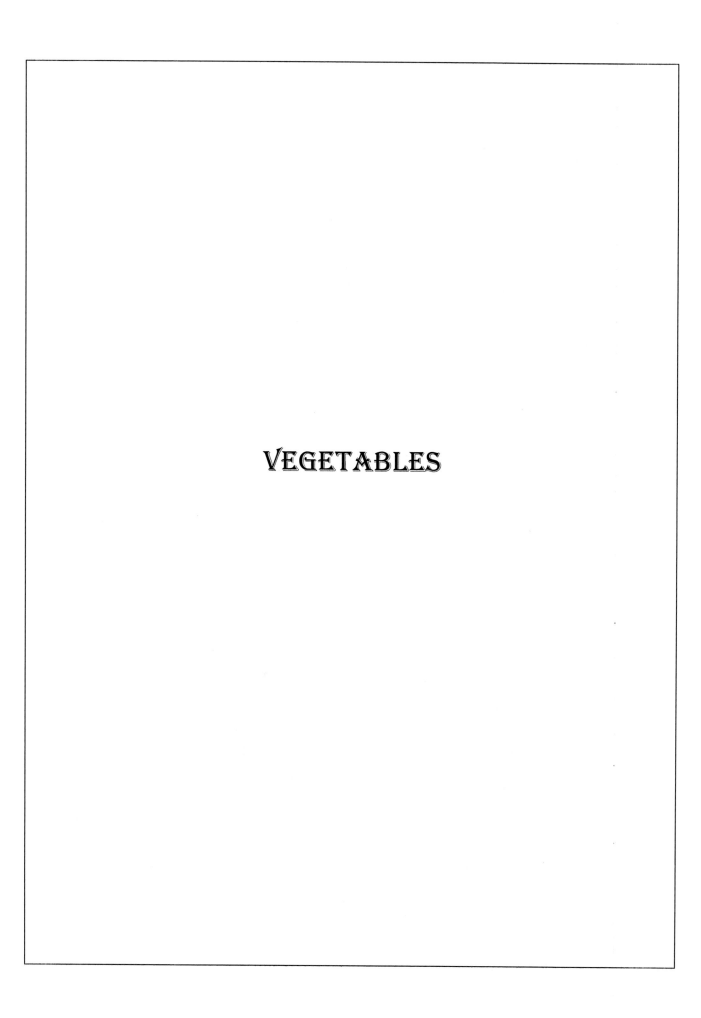

VEGETABLES

Bok Choy (Vegan; GF w/Mod)

This dish will make a green-vegetable-lover out of anyone! Gorgeous and velvety, it is a snap to prepare.

Ingredients

1 tsp of olive oil (canola oil can also be used)

1 tsp of sesame oil

3 medium cloves of garlic- minced (about 1 Tbsp)

8 oz baby bok choy - washed and chopped (keep leaves
 separate from stems) 2 cups stems + 2 cups leaves, chopped

½ tsp of mirin

1 tsp of low-sodium soy sauce (or to taste)

In a medium skillet, heat oils and sauté the garlic for about 1 minute. Add bok choy stems, stirring to coat with garlic & oil; add mirin. After just a couple of minutes, or when stems start to get a little tender, add leaves; add a splash of soy sauce and sauté 30 seconds more. (Do not overcook.)

Yield: 1½ cups cooked (3, ½-cup servings)

~For gluten free, use tamari in place of soy sauce~

Bok Choy: 1 serving = ½ cup

Energy (kcal)	86		
Total Fat (g)	6.3	Calcium (mg)	169
Total Carbohydrate (g)	5.8	Phosphorus (mg)	62
Total Protein (g)	3.2	Magnesium (mg)	21
% Calories from Fat	64.6	Iron (mg)	2.0
% Calories from Carbohydrate	26.0	Zinc (mg)	0.4
% Calories from Protein	9.4	Copper (mg)	0.1
Cholesterol (g)	0	Selenium (mcg)	1.5
Total Saturated Fatty Acids (g) (SFA)	0.9	Sodium (mg)	188
Total Monounsaturated Fatty Acids (g) (MUFA)	3.4	Potassium (mg)	660
Total Polyunsaturated Fatty Acids (g) (PUFA)	1.7		
Omega-3 Fatty Acids (g)	0.1		
% Calories from SFA	9.1	Linoleic Acid - PUFA (18:2) (g)	1.6
% Calories from MUFA	35.0	Linolenic Acid – PUFA (18:3) (g)	0.1
% Calories from PUFA	17.6		
Polyunsaturated to Saturated Fat (P:S) Ratio	1.9	Tryptophan (mg)	3
		Threonine (mg)	10
Total Dietary Fiber (g)	1.8	Isoleucine (mg)	17
Soluble Dietary Fiber (g)	0.2	Leucine (mg)	19
Insoluble Dietary Fiber (g)	1.6	Lysine (mg)	18
		Methionine (mg)	2
Total Vitamin A (mcg) (Retinol Activity Equivalents)	361	Phenylalanine (mg)	10
Vitamin D (calciferol) (mcg)	0.0	Valine (mg)	14
Vitamin E (mg) (Total Alpha-Tocopherol)	0.6	Histidine (mg)	6
Vitamin K (mg) (phylloquinone)	60.1		
Vitamin C (mg) (ascorbic acid)	46.0	Daidzein (mg)	0.0
Thiamin (mg) (vitamin B1)	0.1	Genistein (mg)	0.0
Riboflavin (mg) (vitamin B2)	0.1		
Niacin (mg) (vitamin B3)	0.9	Caffeine (mg)	0
Pantothenic Acid (mg)	0.2	Phytic Acid (mg)	36.7
Vitamin B6 (mg)	0.4	Oxalic Acid (mg)	49.9
Total Folate (mcg)	70	Choline (mg)	23.1
Vitamin B12 (mcg) (cobalamin)	0.		
		Glycemic Index (glucose reference)	54
Beta-Carotene (mcg) (provitamin A carotenoid)	4,334	Glycemic Load (glucose reference)	2
Lutein + Zeaxanthin (mcg)	66		
Lycopene (mcg)	0		

Broccoli Rabe with Garlic (Vegan; GF w/Mod)

Rabe cooked in this traditional style melts in your mouth with incredible flavor. Be sure to make enough, because guests will want seconds..

Ingredients

1 Tbsp olive oil

4 cloves garlic, minced

6 cups broccoli rabe (about half a bunch), washed and chopped (keeping stem separate from everything else)

1 tsp mirin

1 tsp low-sodium soy sauce

Heat oil in a medium skillet, add garlic, and sauté gently for a few minutes to flavor the oil. Add broccoli rabe stems to pan and sauté until almost tender; then add leaves. Add mirin, cover and cook for about 2 minutes over medium heat until leaves are tender (do not overcook). Add in soy sauce, stir. Serve.

NOTE: Regular broccoli can also be used with this recipe.

Yield: 2 cups (4, ½-cup servings)

~For gluten free, use tamari in place of soy sauce~

Broccoli Rabe: 1 serving = ½ cup

Energy (kcal)	61		
Total Fat (g)	3.8	Calcium (mg)	91
Total Carbohydrate (g)	3.9	Phosphorus (mg)	65
Total Protein (g)	3.0	Magnesium (mg)	21
% Calories from Fat	55	Iron (mg)	1.0
% Calories from Carbohydrate	26	Zinc (mg)	0.4
% Calories from Protein	19	Copper (mg)	0.1
Cholesterol (g)	0	Selenium (mcg)	1.4
Total Saturated Fatty Acids (g) (SFA)	0.5	Sodium (mg)	96
Total Monounsaturated Fatty Acids (g) (MUFA)	2.5	Potassium (mg)	261
Total Polyunsaturated Fatty Acids (g) (PUFA)	0.5		
Omega-3 Fatty Acids (g)	0.1		
% Calories from SFA	7.4	Linoleic Acid - PUFA (18:2) (g)	0.4
% Calories from MUFA	36.0	Linolenic Acid – PUFA (18:3) (g)	0.1
% Calories from PUFA	6.8		
Polyunsaturated to Saturated Fat (P:S) Ratio	0.9	Tryptophan (mg)	4
		Threonine (mg)	10
Total Dietary Fiber (g)	2.1	Isoleucine (mg)	10
Soluble Dietary Fiber (g)	0.2	Leucine (mg)	16
Insoluble Dietary Fiber (g)	1.9	Lysine (mg)	18
		Methionine (mg)	5
Total Vitamin A (mcg) (Retinol Activity Equivalents)	163	Phenylalanine (mg)	12
Vitamin D (calciferol) (mcg)	0.0	Valine (mg)	15
Vitamin E (mg) (Total Alpha-Tocopherol)	2.3	Histidine (mg)	6
Vitamin K (mg) (phylloquinone)	186.4		
Vitamin C (mg) (ascorbic acid)	27.6	Daidzein (mg)	0.0
Thiamin (mg) (vitamin B1)	0.1	Genistein (mg)	0.0
Riboflavin (mg) (vitamin B2)	0.1		
Niacin (mg) (vitamin B3)	1.5	Caffeine (mg)	0
Pantothenic Acid (mg)	0.3	Phytic Acid (mg)	13.0
Vitamin B6 (mg)	0.2	Oxalic Acid (mg)	11.3
Total Folate (mcg)	51	Choline (mg)	25.3
Vitamin B12 (mcg) (cobalamin)	0.0		
		Glycemic Index (glucose reference)	59
Beta-Carotene (mcg) (provitamin A carotenoid)	1,959	Glycemic Load (glucose reference)	1
Lutein + Zeaxanthin (mcg)	1,212		
Lycopene (mcg)	0		

Brussels Sprout Sauté (Vegan; GF w/Mod)

This dish captures the essence of Brussels sprouts' sweetness and good nature. Cooked thoroughly and seasoned gently, these little gems are an unexpected delight.

Ingredients

14 oz fresh Brussels sprouts (~4½ cups whole)

2 tsp sesame oil

3 cloves garlic, chopped (4 tsp)

Pinch salt

¼ cup water

1 tsp mirin

1 tsp low-sodium soy sauce (or to taste)

1/8 tsp fresh ground pepper

Wash and drain Brussels sprouts, then trim the ends removing any additional brown leaves. Cut each in half (or if any are very large, cut in quarters, so they are all approximately the same size). Heat the oil in a large sauce pan or wok. Stir in garlic and brown lightly. Add Brussels sprouts and mix to coat well with oil. Add salt to draw out the water. Cover and cook for 2 minutes. Add water and cooking wine; re-cover to steam. Cook over medium high heat for about 5 minutes or until vegetables start to become tender, stirring occasionally. (Note: if vegetables are not yet tender, more water can be added and they can be cooked longer.) Add soy sauce and pepper.

Yield: 2½ cups cooked (5, ½-cup servings)

~For gluten free, use tamari in place of soy sauce~

Inspired by Gretchen DeWire

Brussels Sprouts: 1 serving = ½ cup

Energy (kcal)	52		
Total Fat (g)	2.3	Calcium (mg)	34
Total Carbohydrate (g)	7.2	Phosphorus (mg)	51
Total Protein (g)	2.3	Magnesium (mg)	18
% Calories from Fat	38.1	Iron (mg)	1.1
% Calories from Carbohydrate	50.3	Zinc (mg)	0.3
% Calories from Protein	11.2	Copper (mg)	0.1
Cholesterol (g)	0	Selenium (mcg)	1.5
Total Saturated Fatty Acids (g) (SFA)	0.4	Sodium (mg)	91
Total Monounsaturated Fatty Acids (g) (MUFA)	0.8	Potassium (mg)	277
Total Polyunsaturated Fatty Acids (g) (PUFA)	1.0		
Omega-3 Fatty Acids (g)	0.2		
% Calories from SFA	5.9	Linoleic Acid - PUFA (18:2) (g)	0.8
% Calories from MUFA	12.9	Linolenic Acid – PUFA (18:3) (g)	1.2
% Calories from PUFA	16.5		
Polyunsaturated to Saturated Fat (P:S) Ratio	2.8	Tryptophan (mg)	3
		Threonine (mg)	8
Total Dietary Fiber (g)	2.2	Isoleucine (mg)	9
Soluble Dietary Fiber (g)	0.3	Leucine (mg)	11
Insoluble Dietary Fiber (g)	1.9	Lysine (mg)	11
		Methionine (mg)	2
Total Vitamin A (mcg) (Retinol Activity Equivalents)	33	Phenylalanine (mg)	7
Vitamin D (calciferol) (mcg)	0.0	Valine (mg)	11
Vitamin E (mg) (Total Alpha-Tocopherol)	0.4	Histidine (mg)	5
Vitamin K (mg) (phylloquinone)	118.6		
Vitamin C (mg) (ascorbic acid)	52.8	Daidzein (mg)	0.0
Thiamin (mg) (vitamin B1)	0.1	Genistein (mg)	0.0
Riboflavin (mg) (vitamin B2)	0.1		
Niacin (mg) (vitamin B3)	0.6	Caffeine (mg)	0
Pantothenic Acid (mg)	0.2	Phytic Acid (mg)	7.7
Vitamin B6 (mg)	0.2	Oxalic Acid (mg)	12.1
Total Folate (mcg)	51	Choline (mg)	35.0
Vitamin B12 (mcg) (cobalamin)	0.0		
		Glycemic Index (glucose reference)	53
Beta-Carotene (mcg) (provitamin A carotenoid)	392	Glycemic Load (glucose reference)	3
Lutein + Zeaxanthin (mcg)	1,087		
Lycopene (mcg)	0		

Burdock and Carrots (Vegan; GF w/Mod)

A lovely pairing, a wonderful synergy: hard to believe two root vegetables can pack this much power and taste… Uniquely sweet and savory.

Ingredients

12" piece of burdock root, cut into thin matchsticks (4 oz raw; 1½ cups cut)

2 medium carrots (4½ oz raw, 1½ cups cut)

1 Tbsp sesame oil

1 tsp mirin

1 Tbsp low-sodium soy sauce

(Optional: sesame seeds for garnish)

Slice burdock and carrots in thin matchsticks. Soak burdock in water to cover for 20-30 minutes to get rid of the bitter flavor. Discard water and drain well.

In a medium, seasoned cast-iron skillet, heat oil, add burdock, coating well with oil. Cover and cook over medium heat for about 10 minutes, stirring occasionally and checking to be sure the burdock does not dry out – if so, add a little water to steam).

Add carrot, stir to mix well. Add mirin and cover. Cook for another 10 minutes, or until burdock gets tender. Add soy sauce, stir and cook 2 more minutes. A nice caramel glaze should begin to develop at this point. Serve hot.

Yield: 1-1/3 cup cooked (4, 1/3-cup servings)

~For gluten free, use tamari in place of soy sauce~

Burdock and Carrots: 1 serving = 1/3 cup

Energy (kcal)	91		
Total Fat (g)	3.6	Calcium (mg)	36
Total Carbohydrate (g)	14.3	Phosphorus (mg)	61
Total Protein (g)	1.5	Magnesium (mg)	24
% Calories from Fat	34	Iron (mg)	0.6
% Calories from Carbohydrate	61	Zinc (mg)	0.3
% Calories from Protein	5	Copper (mg)	0.1
Cholesterol (g)	0	Selenium (mcg)	0.8
Total Saturated Fatty Acids (g) (SFA)	0.5	Sodium (mg)	170
Total Monounsaturated Fatty Acids (g) (MUFA)	1.4	Potassium (mg)	275
Total Polyunsaturated Fatty Acids (g) (PUFA)	1.5		
Omega-3 Fatty Acids (g)	0.0		
% Calories from SFA	5.0	Linoleic Acid - PUFA (18:2) (g)	1.5
% Calories from MUFA	13.4	Linolenic Acid – PUFA (18:3) (g)	0.0
% Calories from PUFA	14.5		
Polyunsaturated to Saturated Fat (P:S) Ratio	2.9	Tryptophan (mg)	1
		Threonine (mg)	9
Total Dietary Fiber (g)	2.1	Isoleucine (mg)	6
Soluble Dietary Fiber (g)	0.5	Leucine (mg)	7
Insoluble Dietary Fiber (g)	1.6	Lysine (mg)	9
		Methionine (mg)	2
Total Vitamin A (mcg) (Retinol Activity Equivalents)	359	Phenylalanine (mg)	5
Vitamin D (calciferol) (mcg)	0.0	Valine (mg)	6
Vitamin E (mg) (Total Alpha-Tocopherol)	0.7	Histidine (mg)	4
Vitamin K (mg) (phylloquinone)	7.2		
Vitamin C (mg) (ascorbic acid)	2.7	Daidzein (mg)	0.0
Thiamin (mg) (vitamin B1)	0.0	Genistein (mg)	0.0
Riboflavin (mg) (vitamin B2)	0.1		
Niacin (mg) (vitamin B3)	0.6	Caffeine (mg)	0
Pantothenic Acid (mg)	0.3	Phytic Acid (mg)	46.3
Vitamin B6 (mg)	0.2	Oxalic Acid (mg)	19.6
Total Folate (mcg)	16	Choline (mg)	11.7
Vitamin B12 (mcg) (cobalamin)	0.0		
		Glycemic Index (glucose reference)	62
Beta-Carotene (mcg) (provitamin A carotenoid)	3,509	Glycemic Load (glucose reference)	8
Lutein + Zeaxanthin (mcg)	289		
Lycopene (mcg)	0		

Cabbage with Ginger (Vegan; GF)

Tart, tangy and sweet, this succulent cabbage dish is one to cherish. The preparation time is short and the flavors suit any season.

Ingredients

½ a small head of green cabbage, shredded (about 4 cups)

1 Tbsp sesame oil

1 Tbsp ginger, grated

2 chopped, pitted umeboshi plum

Slice the cabbage into thin shreds, after removing the hard central core. In a skillet, heat oil and add the cabbage, coating the cabbage with oil. Sauté over medium-high heat for about 5 minutes. Squeeze the juice out of the grated ginger and drizzle over the cabbage. Then add the umeboshi (or salt), and mix it evenly to coat the cabbage. Cover and cook over low heat, until the cabbage reaches desired tenderness.

Yield: 2 cups cooked cabbage (4, ½-cup servings)

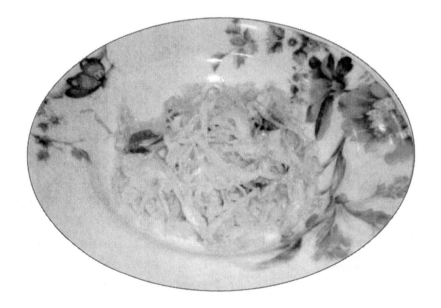

Cabbage with Ginger: 1 serving = ½ cup

Energy (kcal)	49		
Total Fat (g)	3.5	Calcium (mg)	36
Total Carbohydrate (g)	4.4	Phosphorus (mg)	25
Total Protein (g)	1.0	Magnesium (mg)	12
% Calories from Fat	62	Iron (mg)	0.1
% Calories from Carbohydrate	33	Zinc (mg)	0.2
% Calories from Protein	5	Copper (mg)	0.0
Cholesterol (g)	0	Selenium (mcg)	0.5
Total Saturated Fatty Acids (g) (SFA)	0.5	Sodium (mg)	82
Total Monounsaturated Fatty Acids (g) (MUFA)	1.4	Potassium (mg)	154
Total Polyunsaturated Fatty Acids (g) (PUFA)	1.4		
Omega-3 Fatty Acids (g)	0.0		
% Calories from SFA	8.9	Linoleic Acid - PUFA (18:2) (g)	1.4
% Calories from MUFA	24.8	Linolenic Acid – PUFA (18:3) (g)	0.0
% Calories from PUFA	26.1		
Polyunsaturated to Saturated Fat (P:S) Ratio	2.9	Tryptophan (mg)	1
		Threonine (mg)	3
Total Dietary Fiber (g)	1.5	Isoleucine (mg)	2
Soluble Dietary Fiber (g)	0.1	Leucine (mg)	3
Insoluble Dietary Fiber (g)	1.4	Lysine (mg)	3
		Methionine (mg)	1
Total Vitamin A (mcg) (Retinol Activity Equivalents)	3	Phenylalanine (mg)	3
Vitamin D (calciferol) (mcg)	0.0	Valine (mg)	3
Vitamin E (mg) (Total Alpha-Tocopherol)	0.2	Histidine (mg)	2
Vitamin K (mg) (phylloquinone)	82.0		
Vitamin C (mg) (ascorbic acid)	28.2	Daidzein (mg)	0.0
Thiamin (mg) (vitamin B1)	0.0	Genistein (mg)	0.0
Riboflavin (mg) (vitamin B2)	0.0		
Niacin (mg) (vitamin B3)	0.2	Caffeine (mg)	0
Pantothenic Acid (mg)	0.1	Phytic Acid (mg)	1.9
Vitamin B6 (mg)	0.1	Oxalic Acid (mg)	3.8
Total Folate (mcg)	23	Choline (mg)	15.7
Vitamin B12 (mcg) (cobalamin)	0.0		
		Glycemic Index (glucose reference)	51
Beta-Carotene (mcg) (provitamin A carotenoid)	36	Glycemic Load (glucose reference)	2
Lutein + Zeaxanthin (mcg)	20		
Lycopene (mcg)	0		

Carrot-Parsnips (Vegan; GF w/Mod)

Heavenly-sweet parsnips and super-delicious carrots in a glazed pairing that cannot be beat.

Ingredients

3 medium carrots (5 oz [150 g], raw)

3 medium parsnips (5 oz [150 g], raw)

1 tsp sesame oil

1 tsp olive oil

1 cup water

1 tsp mirin

2 tsp low-sodium soy sauce

2 Tbsp fresh Italian parsley, chopped

1 tsp roasted sesame seeds

Wash and peel carrots & parsnips (if either are organic, no need peel them, just scrub with a vegetable brush). Cut on the diagonal in fairly good-size chunks, turning the carrot a half-way around (180-degrees) each time you slice, to get the nice shape.

In a medium skillet or wok, heat the oils; sauté carrots and parsnips over medium heat. Add water to almost cover the vegetables (about 1 cup), then simmer until most of the water is gone. Just before all the water is gone, add mirin and then soy sauce to taste (about 2 tsp), stir and cook until water has evaporated. The sugar from the vegetables should give a nice glaze after the water has evaporated (but be careful at the end not to let this burn!) At the end, add chopped Italian parsley and roasted sesame seeds, mix and serve.

Yield: 2 cups, (4, ½-cup servings)

~For gluten free, use tamari in place of soy sauce~

Inspired by Gretchen DeWire

Carrots with Parsnips: 1 serving = ½ cup

Energy (kcal)	67		
Total Fat (g)	2.8	Calcium (mg)	30
Total Carbohydrate (g)	10.4	Phosphorus (mg)	46
Total Protein (g)	1.1	Magnesium (mg)	19
% Calories from Fat	36	Iron (mg)	0.6
% Calories from Carbohydrate	59	Zinc (mg)	0.3
% Calories from Protein	5	Copper (mg)	0.1
Cholesterol (g)	0	Selenium (mcg)	0.9
Total Saturated Fatty Acids (g) (SFA)	0.4	Sodium (mg)	127
Total Monounsaturated Fatty Acids (g) (MUFA)	1.4	Potassium (mg)	239
Total Polyunsaturated Fatty Acids (g) (PUFA)	0.8		
Omega-3 Fatty Acids (g)	0.0		
% Calories from SFA	5.1	Linoleic Acid - PUFA (18:2) (g)	0.8
% Calories from MUFA	18.8	Linolenic Acid – PUFA (18:3) (g)	0.0
% Calories from PUFA	10.2		
Polyunsaturated to Saturated Fat (P:S) Ratio	2.0	Tryptophan (mg)	1
		Threonine (mg)	9
Total Dietary Fiber (g)	2.6	Isoleucine (mg)	6
Soluble Dietary Fiber (g)	0.6	Leucine (mg)	8
Insoluble Dietary Fiber (g)	2.0	Lysine (mg)	7
		Methionine (mg)	2
Total Vitamin A (mcg) (Retinol Activity Equivalents)	302	Phenylalanine (mg)	5
Vitamin D (calciferol) (mcg)	0.0	Valine (mg)	6
Vitamin E (mg) (Total Alpha-Tocopherol)	0.9	Histidine (mg)	3
Vitamin K (mg) (phylloquinone)	36.7		
Vitamin C (mg) (ascorbic acid)	8.7	Daidzein (mg)	0.0
Thiamin (mg) (vitamin B1)	0.1	Genistein (mg)	0.0
Riboflavin (mg) (vitamin B2)	0.0		
Niacin (mg) (vitamin B3)	0.7	Caffeine (mg)	0
Pantothenic Acid (mg)	0.3	Phytic Acid (mg)	37.6
Vitamin B6 (mg)	0.1	Oxalic Acid (mg)	18.6
Total Folate (mcg)	31	Choline (mg)	14.6
Vitamin B12 (mcg) (cobalamin)	0.0		
		Glycemic Index (glucose reference)	80
Beta-Carotene (mcg) (provitamin A carotenoid)	2,970	Glycemic Load (glucose reference)	6
Lutein + Zeaxanthin (mcg)	341		
Lycopene (mcg)	0		

Cole Slaw (GF)

Homemade cole slaw is quick, simple and better than anything you can buy. Rice vinegar lends a smooth taste and subtlety to this popular side dish.

Ingredients

3 cups fresh green cabbage shredded finely

¼ medium onion, sliced very thinly

1 small carrot, shaved

5 tsp mayonnaise

1 tsp rice vinegar

Pinch salt

Pinch black pepper

1 tsp brown rice syrup (optional)

Wash and dry a head of cabbage. Cut in half, and shred finely. Place in a large mixing bowl and add the onion and carrot, mixing to combine evenly. Add mayonnaise, stir in to blend well. Add vinegar, salt and pepper. Adjust to taste. If needed, a bit of sweetener can be used, such as brown rice syrup.

This is best made in advance and refrigerated for several hours, to allow the tastes to blend well.

Yield: 2¾ cups (5½, ½-cup servings)

~For a vegan dish, use soy mayonnaise~

Cole Slaw: 1 serving = ½ cup

Energy (kcal)	46		
Total Fat (g)	3.4	Calcium (mg)	16
Total Carbohydrate (g)	4.0	Phosphorus (mg)	13
Total Protein (g)	0.5	Magnesium (mg)	5
% Calories from Fat	65	Iron (mg)	0.2
% Calories from Carbohydrate	32	Zinc (mg)	0.1
% Calories from Protein	3	Copper (mg)	0.0
Cholesterol (g)	2	Selenium (mcg)	0.2
Total Saturated Fatty Acids (g) (SFA)	0.5	Sodium (mg)	61
Total Monounsaturated Fatty Acids (g) (MUFA)	0.8	Potassium (mg)	78
Total Polyunsaturated Fatty Acids (g) (PUFA)	1.8		
Omega-3 Fatty Acids (g)	0.2		
% Calories from SFA	9.8	Linoleic Acid - PUFA (18:2) (g)	1.6
% Calories from MUFA	15.8	Linolenic Acid – PUFA (18:3) (g)	0.2
% Calories from PUFA	34.2		
Polyunsaturated to Saturated Fat (P:S) Ratio	3.5	Tryptophan (mg)	1
		Threonine (mg)	2
Total Dietary Fiber (g)	0.9	Isoleucine (mg)	2
Soluble Dietary Fiber (g)	0.2	Leucine (mg)	2
Insoluble Dietary Fiber (g)	0.7	Lysine (mg)	2
		Methionine (mg)	1
Total Vitamin A (mcg) (Retinol Activity Equivalents)	48	Phenylalanine (mg)	2
Vitamin D (calciferol) (mcg)	0.0	Valine (mg)	2
Vitamin E (mg) (Total Alpha-Tocopherol)	0.3	Histidine (mg)	1
Vitamin K (mg) (phylloquinone)	25.7		
Vitamin C (mg) (ascorbic acid)	12.0	Daidzein (mg)	0.0
Thiamin (mg) (vitamin B1)	0.0	Genistein (mg)	0.0
Riboflavin (mg) (vitamin B2)	0.0		
Niacin (mg) (vitamin B3)	0.1	Caffeine (mg)	0
Pantothenic Acid (mg)	0.1	Phytic Acid (mg)	4.0
Vitamin B6 (mg)	0.1	Oxalic Acid (mg)	4.4
Total Folate (mcg)	15	Choline (mg)	5.0
Vitamin B12 (mcg) (cobalamin)	0.0		
		Glycemic Index (glucose reference)	65
Beta-Carotene (mcg) (provitamin A carotenoid)	440	Glycemic Load (glucose reference)	2
Lutein + Zeaxanthin (mcg)	31		
Lycopene (mcg)	0		

Daikon with Greens and Wakame (Vegan; GF w/Mod)

Daikon takes on a whole new twist when paired with wakame seaweed. Nutritious greens bring a splash of color to this energizing dish.

Ingredients

5 g (dry) wakame seaweed

2 c water, divided

1 1/3 cups raw daikon greens (chopped)*

8½ oz daikon radish, sliced on diagonal and cut

      into thick matchsticks (~1½ cups)

1 Tbsp sesame oil

1 Tbsp low-sodium soy sauce

* Your choice of other greens, such as kale or mustard greens, can also be used.

With a scissors, cut the wakame into small pieces. Rinse, drain, and soak in 1 cup water for ~3 minutes to rehydrate (this yields 1/3 cup rehydrated). Drain and squeeze out excess water; discard water.

Heat oil in medium skillet; add daikon greens and sauté for 2 minutes, then add daikon. Sauté briefly, mixing with greens and coating with oil. Add drained wakame, and stir. Add 1 cup of water to the vegetables, cover and simmer for about 15 minutes, add soy sauce, uncover and let water boil away (about 5 minutes).

Yield: 2½ cups (5, ½-cup servings)

~For gluten free, use tamari in place of soy sauce~

Inspired by Gretchen DeWire

146

Daikon with Wakame: 1 serving = ½ cup

Energy (kcal)	38		
Total Fat (g)	2.8	Calcium (mg)	36
Total Carbohydrate (g)	3.1	Phosphorus (mg)	20
Total Protein (g)	0.7	Magnesium (mg)	14
% Calories from Fat	65	Iron (mg)	0.5
% Calories from Carbohydrate	30	Zinc (mg)	0.2
% Calories from Protein	5	Copper (mg)	0.1
Cholesterol (g)	0	Selenium (mcg)	0.5
Total Saturated Fatty Acids (g) (SFA)	0.4	Sodium (mg)	184
Total Monounsaturated Fatty Acids (g) (MUFA)	1.1	Potassium (mg)	151
Total Polyunsaturated Fatty Acids (g) (PUFA)	1.2		
Omega-3 Fatty Acids (g)	0.03		
% Calories from SFA	9.8	Linoleic Acid - PUFA (18:2) (g)	1.1
% Calories from MUFA	25.4	Linolenic Acid – PUFA (18:3) (g)	0.03
% Calories from PUFA	27.2		
Polyunsaturated to Saturated Fat (P:S) Ratio	2.8	Tryptophan (mg)	1
		Threonine (mg)	3
Total Dietary Fiber (g)	1.4	Isoleucine (mg)	3
Soluble Dietary Fiber (g)	0.1	Leucine (mg)	5
Insoluble Dietary Fiber (g)	1.3	Lysine (mg)	4
		Methionine (mg)	1
Total Vitamin A (mcg) (Retinol Activity Equivalents)	49	Phenylalanine (mg)	3
Vitamin D (calciferol) (mcg)	0.0	Valine (mg)	4
Vitamin E (mg) (Total Alpha-Tocopherol)	0.3	Histidine (mg)	2
Vitamin K (mg) (phylloquinone)	42.7		
Vitamin C (mg) (ascorbic acid)	13.8	Daidzein (mg)	0.030
Thiamin (mg) (vitamin B1)	0.0	Genistein (mg)	0.026
Riboflavin (mg) (vitamin B2)	0.0		
Niacin (mg) (vitamin B3)	0.3	Caffeine (mg)	0
Pantothenic Acid (mg)	0.1	Phytic Acid (mg)	6.1
Vitamin B6 (mg)	0.0	Oxalic Acid (mg)	1.1
Total Folate (mcg)	31	Choline (mg)	4.8
Vitamin B12 (mcg) (cobalamin)	0.1		
		Glycemic Index (glucose reference)	61
Beta-Carotene (mcg) (provitamin A carotenoid)	585	Glycemic Load (glucose reference)	1
Lutein + Zeaxanthin (mcg)	938		
Lycopene (mcg)	0		

Green Beans with Soy Crumbles (Vegan)

A most enjoyable way to eat Nature's bounty of green beans. This is a wonderful accompaniment to rice, and is bursting with flavor. Soy crumbles add an extra protein boost.

Ingredients

1½ Tbsp olive oil

4 cloves garlic, minced (about 2 Tbsp)

1 lb fresh green beans – washed and drained, with edges trimmed (~5 cups)

2 tsp mirin

¼ cup water (more or less as needed)

½ cup frozen soy crumbles (optional)

2 tsp low-sodium soy sauce

Heat a frying pan or large saucepan, add oil, and when oil is hot (but not smoking), add minced garlic, sauté gently for about 1 minute. Then add green beans, coating them well with oil, add mirin, turn heat to medium. If beans are on the thicker side, you may need to add about ¼ cup of water to prevent burning; if beans are very fresh and moist, this step can be omitted. Cover for about 3 minutes, stirring occasionally (taking care not to burn them). Add soy crumbles, mix well, and re-cover. When beans are completely cooked, add soy sauce, cook on low for 1 minute and remove from heat.

Yield: 3½ cups (3½, 1-cup servings)

reen Beans with Soy Crumbles: 1 serving = 1 cup

Energy (kcal)	160		
Total Fat (g)	6.6	Calcium (mg)	82
Total Carbohydrate (g)	12.9	Phosphorus (mg)	146
Total Protein (g)	14.6	Magnesium (mg)	28
% Calories from Fat	36	Iron (mg)	3.0
% Calories from Carbohydrate	30	Zinc (mg)	0.9
% Calories from Protein	34	Copper (mg)	0.3
Cholesterol (g)	0	Selenium (mcg)	3.9
Total Saturated Fatty Acids (g) (SFA)	0.9	Sodium (mg)	133
Total Monounsaturated Fatty Acids (g) (MUFA)	4.3	Potassium (mg)	212
Total Polyunsaturated Fatty Acids (g) (PUFA)	1.0		
Omega-3 Fatty Acids (g)	0.2		
% Calories from SFA	5.2	Linoleic Acid - PUFA (18:2) (g)	0.9
% Calories from MUFA	24.0	Linolenic Acid – PUFA (18:3) (g)	0.2
% Calories from PUFA	5.7		
Polyunsaturated to Saturated Fat (P:S) Ratio	1.1	Tryptophan (mg)	19
		Threonine (mg)	57
Total Dietary Fiber (g)	4.3	Isoleucine (mg)	68
Soluble Dietary Fiber (g)	1.0	Leucine (mg)	114
Insoluble Dietary Fiber (g)	3.3	Lysine (mg)	88
		Methionine (mg)	19
Total Vitamin A (mcg) (Retinol Activity Equivalents)	43	Phenylalanine (mg)	72
Vitamin D (calciferol) (mcg)	0.0	Valine (mg)	73
Vitamin E (mg) (Total Alpha-Tocopherol)	1.4	Histidine (mg)	36
Vitamin K (mg) (phylloquinone)	24.0		
Vitamin C (mg) (ascorbic acid)	13.0	Daidzein (mg)	5.4
Thiamin (mg) (vitamin B1)	0.1	Genistein (mg)	8.7
Riboflavin (mg) (vitamin B2)	0.1		
Niacin (mg) (vitamin B3)	1.0	Caffeine (mg)	0
Pantothenic Acid (mg)	0.1	Phytic Acid (mg)	326.1
Vitamin B6 (mg)	0.1	Oxalic Acid (mg)	40.4
Total Folate (mcg)	67	Choline (mg)	35.5
Vitamin B12 (mcg) (cobalamin)	0.0		
		Glycemic Index (glucose reference)	54
Beta-Carotene (mcg) (provitamin A carotenoid)	518	Glycemic Load (glucose reference)	5
Lutein + Zeaxanthin (mcg)	873		
Lycopene (mcg)	0		

Home Fry Pancake (Vegan; GF)

Forget restaurant hash browns! Look no further than you home grater. This is one of the simplest recipes ever, with amazing nutritional returns. Almost as much fun to make as it is to eat!

Ingredients

2 large Yukon Gold potatoes (about 10 ounces each)

2 tsp olive oil, divided

1/8 tsp salt

Pinch black pepper

Wash and peel potatoes. Using a hand-held grater, shred potatoes (makes about 3 cups). Squeeze out excess water. Heat a large skillet (nonstick works well for this recipe) and add 1 tsp of oil. When oil is hot, add shredded potato, completely covering the pan with a thin layer, covering any spaces that show. Press down firmly on surface to help hold the shreds together as they cook, and to allow heat to touch all areas. Cook over medium heat, checking the underside occasionally. After about 10 minutes, or when the underside is a deep golden brown, loosen the edges and underneath the pancake with a large spatula. Trying to keep the pancake in one piece, flip over. Carefully add the other tsp of oil beneath the pancake and twirl pan to coat. Cook until underside is golden brown. (If using a cast iron frying pan, more oil may be needed, and can be added after flipping.) When almost done, add salt and pepper. Serve immediately.

Yield: 1 10"-diameter potato "pancake" or 4 servings

Home Fry Pancake: 1 serving = ¼ pancake

Energy (kcal)	129		
Total Fat (g)	2.4	Calcium (mg)	10
Total Carbohydrate (g)	25.3	Phosphorus (mg)	51
Total Protein (g)	2.2	Magnesium (mg)	25
% Calories from Fat	16	Iron (mg)	0.4
% Calories from Carbohydrate	79	Zinc (mg)	0.3
% Calories from Protein	5	Copper (mg)	0.2
Cholesterol (g)	0	Selenium (mcg)	0.4
Total Saturated Fatty Acids (g) (SFA)	0.3	Sodium (mg)	82
Total Monounsaturated Fatty Acids (g) (MUFA)	1.6	Potassium (mg)	415
Total Polyunsaturated Fatty Acids (g) (PUFA)	0.3		
Omega-3 Fatty Acids (g)	0.0		
% Calories from SFA	2.4	Linoleic Acid - PUFA (18:2) (g)	0.3
% Calories from MUFA	11.3	Linolenic Acid – PUFA (18:3) (g)	0.0
% Calories from PUFA	2.0		
Polyunsaturated to Saturated Fat (P:S) Ratio	0.8	Tryptophan (mg)	3
		Threonine (mg)	8
Total Dietary Fiber (g)	2.6	Isoleucine (mg)	9
Soluble Dietary Fiber (g)	1.3	Leucine (mg)	13
Insoluble Dietary Fiber (g)	1.3	Lysine (mg)	13
		Methionine (mg)	3
Total Vitamin A (mcg) (Retinol Activity Equivalents)	0	Phenylalanine (mg)	10
Vitamin D (calciferol) (mcg)	0.0	Valine (mg)	12
Vitamin E (mg) (Total Alpha-Tocopherol)	0.4	Histidine (mg)	5
Vitamin K (mg) (phylloquinone)	4.1		
Vitamin C (mg) (ascorbic acid)	9.4	Daidzein (mg)	0.0
Thiamin (mg) (vitamin B1)	0.1	Genistein (mg)	0.0
Riboflavin (mg) (vitamin B2)	0.0		
Niacin (mg) (vitamin B3)	1.7	Caffeine (mg)	0
Pantothenic Acid (mg)	0.6	Phytic Acid (mg)	51.9
Vitamin B6 (mg)	0.3	Oxalic Acid (mg)	24.5
Total Folate (mcg)	11	Choline (mg)	16.7
Vitamin B12 (mcg) (cobalamin)	0.0		
		Glycemic Index (glucose reference)	59
Beta-Carotene (mcg) (provitamin A carotenoid)	3	Glycemic Load (glucose reference)	13
Lutein + Zeaxanthin (mcg)	11		
Lycopene (mcg)	0		

Kale with Sunflower Seeds (Vegan: GF)

A light, delicate way to eat a true giant among vegetables! The sautéed onions and seeds add an interesting flavor surprise.

Ingredients

Fresh kale, 7 oz (6 cups sliced)

1 Tbsp sesame oil

1 tsp balsamic vinegar

2 Tbsp sautéed onions (see recipe below)*

4 tsp roasted sunflower seeds

1/8 tsp Kosher salt

Wash and drain kale, trimming any brown or dried ends. Slice stems on the diagonal, about 1/8" thick. Keep separately. Slice leaves and set aside. Steam kale stems for about 2 minutes, then add leaves. When tender (about 5 minutes, depending on the age and type of kale) remove and plate. Sauté onions and set aside to cool - see below.*

In a small saucepan, heat the oil but do not let it smoke. Pour over the cooked kale, then add vinegar, sautéed onions, sunflower seeds, salt and toss gently.

*Sautéed Onion: Dice a large onion (1¾ cups diced), sauté in 1 tsp olive oil, adding a pinch of salt, until translucent. This yield 1 1/8 cups of cooked onion (18 Tbsp).

Yield: 4 cups cooked (4, 1-cup servings)

Kale with Sunflower Seeds: 1 serving = 1 cup

Energy (kcal)	87		
Total Fat (g)	5.4	Calcium (mg)	97
Total Carbohydrate (g)	8.9	Phosphorus (mg)	70
Total Protein (g)	3.1	Magnesium (mg)	28
% Calories from Fat	54	Iron (mg)	1.3
% Calories from Carbohydrate	37	Zinc (mg)	0.5
% Calories from Protein	9	Copper (mg)	0.3
Cholesterol (g)	0	Selenium (mcg)	3.3
Total Saturated Fatty Acids (g) (SFA)	0.7	Sodium (mg)	106
Total Monounsaturated Fatty Acids (g) (MUFA)	1.7	Potassium (mg)	331
Total Polyunsaturated Fatty Acids (g) (PUFA)	2.6		
Omega-3 Fatty Acids (g)	0.1		
% Calories from SFA	7.2	Linoleic Acid - PUFA (18:2) (g)	2.4
% Calories from MUFA	17.5	Linolenic Acid – PUFA (18:3) (g)	0.1
% Calories from PUFA	25.4		
Polyunsaturated to Saturated Fat (P:S) Ratio	3.6	Tryptophan (mg)	4
		Threonine (mg)	13
Total Dietary Fiber (g)	2.9	Isoleucine (mg)	18
Soluble Dietary Fiber (g)	2.4	Leucine (mg)	21
Insoluble Dietary Fiber (g)	0.6	Lysine (mg)	17
		Methionine (mg)	4
Total Vitamin A (mcg) (Retinol Activity Equivalents)	885	Phenylalanine (mg)	16
Vitamin D (calciferol) (mcg)	0.0	Valine (mg)	17
Vitamin E (mg) (Total Alpha-Tocopherol)	1.9	Histidine (mg)	7
Vitamin K (mg) (phylloquinone)	1,063		
Vitamin C (mg) (ascorbic acid)	53.7	Daidzein (mg)	0.0
Thiamin (mg) (vitamin B1)	0.1	Genistein (mg)	0.0
Riboflavin (mg) (vitamin B2)	0.1		
Niacin (mg) (vitamin B3)	0.8	Caffeine (mg)	0
Pantothenic Acid (mg)	0.3	Phytic Acid (mg)	56.4
Vitamin B6 (mg)	0.2	Oxalic Acid (mg)	2.6
Total Folate (mcg)	24	Choline (mg)	2.5
Vitamin B12 (mcg) (cobalamin)	0.0		
		Glycemic Index (glucose reference)	50
Beta-Carotene (mcg) (provitamin A carotenoid)	10,625	Glycemic Load (glucose reference)	3
Lutein + Zeaxanthin (mcg)	23,720		
Lycopene (mcg)	0		

Kohlrabi with Peppercorn (Vegan; GF w/Mod)

These stiff and solid looking bulbs are juicy and crunchy; they make a mouthwatering salad. Simply peel, chop and season. Here is one way to enjoy this mysterious vegetable.

Ingredients

2 tsp whole black peppercorns 4 tsp. olive oil*

3 medium bulbs of kohlrabi no leaves, washed & peeled,
  chopped into small, diced chunks

2 tsp low-sodium soy sauce

Sauté peppercorns in oil until they turn black and crispy. Pour peppercorns & oil over chopped kohlrabi, add soy sauce and mix well.

This is best made ahead to marinate for at least one hour, stirring occasionally.

*Note: 1 tsp ground is ~2 tsp whole peppercorns

Yield. 5 cups (10, ½ cup servings)

~For gluten free, use tamari in place of soy sauce~

154

Kohlrabi with Peppercorn: 1 serving = ½ cup

Energy (kcal)	35		
Total Fat (g)	1.9	Calcium (mg)	17
Total Carbohydrate (g)	4.4	Phosphorus (mg)	33
Total Protein (g)	1.2	Magnesium (mg)	14
% Calories from Fat	47	Iron (mg)	0.4
% Calories from Carbohydrate	45	Zinc (mg)	0.0
% Calories from Protein	8	Copper (mg)	0.1
Cholesterol (g)	0	Selenium (mcg)	0.5
Total Saturated Fatty Acids (g) (SFA)	0.3	Sodium (mg)	49
Total Monounsaturated Fatty Acids (g) (MUFA)	1.3	Potassium (mg)	241
Total Polyunsaturated Fatty Acids (g) (PUFA)	0.2		
Omega-3 Fatty Acids (g)	0.03		
% Calories from SFA	6.5	Linoleic Acid - PUFA (18:2) (g)	0.19
% Calories from MUFA	33.1	Linolenic Acid – PUFA (18:3) (g)	0.03
% Calories from PUFA	5.6		
Polyunsaturated to Saturated Fat (P:S) Ratio	0.9	Tryptophan (mg)	1
		Threonine (mg)	4
Total Dietary Fiber (g)	2.5	Isoleucine (mg)	6
Soluble Dietary Fiber (g)	1.7	Leucine (mg)	5
Insoluble Dietary Fiber (g)	0.8	Lysine (mg)	4
		Methionine (mg)	1
Total Vitamin A (mcg) (Retinol Activity Equivalents)	1	Phenylalanine (mg)	3
Vitamin D (calciferol) (mcg)	0.0	Valine (mg)	4
Vitamin E (mg) (Total Alpha-Tocopherol)	0.6	Histidine (mg)	1
Vitamin K (mg) (phylloquinone)	1.5		
Vitamin C (mg) (ascorbic acid)	41.9	Daidzein (mg)	0.0
Thiamin (mg) (vitamin B1)	0.0	Genistein (mg)	0.0
Riboflavin (mg) (vitamin B2)	0.0		
Niacin (mg) (vitamin B3)	0.3	Caffeine (mg)	0
Pantothenic Acid (mg)	0.1	Phytic Acid (mg)	2.1
Vitamin B6 (mg)	0.1	Oxalic Acid (mg)	3.5
Total Folate (mcg)	11	Choline (mg)	8.7
Vitamin B12 (mcg) (cobalamin)	0.0		
		Glycemic Index (glucose reference)	50
Beta-Carotene (mcg) (provitamin A carotenoid)	15	Glycemic Load (glucose reference)	1
Lutein + Zeaxanthin (mcg)	0		
Lycopene (mcg)	0		

Lemony Lotus Root (Vegan: GF)

Truly a unique vegetable, in texture, appearance and taste, lotus root is amazingly easy to prepare.
Well cooked, it is delicate and satisfying. Great by itself, it also shines in groups – so try it in your
favorite vegetable stew.

Ingredients

1 tsp sesame oil

Lotus root, 4 ounces, cut in paper-thin slices (1½ cups sliced)

¾ cup water

½ tsp fresh-squeezed lemon juice

1/8 tsp Kosher salt

1 small scallion (20 g), chopped

Heat the oil in a small skillet; then add the lotus slices and sauté for 2 minutes. Add water to just cover
(about ¾ cup) and cover, simmering on medium heat for 5 minutes. Stir in lemon juice and salt,
recover and cook for another 5 minutes or until all water has cooked away. Mix in chopped scallion,
heat one minute, and serve.

Yield: 1-1/3 cups (4, 1/3 cup servings)

Inspired by Lima Ohsawa, *The Art of Just Cooking*, Hayama, *Japan:* Autumn Press, 1974

Lemony Lotus Root: 1 serving = 1/3 cup

Energy (kcal)	36		
Total Fat (g)	1.2	Calcium (mg)	12
Total Carbohydrate (g)	6.4	Phosphorus (mg)	31
Total Protein (g)	0.6	Magnesium (mg)	9
% Calories from Fat	28	Iron (mg)	0.4
% Calories from Carbohydrate	67	Zinc (mg)	0.1
% Calories from Protein	5	Copper (mg)	0.1
Cholesterol (g)	0	Selenium (mcg)	0.2
Total Saturated Fatty Acids (g) (SFA)	0.2	Sodium (mg)	96
Total Monounsaturated Fatty Acids (g) (MUFA)	0.5	Potassium (mg)	146
Total Polyunsaturated Fatty Acids (g) (PUFA)	0.5		
Omega-3 Fatty Acids (g)	0.0		
% Calories from SFA	4.2	Linoleic Acid - PUFA (18:2) (g)	0.5
% Calories from MUFA	11.1	Linolenic Acid – PUFA (18:3) (g)	0.0
% Calories from PUFA	11.7		
Polyunsaturated to Saturated Fat (P:S) Ratio	2.8	Tryptophan (mg)	1
		Threonine (mg)	1
Total Dietary Fiber (g)	1.2	Isoleucine (mg)	1
Soluble Dietary Fiber (g)	0.7	Leucine (mg)	2
Insoluble Dietary Fiber (g)	0.5	Lysine (mg)	2
		Methionine (mg)	1
Total Vitamin A (mcg) (Retinol Activity Equivalents)	1	Phenylalanine (mg)	1
Vitamin D (calciferol) (mcg)	0.0	Valine (mg)	1
Vitamin E (mg) (Total Alpha-Tocopherol)	0.0	Histidine (mg)	1
Vitamin K (mg) (phylloquinone)	2.8		
Vitamin C (mg) (ascorbic acid)	11.2	Daidzein (mg)	0.0
Thiamin (mg) (vitamin B1)	0.1	Genistein (mg)	0.0
Riboflavin (mg) (vitamin B2)	0.0		
Niacin (mg) (vitamin B3)	0.1	Caffeine (mg)	0
Pantothenic Acid (mg)	0.1	Phytic Acid (mg)	27.2
Vitamin B6 (mg)	0.1	Oxalic Acid (mg)	7.1
Total Folate (mcg)	4	Choline (mg)	10.0
Vitamin B12 (mcg) (cobalamin)	0.0		
		Glycemic Index (glucose reference)	67
Beta-Carotene (mcg) (provitamin A carotenoid)	7	Glycemic Load (glucose reference)	3
Lutein + Zeaxanthin (mcg)	14		
Lycopene (mcg)	0		

Onion Rings <small>(Vegan; GF w/Mod)</small>

Here is another way to showcase this versatile vegetable. Making onion rings at home can be rewarding and a real treat. Include other vegetables for a plate of vegetable tempura!

Ingredients

1 medium onion, 7 ounces, sliced into rings

1 cup whole wheat pastry flour

¼ cup corn flour

1 Tbsp arrowroot flour (or cornstarch)

½ tsp salt

1 cup water

Canola oil for deep-frying*

*Start with about 3 cups of oil, or enough so that the oil is about 1-inch deep.

Slice onion horizontally into ¼-inch rings, and separate into individual circles. Prepare batter in a medium mixing bowl, by combining pastry flour, corn flour, arrowroot flour, and salt. Add enough water (about 1 cup) to make a pancake-batter consistency. Let sit for about 30 minutes.

Place raw rings into batter, stir to coat lightly.

Into a wok or high-sided, stainless steel pot, place canola oil (or safflower) and heat on medium-high. Oil is ready when a kernel or cooked rice or a small amount of batter dropped in comes back up quickly to the surface. Drop batter-dipped vegetables into hot oil. Be careful not to overload the pan. Cook awhile, then turn over. Turn and fry other side until ring becomes golden brown and crispy. Remove carefully with a strainer or tongs. Drain well on a plate lined with paper towel. (Serve with grated daikon.)

Yield: 48 onion rings (8 servings of 6 rings each)

~For gluten-free, use 1 cup gluten-free flour mix in place of whole wheat pastry flour ~

Onion Rings: 1 serving = 6 rings

Energy (kcal)	208		
Total Fat (g)	12.5	Calcium (mg)	14
Total Carbohydrate (g)	22.2	Phosphorus (mg)	95
Total Protein (g)	3.6	Magnesium (mg)	37
% Calories from Fat	53	Iron (mg)	1.0
% Calories from Carbohydrate	41	Zinc (mg)	0.8
% Calories from Protein	6	Copper (mg)	0.1
Cholesterol (g)	0	Selenium (mcg)	16.6
Total Saturated Fatty Acids (g) (SFA)	10.0	Sodium (mg)	151
Total Monounsaturated Fatty Acids (g) (MUFA)	7.6	Potassium (mg)	138
Total Polyunsaturated Fatty Acids (g) (PUFA)	3.6		
Omega-3 Fatty Acids (g)	1.1		
% Calories from SFA	4.1	Linoleic Acid - PUFA (18:2) (g)	2.5
% Calories from MUFA	32.5	Linolenic Acid – PUFA (18:3) (g)	1.1
% Calories from PUFA	15.3		
Polyunsaturated to Saturated Fat (P:S) Ratio	3.7	Tryptophan (mg)	5
		Threonine (mg)	11
Total Dietary Fiber (g)	3.3	Isoleucine (mg)	13
Soluble Dietary Fiber (g)	0.4	Leucine (mg)	25
Insoluble Dietary Fiber (g)	2.9	Lysine (mg)	11
		Methionine (mg)	6
Total Vitamin A (mcg) (Retinol Activity Equivalents)	1	Phenylalanine (mg)	17
Vitamin D (calciferol) (mcg)	0.0	Valine (mg)	16
Vitamin E (mg) (Total Alpha-Tocopherol)	2.3	Histidine (mg)	8
Vitamin K (mg) (phylloquinone)	9.1		
Vitamin C (mg) (ascorbic acid)	1.1	Daidzein (mg)	0.0
Thiamin (mg) (vitamin B1)	0.1	Genistein (mg)	0.0
Riboflavin (mg) (vitamin B2)	0.1		
Niacin (mg) (vitamin B3)	1.5	Caffeine (mg)	0
Pantothenic Acid (mg)	0.3	Phytic Acid (mg)	203.6
Vitamin B6 (mg)	0.1	Oxalic Acid (mg)	18.6
Total Folate (mcg)	14	Choline (mg)	9.8
Vitamin B12 (mcg) (cobalamin)	0.0		
		Glycemic Index (glucose reference)	53
Beta-Carotene (mcg) (provitamin A carotenoid)	5	Glycemic Load (glucose reference)	10
Lutein + Zeaxanthin (mcg)	100		
Lycopene (mcg)	0		

Pan-Fried Zucchini (Vegan: GF w/Mod)

Mouthwatering, rich, sweet, indulgent. Zucchini at its best.

Ingredients

1 medium zucchini, ~8 oz, sliced

5 Tbsp vanilla soymilk

3 Tbsp whole wheat pastry flour

5 Tbsp breadcrumbs

2 Tbsp olive oil

Pinch salt

Pinch fresh-ground black pepper

Wash zucchini and slice ¼" thick on the diagonal. Place the soymilk in a shallow bowl. Cut two pieces of wax paper, and place the flour on one and bread crumbs on the other. Dip the zucchini slices in the soymilk, then into the flour to coat both sides lightly. Tap the zucchini so any excess flour falls off. Then very quickly dip the slices again into the soymilk, and remove. Place on the breadcrumbs and press firmly so breadcrumbs will cover entire piece. Turn over slice and repeat.

After all slices have been breaded, heat a nonstick skillet and add olive oil. When oil is nice and hot, add breaded zucchini slices. Cook on medium heat (so inside will cook before outer coating browns) for about 7 minutes on each side. When bottom is deep golden brown, turn over carefully and cook the other side until golden. At the end, add a pinch of salt and pepper.

Yield: 14 slices (3-4 slices per serving)

~For gluten-free, use gluten-free flour mix in place of whole wheat pastry flour and gluten-free breadcrumbs in place of regular; use soymilk which does not contain malted wheat or barley~

Pan Fried Zucchini: 1 serving = 3 slices

Energy (kcal)	121		
Total Fat (g)	6.6	Calcium (mg)	41
Total Carbohydrate (g)	13.6	Phosphorus (mg)	65
Total Protein (g)	2.8	Magnesium (mg)	26
% Calories from Fat	48	Iron (mg)	1.0
% Calories from Carbohydrate	44	Zinc (mg)	0.4
% Calories from Protein	8	Copper (mg)	0.1
Cholesterol (g)	0	Selenium (mcg)	7.4
Total Saturated Fatty Acids (g) (SFA)	1.0	Sodium (mg)	94
Total Monounsaturated Fatty Acids (g) (MUFA)	4.4	Potassium (mg)	169
Total Polyunsaturated Fatty Acids (g) (PUFA)	1.0		
Omega-3 Fatty Acids (g)	0.1		
% Calories from SFA	6.9	Linoleic Acid - PUFA (18:2) (g)	0.9
% Calories from MUFA	31.8	Linolenic Acid – PUFA (18:3) (g)	0.1
% Calories from PUFA	7.0		
Polyunsaturated to Saturated Fat (P:S) Ratio	1.0	Tryptophan (mg)	4
		Threonine (mg)	9
Total Dietary Fiber (g)	2.0	Isoleucine (mg)	11
Soluble Dietary Fiber (g)	0.4	Leucine (mg)	20
Insoluble Dietary Fiber (g)	1.6	Lysine (mg)	11
		Methionine (mg)	4
Total Vitamin A (mcg) (Retinol Activity Equivalents)	33	Phenylalanine (mg)	13
Vitamin D (calciferol) (mcg)	0.2	Valine (mg)	13
Vitamin E (mg) (Total Alpha-Tocopherol)	1.2	Histidine (mg)	7
Vitamin K (mg) (phylloquinone)	6.5		
Vitamin C (mg) (ascorbic acid)	2.0	Daidzein (mg)	0.8
Thiamin (mg) (vitamin B1)	0.1	Genistein (mg)	0.9
Riboflavin (mg) (vitamin B2)	0.1		
Niacin (mg) (vitamin B3)	1.3	Caffeine (mg)	0
Pantothenic Acid (mg)	0.2	Phytic Acid (mg)	70.4
Vitamin B6 (mg)	0.1	Oxalic Acid (mg)	9.0
Total Folate (mcg)	20	Choline (mg)	8.6
Vitamin B12 (mcg) (cobalamin)	0.2		
		Glycemic Index (glucose reference)	65
Beta-Carotene (mcg) (provitamin A carotenoid)	277	Glycemic Load (glucose reference)	8
Lutein + Zeaxanthin (mcg)	491		
Lycopene (mcg)	0		

Roasted Potatoes (Vegan; GF)

Hints of rosemary and oregano provide the background for this sweet and white potato mixture. Baking accentuates the sweetness of these heavenly tubers.

Ingredients

4 medium Yukon gold potatoes

2 large sweet potatoes (12 oz each)

2 Tbsp olive oil

3/8 tsp salt

½ tsp black pepper

6 sprigs fresh rosemary

½ tsp dried oregano

Preheat oven to 450°F. Wash and peel potatoes. Cut in quarter-moons about ½" thick. In large mixing bowl, combine potatoes and olive oil, making sure all potato chunks are well coated. Add salt and pepper, oregano and rosemary (peeled off stems). Place in ceramic or glass baking pan and bake for 20 minutes. Turn with a spatula. Lower the heat to 350°F and cook another 10 to 20 minutes until potatoes are well done.

Note: Many other vegetables work in this recipe: onion, garlic, carrots, parsnips, peppers, zucchini, summer squash and turnips.

Yield: 7 cups (7, 1-cup servings)

Roasted Potatoes: 1 serving = 1 cup

Energy (kcal)	173		
Total Fat (g)	4.1	Calcium (mg)	34
Total Carbohydrate (g)	32.0	Phosphorus (mg)	79
Total Protein (g)	3.0	Magnesium (mg)	40
% Calories from Fat	21	Iron (mg)	0.9
% Calories from Carbohydrate	74	Zinc (mg)	0.5
% Calories from Protein	5	Copper (mg)	0.3
Cholesterol (g)	0	Selenium (mcg)	0.4
Total Saturated Fatty Acids (g) (SFA)	0.6	Sodium (mg)	158
Total Monounsaturated Fatty Acids (g) (MUFA)	2.8	Potassium (mg)	656
Total Polyunsaturated Fatty Acids (g) (PUFA)	0.5		
Omega-3 Fatty Acids (g)	0.0		
% Calories from SFA	3.0	Linoleic Acid - PUFA (18:2) (g)	0.4
% Calories from MUFA	14.3	Linolenic Acid – PUFA (18:3) (g)	0.0
% Calories from PUFA	2.5		
Polyunsaturated to Saturated Fat (P:S) Ratio	0.8	Tryptophan (mg)	5
		Threonine (mg)	13
Total Dietary Fiber (g)	3.7	Isoleucine (mg)	11
Soluble Dietary Fiber (g)	0.9	Leucine (mg)	18
Insoluble Dietary Fiber (g)	2.8	Lysine (mg)	15
		Methionine (mg)	05
Total Vitamin A (mcg) (Retinol Activity Equivalents)	729	Phenylalanine (mg)	15
Vitamin D (calciferol) (mcg)	0.0	Valine (mg)	17
Vitamin E (mg) (Total Alpha-Tocopherol)	1.1	Histidine (mg)	6
Vitamin K (mg) (phylloquinone)	4.8		
Vitamin C (mg) (ascorbic acid)	24.5	Daidzein (mg)	0.0
Thiamin (mg) (vitamin B1)	0.2	Genistein (mg)	0.0
Riboflavin (mg) (vitamin B2)	0.1		
Niacin (mg) (vitamin B3)	2.2	Caffeine (mg)	0
Pantothenic Acid (mg)	1.1	Phytic Acid (mg)	37.3
Vitamin B6 (mg)	0.4	Oxalic Acid (mg)	90.5
Total Folate (mcg)	12	Choline (mg)	20.8
Vitamin B12 (mcg) (cobalamin)	0.0		
		Glycemic Index (glucose reference)	84
Beta-Carotene (mcg) (provitamin A carotenoid)	8,730	Glycemic Load (glucose reference)	24
Lutein + Zeaxanthin (mcg)	2		
Lycopene (mcg)	0		

Salad with Green Beans (Vegan; GF w/Mod)

Adding a steamed or lightly parboiled vegetable to a green salad adds color, interest and nutrition. Lemon-tahini dressing melds the mixture together softly, and the result is a pleasantly satisfying side dish.

Ingredients

4½ Tbsp Lemon Tahini Salad Dressing (see below)*

1 cup green beans (washed, ends trimmed)

2 cups chopped Romaine lettuce

1/3 cucumber (4 oz), sliced thinly

1 medium tomato, chopped

¼ medium red onion (2 oz), sliced thinly

½ carrot, shaved (1 oz)

Make salad dressing and set aside.

Parboil green beans until softened, but still bright green. Let cool. Wash lettuce and spin dry in a salad spinner. Combine with cucumber, tomato, red onion, and carrot. Mix in cooled green beans and dress with your favorite salad dressing (recommend: lemon tahini dressing).

Yield: 6 cups of salad (3, 2-cup servings)

*Lemon-Tahini Dressing *(Makes 9 Tbsp of dressing)*

4 Tbsp Tahini
3 Tbsp water (more or less for desired consistency)
1 Tbsp low-sodium soy sauce
2 Tbsp fresh lemon juice

Put tahini, water, soy sauce and lemon juice into a food processor and blend until smooth. This is especially good with boiled vegetables and salad that contains them.

~For gluten free, use tamari in place of soy sauce~

Salad with Green Beans: 1 serving = 2 cup

Energy (kcal)	50		
Total Fat (g)	2.9	Calcium (mg)	44
Total Carbohydrate (g)	5.6	Phosphorus (mg)	59
Total Protein (g)	1.8	Magnesium (mg)	16
% Calories from Fat	47	Iron (mg)	0.9
% Calories from Carbohydrate	42	Zinc (mg)	0.4
% Calories from Protein	11	Copper (mg)	0.1
Cholesterol (g)	0	Selenium (mcg)	0.3
Total Saturated Fatty Acids (g) (SFA)	0.4	Sodium (mg)	56
Total Monounsaturated Fatty Acids (g) (MUFA)	1.0	Potassium (mg)	160
Total Polyunsaturated Fatty Acids (g) (PUFA)	1.3		
Omega-3 Fatty Acids (g)	0.1		
% Calories from SFA	6.9	Linoleic Acid - PUFA (18:2) (g)	1.2
% Calories from MUFA	17.1	Linolenic Acid – PUFA (18:3) (g)	0.1
% Calories from PUFA	20.9		
Polyunsaturated to Saturated Fat (P:S) Ratio	3.1	Tryptophan (mg)	3
		Threonine (mg)	8
Total Dietary Fiber (g)	2.1	Isoleucine (mg)	7
Soluble Dietary Fiber (g)	0.4	Leucine (mg)	12
Insoluble Dietary Fiber (g)	1.7	Lysine (mg)	8
		Methionine (mg)	4
Total Vitamin A (mcg) (Retinol Activity Equivalents)	118	Phenylalanine (mg)	8
Vitamin D (calciferol) (mcg)	0.0	Valine (mg)	9
Vitamin E (mg) (Total Alpha-Tocopherol)	0.2	Histidine (mg)	4
Vitamin K (mg) (phylloquinone)	23.2		
Vitamin C (mg) (ascorbic acid)	8.9	Daidzein (mg)	0.0
Thiamin (mg) (vitamin B1)	0.1	Genistein (mg)	0.0
Riboflavin (mg) (vitamin B2)	0.1		
Niacin (mg) (vitamin B3)	0.6	Caffeine (mg)	0
Pantothenic Acid (mg)	0.2	Phytic Acid (mg)	91.9
Vitamin B6 (mg)	0.1	Oxalic Acid (mg)	24.0
Total Folate (mcg)	38	Choline (mg)	9.3
Vitamin B12 (mcg) (cobalamin)	0.0		
		Glycemic Index (glucose reference)	48
Beta-Carotene (mcg) (provitamin A carotenoid)	1,323	Glycemic Load (glucose reference)	2
Lutein + Zeaxanthin (mcg)	531		
Lycopene (mcg)	86		

Seasoned Broccoli (Vegan; GF)

This cooking style combines flavorful sauté with the ease of steaming. Pop the lid on and let the ingredients work their magic! The oil provides richness, but only a little is needed, as the added water keeps the broccoli tender and succulent.

Ingredients

3 stalks (stem & flowerets) of fresh broccoli,
   cut into bit-sized pieces (~6 cups chopped)

½ cup water

1½ Tbsp olive oil

¼ tsp Kosher salt

1/8 tsp garlic powder

1/8 tsp oregano

1/8 tsp dried basil

1/8 tsp crushed red pepper

1/8 tsp ground black pepper

Wash and cut broccoli. Chop any tough ends off the stems. Chop the broccoli tops into medium-sized flowerets, then slice the stems in half, lengthwise, and slice each on the diagonal into thin slices.

In a small bowl, whisk together the water, olive oil, salt, garlic powder, oregano, basil, red and black pepper. In a large saucepan, bring this mixture to a boil. Add broccoli and cover, letting it steam for 3 minutes over high heat. Remove cover, reduce heat to medium and let cook just long enough so that all the remaining juices get absorbed (about 4 minutes).

Yield: 4 cups (4, 1-cup servings)

Seasoned Broccoli: 1 serving = 1 cup

Energy (kcal)	80		
Total Fat (g)	5.5	Calcium (mg)	42
Total Carbohydrate (g)	71	Phosphorus (mg)	66
Total Protein (g)	2.3	Magnesium (mg)	21
% Calories from Fat	61	Iron (mg)	0.7
% Calories from Carbohydrate	32	Zinc (mg)	0.4
% Calories from Protein	7	Copper (mg)	0.1
Cholesterol (g)	0	Selenium (mcg)	1.6
Total Saturated Fatty Acids (g) (SFA)	0.8	Sodium (mg)	187
Total Monounsaturated Fatty Acids (g) (MUFA)	3.7	Potassium (mg)	289
Total Polyunsaturated Fatty Acids (g) (PUFA)	0.7		
Omega-3 Fatty Acids (g)	0.2		
% Calories from SFA	8.6	Linoleic Acid - PUFA (18:2) (g)	0.6
% Calories from MUFA	41.5	Linolenic Acid – PUFA (18:3) (g)	0.2
% Calories from PUFA	7.7		
Polyunsaturated to Saturated Fat (P:S) Ratio	0.9	Tryptophan (mg)	3
		Threonine (mg)	9
Total Dietary Fiber (g)	3.3	Isoleucine (mg)	9
Soluble Dietary Fiber (g)	0.4	Leucine (mg)	14
Insoluble Dietary Fiber (g)	3.0	Lysine (mg)	15
		Methionine (mg)	4
Total Vitamin A (mcg) (Retinol Activity Equivalents)	77	Phenylalanine (mg)	11
Vitamin D (calciferol) (mcg)	0.0	Valine (mg)	14
Vitamin E (mg) (Total Alpha-Tocopherol)	2.7	Histidine (mg)	6
Vitamin K (mg) (phylloquinone)	140.6		
Vitamin C (mg) (ascorbic acid)	63.1	Daidzein (mg)	0.0
Thiamin (mg) (vitamin B1)	0.1	Genistein (mg)	0.0
Riboflavin (mg) (vitamin B2)	0.1		
Niacin (mg) (vitamin B3)	0.5	Caffeine (mg)	0
Pantothenic Acid (mg)	0.6	Phytic Acid (mg)	17.9
Vitamin B6 (mg)	0.2	Oxalic Acid (mg)	6.4
Total Folate (mcg)	105	Choline (mg)	39.0
Vitamin B12 (mcg) (cobalamin)	0.0		
		Glycemic Index (glucose reference)	50
Beta-Carotene (mcg) (provitamin A carotenoid)	916	Glycemic Load (glucose reference)	2
Lutein + Zeaxanthin (mcg)	1,056		
Lycopene (mcg)	0		

Spinach Sauté (Vegan; GF w/Mod)

Luscious, garlicky and tender. Who knew spinach could be so divine?!

Ingredients

2 tsp olive oil

3 cloves garlic

8 cups raw spinach, washed and chopped into bit-sized pieces

1 tsp mirin

Pinch salt

½ tsp low-sodium soy sauce

Heat a medium nonstick skillet and add olive oil to heat. Cook garlic in oil briefly (about 1 minute), then add in all the spinach. Mix with garlic and cook over medium-high heat until spinach starts to wilt. Add mirin, salt, and soy sauce; cook briefly (without overcooking).

Yield: 1½ cups (3, ½ cup servings)

~For gluten free, use tamari in place of soy sauce~

Spinach Sauté: 1 serving = ½ cup

Energy (kcal)	55		
Total Fat (g)	3.3	Calcium (mg)	128
Total Carbohydrate (g)	5.2	Phosphorus (mg)	56
Total Protein (g)	2.9	Magnesium (mg)	79
% Calories from Fat	52	Iron (mg)	3.3
% Calories from Carbohydrate	35	Zinc (mg)	0.7
% Calories from Protein	13	Copper (mg)	0.2
Cholesterol (g)	0	Selenium (mcg)	1.8
Total Saturated Fatty Acids (g) (SFA)	0.5	Sodium (mg)	155
Total Monounsaturated Fatty Acids (g) (MUFA)	2.2	Potassium (mg)	433
Total Polyunsaturated Fatty Acids (g) (PUFA)	0.4		
Omega-3 Fatty Acids (g)	0.1		
% Calories from SFA	7.3	Linoleic Acid - PUFA (18:2) (g)	0.3
% Calories from MUFA	35.1	Linolenic Acid – PUFA (18:3) (g)	0.1
% Calories from PUFA	6.7		
Polyunsaturated to Saturated Fat (P:S) Ratio	0.9	Tryptophan (mg)	4
		Threonine (mg)	12
Total Dietary Fiber (g)	2.2	Isoleucine (mg)	15
Soluble Dietary Fiber (g)	0.3	Leucine (mg)	22
Insoluble Dietary Fiber (g)	1.9	Lysine (mg)	18
		Methionine (mg)	5
Total Vitamin A (mcg) (Retinol Activity Equivalents)	472	Phenylalanine (mg)	13
Vitamin D (calciferol) (mcg)	0.0	Valine (mg)	16
Vitamin E (mg) (Total Alpha-Tocopherol)	2.3	Histidine (mg)	6
Vitamin K (mg) (phylloquinone)	446.1		
Vitamin C (mg) (ascorbic acid)	9.8	Daidzein (mg)	0.0
Thiamin (mg) (vitamin B1)	0.1	Genistein (mg)	0.0
Riboflavin (mg) (vitamin B2)	0.2		
Niacin (mg) (vitamin B3)	0.5	Caffeine (mg)	0
Pantothenic Acid (mg)	0.2	Phytic Acid (mg)	16.3
Vitamin B6 (mg)	0.3	Oxalic Acid (mg)	425.1
Total Folate (mcg)	132	Choline (mg)	18.7
Vitamin B12 (mcg) (cobalamin)	0.0		
		Glycemic Index (glucose reference)	57
Beta-Carotene (mcg) (provitamin A carotenoid)	5,659	Glycemic Load (glucose reference)	2
Lutein + Zeaxanthin (mcg)	10,178		
Lycopene (mcg)	0		

Squash-Cabbage-Onion Medley (Vegan; GF)

Each one of these sweet vegetables contributes a uniqueness that supports the others. The result is a rare synergy that defies definition.

Ingredients

Half a small buttercup squash, peeled and cut into bit-size chunks (12 oz)

1 medium onion (6 oz), cut into thick slices

Quarter head of cabbage (12 oz), cut into wedges

Half of a vegetable (sodium-free) bouillon cube

1 cup boiling water

1/8 tsp salt

Pinch pepper

Wash and prepare squash, using a vegetable peeler to peel the outer surface. Wash and cut onions and cabbage. In a glass measuring cup, place half bouillon cube and pour hot water over it. Whisk to dissolve.

In a medium soup pot, layer the cabbage, onions, and squash. Add the broth. Bring to a boil, cover and simmer, undisturbed, on medium heat for 15 minutes. Then mix gently to combine vegetables, and check to see that squash is softened. Add salt and pepper; simmer 5 minutes more.

Yield: 5½ cups (5½, 1-cup servings)

Squash-Cabbage-Onion Medley: 1 serving = 1 cup

Energy (kcal)	45		
Total Fat (g)	0.3	Calcium (mg)	48
Total Carbohydrate (g)	10.7	Phosphorus (mg)	39
Total Protein (g)	1.6	Magnesium (mg)	19
% Calories from Fat	5	Iron (mg)	0.4
% Calories from Carbohydrate	86	Zinc (mg)	0.3
% Calories from Protein	9	Copper (mg)	0.1
Cholesterol (g)	0	Selenium (mcg)	0.7
Total Saturated Fatty Acids (g) (SFA)	0.0	Sodium (mg)	42
Total Monounsaturated Fatty Acids (g) (MUFA)	0.0	Potassium (mg)	290
Total Polyunsaturated Fatty Acids (g) (PUFA)	0.1		
Omega-3 Fatty Acids (g)	0.1		
% Calories from SFA	0.9	Linoleic Acid - PUFA (18:2) (g)	0.1
% Calories from MUFA	0.6	Linolenic Acid – PUFA (18:3) (g)	0.1
% Calories from PUFA	2.1		
Polyunsaturated to Saturated Fat (P:S) Ratio	2.4	Tryptophan (mg)	2
		Threonine (mg)	4
Total Dietary Fiber (g)	3.0	Isoleucine (mg)	5
Soluble Dietary Fiber (g)	1.0	Leucine (mg)	6
Insoluble Dietary Fiber (g)	2.0	Lysine (mg)	6
		Methionine (mg)	2
Total Vitamin A (mcg) (Retinol Activity Equivalents)	143	Phenylalanine (mg)	5
Vitamin D (calciferol) (mcg)	0.0	Valine (mg)	5
Vitamin E (mg) (Total Alpha-Tocopherol)	0.2	Histidine (mg)	3
Vitamin K (mg) (phylloquinone)	67.1		
Vitamin C (mg) (ascorbic acid)	28.8	Daidzein (mg)	0.0
Thiamin (mg) (vitamin B1)	0.1	Genistein (mg)	0.0
Riboflavin (mg) (vitamin B2)	0.1		
Niacin (mg) (vitamin B3)	0.5	Caffeine (mg)	0
Pantothenic Acid (mg)	0.3	Phytic Acid (mg)	14.2
Vitamin B6 (mg)	0.2	Oxalic Acid (mg)	2.6
Total Folate (mcg)	33	Choline (mg)	19.5
Vitamin B12 (mcg) (cobalamin)	0.0		
		Glycemic Index (glucose reference)	66
Beta-Carotene (mcg) (provitamin A carotenoid)	1,532	Glycemic Load (glucose reference)	5
Lutein + Zeaxanthin (mcg)	779		
Lycopene (mcg)	0		

Steamed Cauliflower with Sesame-Miso-Scallion Dressing

(Vegan; GF w/Mod)

Bringing out the best in cauliflower can mean simply steaming and letting the subtle natural flavors emerge. Frosted with a sturdy and sensuous dressing, spruced up with sliced scallions, this is a beautiful and satisfying tribute to an often-under-appreciated vegetable.

Ingredients

4 cups cauliflower flowerets

4 Tbsp sesame miso scallion dressing (see below)*

Bring water to boil in the bottom half of a steamer.

Wash and separate cauliflower flowerets.

Place in steamer and steam for approximately 5 minutes (until cauliflower reaches desired tenderness). Set on a plate.

*Sesame Miso Scallion Dressing (*makes 4 Tbsp of dressing*)

4 Tbsp roasted sesame butter (or fresh roasted, ground sesame seeds)

1 Tbsp white miso

½ tsp rice vinegar

½ cup boiling water

3 large stalks scallions, chopped (3/4 cup chopped)

Cooking spray

In a small mixing bowl, blend 4 Tbsp of sesame butter, miso and vinegar together. Gently add in the hot water and mix well, eventually usually a small whisk, for a smooth sauce.

Heat a small skillet, spray with cooking oil and sauté scallions until just tender. Add to sauce, blend well and spoon over cauliflower. [Alternatively, serve on side for individual additions.]

Yield: 4 cups cauliflower (4, 1-cup servings, each with 1 Tbsp of dressing)

~For gluten-free use brown-rice miso in place of white miso~

Steamed Cauliflower with Sesame Dressing: 1 serving = ½ cup

Energy (kcal)	64		
Total Fat (g)	3.4	Calcium (mg)	46
Total Carbohydrate (g)	7.1	Phosphorus (mg)	80
Total Protein (g)	3.3	Magnesium (mg)	18
% Calories from Fat	45	Iron (mg)	1.0
% Calories from Carbohydrate	41	Zinc (mg)	0.5
% Calories from Protein	14	Copper (mg)	0.1
Cholesterol (g)	0	Selenium (mcg)	0.9
Total Saturated Fatty Acids (g) (SFA)	0.5	Sodium (mg)	53
Total Monounsaturated Fatty Acids (g) (MUFA)	1.1	Potassium (mg)	215
Total Polyunsaturated Fatty Acids (g) (PUFA)	1.5		
Omega-3 Fatty Acids (g)	0.2		
% Calories from SFA	6.3	Linoleic Acid - PUFA (18:2) (g)	1.3
% Calories from MUFA	15.0	Linolenic Acid – PUFA (18:3) (g)	0.2
% Calories from PUFA	19.8		
Polyunsaturated to Saturated Fat (P:S) Ratio	3.2	Tryptophan (mg)	5
		Threonine (mg)	13
Total Dietary Fiber (g)	3.5	Isoleucine (mg)	13
Soluble Dietary Fiber (g)	0.6	Leucine (mg)	21
Insoluble Dietary Fiber (g)	2.9	Lysine (mg)	16
		Methionine (mg)	6
Total Vitamin A (mcg) (Retinol Activity Equivalents)	4	Phenylalanine (mg)	13
Vitamin D (calciferol) (mcg)	0.0	Valine (mg)	17
Vitamin E (mg) (Total Alpha-Tocopherol)	0.2	Histidine (mg)	8
Vitamin K (mg) (phylloquinone)	30.3		
Vitamin C (mg) (ascorbic acid)	56.1	Daidzein (mg)	0.1
Thiamin (mg) (vitamin B1)	0.1	Genistein (mg)	0.2
Riboflavin (mg) (vitamin B2)	0.1		
Niacin (mg) (vitamin B3)	0.8	Caffeine (mg)	0
Pantothenic Acid (mg)	0.7	Phytic Acid (mg)	90.6
Vitamin B6 (mg)	0.2	Oxalic Acid (mg)	28.7
Total Folate (mcg)	64	Choline (mg)	50.6
Vitamin B12 (mcg) (cobalamin)	0.0		
		Glycemic Index (glucose reference)	46
Beta-Carotene (mcg) (provitamin A carotenoid)	48	Glycemic Load (glucose reference)	2
Lutein + Zeaxanthin (mcg)	107		
Lycopene (mcg)	0		

Steamed Collard Greens with Creamy Pine Nut Dressing

(Vegan; GF)

A sublime way to enjoy these amazingly nutritious, green, leafy vegetables.

Ingredients

Fresh collard greens, 3 cups sliced

2 Tbsp roasted pine nuts

2 Tbsp of pine nut dressing (see below)*

Wash and slice collard greens– cutting stems fairly thinly to cook at the same rate as the leaves. Steam for approximately 3 minutes, or just long enough for greens to become tender while maintaining their bright green color. Shake dressing well before spooning over collard greens. Use about 2 tsp per ½-cup serving of cooked collard greens.

Add roasted pine nuts to garnish.

*Pine nut dressing *(Makes ~6 Tbsp of dressing)*
3½ Tbsp pine nuts, roasted

1 small clove of garlic (about 1 tsp), minced

1/8 cup fresh basil, sliced (packed)

2 Tbsp rice vinegar

2 Tbsp water

1½ tsp. apple juice

¼ tsp Kosher salt

Roast pine nuts in oven at 300°F for about 10 minutes or until lightly browned. Alternatively, place in skillet and heat on low for about 10 minutes stirring often and watching carefully to prevent burning.

Place pine nuts, garlic, basil, vinegar, water, apple juice and salt into a food processor (or blender) and mix until smooth. Chill for 3 hours or more in the refrigerator to increase the flavor depth.

Yield: 1½ cups (3, ½-cup servings)

Pine Nut Dressing adapted from Brother Ron Pickarski, author of *Friendly Foods* (Ten Speed Press, 1991), printed in *Natural Health magazine*, July/August 1993

Steamed Collards with Pine Nut Dressing: 1 serving = ½ cup

Energy (kcal)	86		
Total Fat (g)	6.4	Calcium (mg)	137
Total Carbohydrate (g)	6.0	Phosphorus (mg)	81
Total Protein (g)	3.3	Magnesium (mg)	42
% Calories from Fat	63	Iron (mg)	1.6
% Calories from Carbohydrate	26	Zinc (mg)	0.8
% Calories from Protein	11	Copper (mg)	0.2
Cholesterol (g)	0	Selenium (mcg)	0.6
Total Saturated Fatty Acids (g) (SFA)	0.5	Sodium (mg)	81
Total Monounsaturated Fatty Acids (g) (MUFA)	1.7	Potassium (mg)	167
Total Polyunsaturated Fatty Acids (g) (PUFA)	3.2		
Omega-3 Fatty Acids (g)	0.1		
% Calories from SFA	4.7	Linoleic Acid - PUFA (18:2) (g)	3.0
% Calories from MUFA	16.5	Linolenic Acid – PUFA (18:3) (g)	0.1
% Calories from PUFA	31.1		
Polyunsaturated to Saturated Fat (P:S) Ratio	6.6	Tryptophan (mg)	4
		Threonine (mg)	11
Total Dietary Fiber (g)	3.0	Isoleucine (mg)	13
Soluble Dietary Fiber (g)	0.2	Leucine (mg)	21
Insoluble Dietary Fiber (g)	2.8	Lysine (mg)	15
		Methionine (mg)	5
Total Vitamin A (mcg) (Retinol Activity Equivalents)	387	Phenylalanine (mg)	12
Vitamin D (calciferol) (mcg)	0.0	Valine (mg)	16
Vitamin E (mg) (Total Alpha-Tocopherol)	1.7	Histidine (mg)	7
Vitamin K (mg) (phylloquinone)	425.0		
Vitamin C (mg) (ascorbic acid)	17.6	Daidzein (mg)	0.0
Thiamin (mg) (vitamin B1)	0.1	Genistein (mg)	0.0
Riboflavin (mg) (vitamin B2)	0.1		
Niacin (mg) (vitamin B3)	1.0	Caffeine (mg)	0
Pantothenic Acid (mg)0.2	0.2	Phytic Acid (mg)	27.3
Vitamin B6 (mg)	0.1	Oxalic Acid (mg)	28.2
Total Folate (mcg)	92	Choline (mg)	35.3
Vitamin B12 (mcg) (cobalamin)	0.0		
		Glycemic Index (glucose reference)	41
Beta-Carotene (mcg) (provitamin A carotenoid)	4,593	Glycemic Load (glucose reference)	1
Lutein + Zeaxanthin (mcg)	7,344		
Lycopene (mcg)	0		

Watercress and Garlic (Vegan; GF w/Mod)

This recipe is so easy and quick! The olive gives a buttery taste, and the garlic makes everything special!

Ingredients

2 bunches of watercress – washed* and cut in half

4 tsp of olive (canola oil could also be used)

1 tsp of sesame oil

4 medium cloves of garlic- chopped

1 tsp of mirin

1 Tbsp low-sodium soy sauce

* This is about 9 cups raw. [This really cooks down; if you like watercress, you might want to figure on at least 1 bunch for every 3-4 people.]

You can conveniently cut each bunch in half, crosswise, while still bundled, then discard the twist-tie or elastic band. Wash pieces in a large basin of water. (Fill a large, clean basin of water and completely submerge the watercress to rinse away any debris.) Drain well (or spin in a salad spinner).

In a large frying pan, heat oils, and add garlic. Sauté the garlic in oil for about 1 minute, then add watercress, stirring to coat with garlic and oil. Sauté briefly, add mirin, stir and cover. After just a minute or two, the leaves & stems will have wilted, the color will be darker, and the watercress will be nearly done. Add soy sauce and sauté a few seconds more. (Be careful not to overcook.)

Yield: 3 cups (2¼, ¾-cup servings)

~For gluten free, use tamari in place of soy sauce~

Watercress with Garlic: 1 serving = ¾ cup

Energy (kcal)	70		
Total Fat (g)	5.8	Calcium (mg)	129
Total Carbohydrate (g)	3.2	Phosphorus (mg)	71
Total Protein (g)	2.8	Magnesium (mg)	24
% Calories from Fat	73	Iron (mg)	0.4
% Calories from Carbohydrate	17	Zinc (mg)	0.2
% Calories from Protein	10	Copper (mg)	0.1
Cholesterol (g)	0	Selenium (mcg)	1.4
Total Saturated Fatty Acids (g) (SFA)	0.8	Sodium (mg)	186
Total Monounsaturated Fatty Acids (g) (MUFA)	3.7	Potassium (mg)	358
Total Polyunsaturated Fatty Acids (g) (PUFA)	1.0		
Omega-3 Fatty Acids (g)	0.1		
% Calories from SFA	10.3	Linoleic Acid - PUFA (18:2) (g)	0.9
% Calories from MUFA	49.3	Linolenic Acid - PUFA (18:3) (g)	0.1
% Calories from PUFA	12.5		
Polyunsaturated to Saturated Fat (P:S) Ratio	1.2	Tryptophan (mg)	4
		Threonine (mg)	15
Total Dietary Fiber (g)	0.6	Isoleucine (mg)	11
Soluble Dietary Fiber (g)	0.3	Leucine (mg)	20
Insoluble Dietary Fiber (g)	0.3	Lysine (mg)	16
		Methionine (mg)	3
Vitamin A (mcg) (Retinol Activity Equivalents)	164	Phenylalanine (mg)	13
Vitamin D (calciferol) (mcg)	0.0	Valine (mg)	16
Vitamin E (mg) (Total Alpha-Tocopherol)	1.7	Histidine (mg)	5
Vitamin K (mg) (phylloquinone)	259.8		
Vitamin C (mg) (ascorbic acid)	31.8	Daidzein (mg)	0.0
Thiamin (mg) (vitamin B1)	0.1	Genistein (mg)	0.0
Riboflavin (mg) (vitamin B2)	0.1		
Niacin (mg) (vitamin B3)	0.4	Caffeine (mg)	0
Pantothenic Acid (mg)	0.3	Phytic Acid (mg)	10.0
Vitamin B6 (mg)	0.2	Oxalic Acid (mg)	11.6
Total Folate (mcg)	10	Choline (mg)	11.3
Vitamin B12 (mcg) (cobalamin)	0.0		
		Glycemic Index (glucose reference)	56
Beta-Carotene (mcg) (provitamin A carotenoid)	1,967	Glycemic Load (glucose reference)	1
Lutein + Zeaxanthin (mcg)	5,926		
Lycopene (mcg)	0		

SAUCES AND DRESSINGS

Carrot Ginger Salad Dressing (Vegan; GF w/Mod)

This is a unique dressing that will brighten any salad. A memorable taste sensation!

Ingredients

½ cup shredded carrot (1 medium carrot)

3 oz. silken tofu (for creamier texture) this is about 3/8 of a cup

2 Tbsp mirin

2 Tbsp rice vinegar

1 Tbsp low-sodium soy sauce

½ Tbsp fresh grated ginger

½ tsp sesame oil

Blend carrot, tofu, mirin, vinegar, soy sauce, ginger and sesame oil in a food processor until smooth. Best if chilled one or two hours before serving.

Yield: ¾ cup of salad dressing, 12, 1-Tbsp servings (without tofu, yields 1/3 cup).

~For gluten free, use tamari in place of soy sauce~

180

Carrot Ginger Dressing: 1 serving = 1 Tbsp.

Energy (kcal)	14		
Total Fat (g)	0.4	Calcium (mg)	4
Total Carbohydrate (g)	2.0	Phosphorus (mg)	10
Total Protein (g)	0.6	Magnesium (mg)	3
% Calories from Fat	25	Iron (mg)	0.1
% Calories from Carbohydrate	58	Zinc (mg)	0.1
% Calories from Protein	17	Copper (mg)	0.0
Cholesterol (g)	0	Selenium (mcg)	0.7
Total Saturated Fatty Acids (g) (SFA)	0.1	Sodium (mg)	72
Total Monounsaturated Fatty Acids (g) (MUFA)	0.1	Potassium (mg)	34
Total Polyunsaturated Fatty Acids (g) (PUFA)	0.2		
Omega-3 Fatty Acids (g)	0.01		
% Calories from SFA	3.7	Linoleic Acid - PUFA (18:2) (g)	0.2
% Calories from MUFA	7.2	Linolenic Acid – PUFA (18:3) (g)	0.01
% Calories from PUFA	12.0		
Polyunsaturated to Saturated Fat (P:S) Ratio	3.3	Tryptophan (mg)	1
		Threonine (mg)	3
Total Dietary Fiber (g)	0.1	Isoleucine (mg)	3
Soluble Dietary Fiber (g)	0.0	Leucine (mg)	5
Insoluble Dietary Fiber (g)	0.1	Lysine (mg)	4
		Methionine (mg)	1
Total Vitamin A (mcg) (Retinol Activity Equivalents)	42	Phenylalanine (mg)	4
Vitamin D (calciferol) (mcg)	0.0	Valine (mg)	3
Vitamin E (mg) (Total Alpha-Tocopherol)	0.1	Histidine (mg)	2
Vitamin K (mg) (phylloquinone)	0.6		
Vitamin C (mg) (ascorbic acid)	0.3	Daidzein (mg)	0.8
Thiamin (mg) (vitamin B1)	0.0	Genistein (mg)	1.1
Riboflavin (mg) (vitamin B2)	0.0		
Niacin (mg) (vitamin B3)	0.1	Caffeine (mg)	0
Pantothenic Acid (mg)	0.0	Phytic Acid (mg)	14.3
Vitamin B6 (mg)	0.0	Oxalic Acid (mg)	3.1
Total Folate (mcg)	4	Choline (mg)	3.0
Vitamin B12 (mcg) (cobalamin)	0.0		
		Glycemic Index (glucose reference)	67
Beta-Carotene (mcg) (provitamin A carotenoid)	421	Glycemic Load (glucose reference)	1
Lutein + Zeaxanthin (mcg)	13		
Lycopene (mcg)	0		

Lemon-Tahini Dressing (Vegan; GF w/Mod)

A thick and creamy dressing for salad or cooked vegetables ~ simple and cholesterol-free!

Ingredients

4 Tbsp tahini

3 Tbsp water (more or less for desired consistency)

1 Tbsp low-sodium soy sauce

2 Tbsp fresh lemon juice

Put tahini, water, soy sauce and lemon juice in a food processor and blend until smooth. This is especially good with boiled vegetables and salad that contains them.

Yield: 9 Tbsp of dressing (6, 1½ -Tbsp servings)

~For gluten free, use tamari in place of soy sauce~

Lemon Tahini Dressing: 1 serving = 1½ Tbsp.

Energy (kcal)	62		
Total Fat (g)	5.4	Calcium (mg)	44
Total Carbohydrate (g)	2.7	Phosphorus (mg)	77
Total Protein (g)	1.9	Magnesium (mg)	11
% Calories from Fat	73	Iron (mg)	1.0
% Calories from Carbohydrate	17	Zinc (mg)	0.5
% Calories from Protein	10	Copper (mg)	0.2
Cholesterol (g)	0	Selenium (mcg)	0.2
Total Saturated Fatty Acids (g) (SFA)	0.8	Sodium (mg)	100
Total Monounsaturated Fatty Acids (g) (MUFA)	2.0	Potassium (mg)	52
Total Polyunsaturated Fatty Acids (g) (PUFA)	2.4		
Omega-3 Fatty Acids (g)	0.04		
% Calories from SFA	10.2	Linoleic Acid - PUFA (18:2) (g)	2.3
% Calories from MUFA	27.4	Linolenic Acid – PUFA (18:3) (g)	0.04
% Calories from PUFA	31.9		
Polyunsaturated to Saturated Fat (P:S) Ratio	3.1	Tryptophan (mg)	4
		Threonine (mg)	8
Total Dietary Fiber (g)	1.0	Isoleucine (mg)	8
Soluble Dietary Fiber (g)	0.2	Leucine (mg)	14
Insoluble Dietary Fiber (g)	0.8	Lysine (mg)	6
		Methionine (mg)	6
Total Vitamin A (mcg) (Retinol Activity Equivalents)	0	Phenylalanine (mg)	10
Vitamin D (calciferol) (mcg)	0.0	Valine (mg)	10
Vitamin E (mg) (Total Alpha-Tocopherol)	0.0	Histidine (mg)	5
Vitamin K (mg) (phylloquinone)	0.0		
Vitamin C (mg) (ascorbic acid)	2.3	Daidzein (mg)	0.0
Thiamin (mg) (vitamin B1)	0.1	Genistein (mg)	0.0
Riboflavin (mg) (vitamin B2)	0.1		
Niacin (mg) (vitamin B3)	0.6	Caffeine (mg)	0
Pantothenic Acid (mg)	0.1	Phytic Acid (mg)	163.1
Vitamin B6 (mg)	0.0	Oxalic Acid (mg)	39.4
Total Folate (mcg)	11	Choline (mg)	3.7
Vitamin B12 (mcg) (cobalamin)	0.0		
		Glycemic Index (glucose reference)	24
Beta-Carotene (mcg) (provitamin A carotenoid)	4	Glycemic Load (glucose reference)	0
Lutein + Zeaxanthin (mcg)	1		
Lycopene (mcg)	0		

Peanut Sauce (Vegan; GF w/Mod)

This smooth, rich, sensational sauce can be used for salads, cooked vegetables, noodle dishes, tofu, and others. Simply spoon sauce over the finished product or keep aside as an add-on dressing. Cover tightly and it will keep in the refrigerator for several days.

Ingredients

½ cup (8 Tbsp) peanut butter (creamy or crunchy)

2 Tbsp lime juice

2 Tbsp brown rice syrup{or maple syrup}

2 Tbsp hot water

1½ Tbsp low-sodium soy sauce

1 Tbsp chopped garlic

1 Tbsp mirin

2 tsp rice vinegar

Place peanut butter, lime juice, brown rice syrup, water, soy sauce, garlic, mirin and vinegar in a food processor and whip until smooth and creamy (more liquid can be added to modify consistency).

Add to pasta dishes or cooked vegetables; top a serving of simple, steamed tofu.

Note: You can use less syrup (e.g., 1 Tbsp instead of 2 Tbsp) for a more robust taste.

Yield: 10 Tbsp (15, 2-tsp servings)

~For gluten free, use tamari in place of soy sauce~

Peanut Sauce: 1 serving = 2 tsp.

Energy (kcal)	64		
Total Fat (g)	4.3	Calcium (mg)	6
Total Carbohydrate (g)	5.0	Phosphorus (mg)	34
Total Protein (g)	2.3	Magnesium (mg)	14
% Calories from Fat	57	Iron (mg)	0.2
% Calories from Carbohydrate	31	Zinc (mg)	0.3
% Calories from Protein	12	Copper (mg)	0.0
Cholesterol (g)	0	Selenium (mcg)	0.6
Total Saturated Fatty Acids (g) (SFA)	0.9	Sodium (mg)	106
Total Monounsaturated Fatty Acids (g) (MUFA)	2.1	Potassium (mg)	64
Total Polyunsaturated Fatty Acids (g) (PUFA)	1.2		
Omega-3 Fatty Acids (g)	0.0		
% Calories from SFA	11.9	Linoleic Acid - PUFA (18:2) (g)	1.2
% Calories from MUFA	27.3	Linolenic Acid – PUFA (18:3) (g)	0.0
% Calories from PUFA	16.0		
Polyunsaturated to Saturated Fat (P:S) Ratio	1.3	Tryptophan (mg)	2
		Threonine (mg)	5
Total Dietary Fiber (g)	0.55	Isoleucine (mg)	6
Soluble Dietary Fiber (g)	0.05	Leucine (mg)	14
Insoluble Dietary Fiber (g)	0.5	Lysine (mg)	6
		Methionine (mg)	2
Total Vitamin A (mcg) (Retinol Activity Equivalents)	0	Phenylalanine (mg)	11
Vitamin D (calciferol) (mcg)	0.0	Valine (mg)	7
Vitamin E (mg) (Total Alpha-Tocopherol)	0.8	Histidine (mg)	5
Vitamin K (mg) (phylloquinone)	0.1		
Vitamin C (mg) (ascorbic acid)	0.8	Daidzein (mg)	0.0
Thiamin (mg) (vitamin B1)	0.0	Genistein (mg)	0.0
Riboflavin (mg) (vitamin B2)	0.0		
Niacin (mg) (vitamin B3)	1.2	Caffeine (mg)	0
Pantothenic Acid (mg)	0.1	Phytic Acid (mg)	40.1
Vitamin B6 (mg)	0.1	Oxalic Acid (mg)	16.0
Total Folate (mcg)	7	Choline (mg)	6.2
Vitamin B12 (mcg) (cobalamin)	0.0		
		Glycemic Index (glucose reference)	68
Beta-Carotene (mcg) (provitamin A carotenoid)	0	Glycemic Load (glucose reference)	3
Lutein + Zeaxanthin (mcg)	0		
Lycopene (mcg)	0		

Pine nut dressing (Vegan: GF)

This is an interesting and unusual dressing that will spruce up a raw salad or cooked vegetable dish. Pine nuts lend both a gentleness and depth to surprise and satisfy.

Ingredients

3½ Tbsp pine nuts, roasted

1 small clove of garlic (about 1 tsp), minced

1/8 cup fresh basil, sliced (packed)

2 Tbsp rice vinegar

2 Tbsp water

1½ tsp apple juice

¼ tsp Kosher salt

Roast pine nuts in oven at 300°F for about 10 minutes or until lightly browned. Alternatively, place in skillet and heat on low for about 10 minutes stirring often and watching carefully to prevent burning. Add pine nuts, garlic, basil, vinegar, water, apple juice and salt to a food processor (or blender) and mix until smooth. Chill for 3 hours or more in the refrigerator to increase the flavor depth. Shake well before spooning over collard greens.

Yield: ~6 Tbsp (9, 2-tsp servings)

Adapted from Brother Ron Pickarski, author of *Friendly Foods* (Ten Speed Press, 1991), July/August 1993 Natural Health magazine

Pine Nut Dressing: 1 serving = 2 tsp

Energy (kcal)	24		
Total Fat (g)	2.3	Calcium (mg)	3
Total Carbohydrate (g)	0.6	Phosphorus (mg)	20
Total Protein (g)	0.5	Magnesium (mg)	9
% Calories from Fat	80	Iron (mg)	0.2
% Calories from Carbohydrate	13	Zinc (mg)	0.2
% Calories from Protein	17	Copper (mg)	0.0
Cholesterol (g)	0	Selenium (mcg)	0.1
Total Saturated Fatty Acids (g) (SFA)	0.2	Sodium (mg)	65
Total Monounsaturated Fatty Acids (g) (MUFA)	0.6	Potassium (mg)	24
Total Polyunsaturated Fatty Acids (g) (PUFA)	1.1		
Omega-3 Fatty Acids (g)	0.0		
% Calories from SFA	5.7	Linoleic Acid - PUFA (18:2) (g)	1.1
% Calories from MUFA	21.8	Linolenic Acid – PUFA (18:3) (g)	0.0
% Calories from PUFA	39.6		
Polyunsaturated to Saturated Fat (P:S) Ratio	6.9	Tryptophan (mg)	0.4
		Threonine (mg)	1
Total Dietary Fiber (g)	0.1	Isoleucine (mg)	2
Soluble Dietary Fiber (g)	0.0	Leucine (mg)	4
Insoluble Dietary Fiber (g)	0.1	Lysine (mg)	2
		Methionine (mg)	1
Total Vitamin A (mcg) (Retinol Activity Equivalents)	2	Phenylalanine (mg)	2
Vitamin D (calciferol) (mcg)	0.0	Valine (mg)	3
Vitamin E (mg) (Total Alpha-Tocopherol)	0.3	Histidine (mg)	1
Vitamin K (mg) (phylloquinone)	4.2		
Vitamin C (mg) (ascorbic acid)	0.2	Daidzein (mg)	0.0
Thiamin (mg) (vitamin B1)	0.0	Genistein (mg)	0.0
Riboflavin (mg) (vitamin B2)	0.0		
Niacin (mg) (vitamin B3)	0.2	Caffeine (mg)	0
Pantothenic Acid (mg)	0.0	Phytic Acid (mg)	7.6
Vitamin B6 (mg)	0.0	Oxalic Acid (mg)	8.3
Total Folate (mcg)	2	Choline (mg)	2.0
Vitamin B12 (mcg) (cobalamin)	0.0		
		Glycemic Index (glucose reference)	28
Beta-Carotene (mcg) (provitamin A carotenoid)	19	Glycemic Load (glucose reference)	0
Lutein + Zeaxanthin (mcg)	34		
Lycopene (mcg)	0		

Sesame Miso Scallion Dressing (Vegan; GF w/Mod)

The combination of sesame, miso and cooked green onions is indescribable! Wonderful for simply steamed or boiled vegetables, noodles or pasta salads, it also makes a great sandwich spread.

Ingredients

4 Tbsp roasted sesame butter (or fresh roasted, ground sesame seeds)

1 Tbsp white miso

½ tsp rice vinegar

½ cup boiling water

3 large stalks scallions, chopped (3/4 cup chopped)

Cooking spray

In a small mixing bowl, blend 4 Tbsp of sesame butter, miso and vinegar together. Gently add in the hot water and mix well, eventually usually a small whisk, for a smooth sauce.

Heat a small skillet, spray with cooking oil and sauté scallions until just tender. Add to sauce, blend well and spoon over vegetables or cooked pasta. [Alternatively, serve on side for individual additions.]

Yield: 4 Tbsp (4, 1-Tbsp servings)

~For gluten-free, use brown rice miso instead of white miso~

Sesame Miso Dressing: 1 serving = 1 Tbsp.

Energy (kcal)	35		
Total Fat (g)	2.9	Calcium (mg)	27
Total Carbohydrate (g)	2.0	Phosphorus (mg)	40
Total Protein (g)	1.0	Magnesium (mg)	6
% Calories from Fat	68	Iron (mg)	0.6
% Calories from Carbohydrate	22	Zinc (mg)	0.3
% Calories from Protein	10	Copper (mg)	0.1
Cholesterol (g)	0	Selenium (mcg)	0.2
Total Saturated Fatty Acids (g) (SFA)	0.4	Sodium (mg)	35
Total Monounsaturated Fatty Acids (g) (MUFA)	1.1	Potassium (mg)	9
Total Polyunsaturated Fatty Acids (g) (PUFA)	1.2		
Omega-3 Fatty Acids (g)	0.04		
% Calories from SFA	9.4	Linoleic Acid - PUFA (18:2) (g)	1.2
% Calories from MUFA	26.2	Linolenic Acid - PUFA (18:3) (g)	0.04
% Calories from PUFA	29.4		
Polyunsaturated to Saturated Fat (P:S) Ratio	3.1	Tryptophan (mg)	2
		Threonine (mg)	4
Total Dietary Fiber (g)	0.7	Isoleucine (mg)	5
Soluble Dietary Fiber (g)	0.1	Leucine (mg)	8
Insoluble Dietary Fiber (g)	0.6	Lysine (mg)	4
		Methionine (mg)	3
Total Vitamin A (mcg) (Retinol Activity Equivalents)	3	Phenylalanine (mg)	5
Vitamin D (calciferol) (mcg)	0.0	Valine (mg)	6
Vitamin E (mg) (Total Alpha-Tocopherol)	0.1	Histidine (mg)	3
Vitamin K (mg) (phylloquinone)	13.2		
Vitamin C (mg) (ascorbic acid)	1.2	Daidzein (mg)	0.1
Thiamin (mg) (vitamin B1)	0.1	Genistein (mg)	0.2
Riboflavin (mg) (vitamin B2)	0.0		
Niacin (mg) (vitamin B3)	0.3	Caffeine (mg)	0
Pantothenic Acid (mg)	0.0	Phytic Acid (mg)	85.4
Vitamin B6 (mg)	0.0	Oxalic Acid (mg)	24.6
Total Folate (mcg)	9	Choline (mg)	2.1
Vitamin B12 (mcg) (cobalamin)	0.0		
		Glycemic Index (glucose reference)	40
Beta-Carotene (mcg) (provitamin A carotenoid)	40	Glycemic Load (glucose reference)	1
Lutein + Zeaxanthin (mcg)	71		
Lycopene (mcg)	0		

Sesame Salt (Gomasio) (Vegan; GF)

A tasty condiment to perk up a grain or vegetable dish.

Ingredients

1 tsp sea salt

½ cup (8 Tbsp) raw sesame seeds

Note: A pestle with suribachi is needed to make this

condiment. If necessary, a coffee grinder can be used, but

be careful not to over-grind the seeds.

In a medium saucepan or skillet, roast salt over medium heat for about 2 minutes to heat thoroughly. Transfer to suribachi. Wash and drain sesame seeds, using a fine, wire-mesh strainer. Shake out excess water. Add seeds to pan and dry roast over medium heat, stirring frequently until seeds first dry out, then start to turn a golden brown. They will start to give off a wonderful fragrance, and at this point they are almost done. Check by using thumb and 4th (ring) finger to see if they crush easily. This means they are done. Add seeds to suribachi and grind with the salt, until about 80% of the seeds are crushed. Store in an air-tight glass container and keep in a cool place.

Yield: 12 Tbsp; 1 serving = ½ tsp (72 servings)

From: Kushi M and Jack A: *The Macrobiotic Path to Total Health*, NY: Ballantine Books, 2003, with permission from Alex Jack.

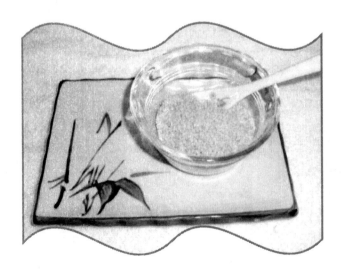

Sesame Salt: 1 serving = ½ tsp.

Energy (kcal)	15		
Total Fat (g)	1.3	Calcium (mg)	4
Total Carbohydrate (g)	0.7	Phosphorus (mg)	21
Total Protein (g)	0.5	Magnesium (mg)	9
% Calories from Fat	71	Iron (mg)	0.2
% Calories from Carbohydrate	19	Zinc (mg)	0.3
% Calories from Protein	10	Copper (mg)	0.0
Cholesterol (g)	0	Selenium (mcg)	0.0
Total Saturated Fatty Acids (g) (SFA)	0.2	Sodium (mg)	98
Total Monounsaturated Fatty Acids (g) (MUFA)	0.5	Potassium (mg)	11
Total Polyunsaturated Fatty Acids (g) (PUFA)	0.6		
Omega-3 Fatty Acids (g)	0.01		
% Calories from SFA	9.9	Linoleic Acid - PUFA (18:2) (g)	0.551
% Calories from MUFA	26.8	Linolenic Acid – PUFA (18:3) (g)	0.01
% Calories from PUFA	31.1		
Polyunsaturated to Saturated Fat (P:S) Ratio	3.1	Tryptophan (mg)	1
		Threonine (mg)	2
Total Dietary Fiber (g)	0.4	Isoleucine (mg)	2
Soluble Dietary Fiber (g)	0.1	Leucine (mg)	4
Insoluble Dietary Fiber (g)	0.3	Lysine (mg)	2
		Methionine (mg)	2
Total Vitamin A (mcg) (Retinol Activity Equivalents)	0	Phenylalanine (mg)	2
Vitamin D (calciferol) (mcg)	0.0	Valine (mg)	3
Vitamin E (mg) (Total Alpha-Tocopherol)	0.0	Histidine (mg)	1
Vitamin K (mg) (phylloquinone)	0.0		
Vitamin C (mg) (ascorbic acid)	0.0	Daidzein (mg)	0.0
Thiamin (mg) (vitamin B1)	0.0	Genistein (mg)	0.0
Riboflavin (mg) (vitamin B2)	0.0		
Niacin (mg) (vitamin B3)	0.1	Caffeine (mg)	0
Pantothenic Acid (mg)	0.0	Phytic Acid (mg)	43.3
Vitamin B6 (mg)	0.0	Oxalic Acid (mg)	21.0
Total Folate (mcg)	3	Choline (mg)	0.7
Vitamin B12 (mcg) (cobalamin)	0.0		
		Glycemic Index (glucose reference)	18
Beta-Carotene (mcg) (provitamin A carotenoid)	1	Glycemic Load (glucose reference)	0
Lutein + Zeaxanthin (mcg)	0		
Lycopene (mcg)	0		

Vegetarian Bolognese Sauce (Vegan)

It might surprise your dinner guests that there is no meat in this sauce. Generous amounts of flavorful garlic and onion paired with seasoned tomato sauce make this sauce a memorable pasta accompaniment.

Ingredients

2 Tbsp olive oil

5 cloves garlic

½ large onion (1 cup, chopped)

1 cup soy crumbles (frozen)

2 plum tomatoes, chopped

2 cups tomato sauce

½ tsp oregano

2 Tbsp brown rice syrup (or to taste)

¼ cup chopped fresh basil

Heat a medium saucepan and add olive oil. When oil becomes hot, add garlic and sauté for 1 minute. Add onions and stir-fry for another 2 minutes. Add soy crumbles and mix well, and continue to cook over medium-high heat for 3 minutes, stirring regularly. Add in chopped tomato, mix again, cover and let this cook for 5 more minutes. Add sauce and oregano, stir, re-cover and simmer for 10 minutes. Add brown rice syrup (to taste, and only if needed, depending upon the sweetness of the tomato sauce used). Right before serving, add chopped basil and heat for one more minute.

Yield: 4 cups sauce (4, 1-cup servings)

Adapted from: DuPont Company Soy Recipes, 2000; used with permission

Vegetarian Bolognese Sauce: 1 serving = 1 cup

Energy (kcal)	224		
Total Fat (g)	3.4	Calcium (mg)	78
Total Carbohydrate (g)	26.1	Phosphorus (mg)	243
Total Protein (g)	23.4	Magnesium (mg)	39
% Calories from Fat	13.4	Iron (mg)	5.0
% Calories from Carbohydrate	45.3	Zinc (mg)	1.4
% Calories from Protein	41.2	Copper (mg)	0.7
Cholesterol (g)	0	Selenium (mcg)	7.1
Total Saturated Fatty Acids (g) (SFA)	0.5	Sodium (mg)	43
Total Monounsaturated Fatty Acids (g) (MUFA)	1.9	Potassium (mg)	606
Total Polyunsaturated Fatty Acids (g) (PUFA)	0.8		
Omega-3 Fatty Acids (g)	0.1		
% Calories from SFA	1.9	Linoleic Acid - PUFA (18:2) (g)	0.7
% Calories from MUFA	7.3	Linolenic Acid – PUFA (18:3) (g)	0.1
% Calories from PUFA	3.2		
Polyunsaturated to Saturated Fat (P:S) Ratio	1.7	Tryptophan (mg)	30
		Threonine (mg)	86
Total Dietary Fiber (g)	3.1	Isoleucine (mg)	110
Soluble Dietary Fiber (g)	1.3	Leucine (mg)	181
Insoluble Dietary Fiber (g)	1.8	Lysine (mg)	142
		Methionine (mg)	30
Total Vitamin A (mcg) (Retinol Activity Equivalents)	45	Phenylalanine (mg)	116
Vitamin D (calciferol) (mcg)	0.0	Valine (mg)	111
Vitamin E (mg) (Total Alpha-Tocopherol)	2.6	Histidine (mg)	58
Vitamin K (mg) (phylloquinone)	19.6		
Vitamin C (mg) (ascorbic acid)	24.2	Daidzein (mg)	9.4
Thiamin (mg) (vitamin B1)	0.2	Genistein (mg)	15.3
Riboflavin (mg) (vitamin B2)	0.1		
Niacin (mg) (vitamin B3)	1.8	Caffeine (mg)	0
Pantothenic Acid (mg)	0.6	Phytic Acid (mg)	490.8
Vitamin B6 (mg)	0.3	Oxalic Acid (mg)	64.8
Total Folate (mcg)	66	Choline (mg)	42.3
Vitamin B12 (mcg) (cobalamin)	0.0		
		Glycemic Index (glucose reference)	66
Beta-Carotene (mcg) (provitamin A carotenoid)	537	Glycemic Load (glucose reference)	15
Lutein + Zeaxanthin (mcg)	206		
Lycopene (mcg)	21,572		

SEA VEGETABLES

Arame with carrot and onion (Vegan; GF w/Mod)

A true gift-from-the-sea, arame is a delicate and subtle sea vegetable, remarkable when paired with sweet carrots and onions.

Ingredients

1 oz dry arame seaweed (30 g)

1 cup water

1 tsp sesame oil

1 small onion (3½ oz), sliced thinly (1 cup)

2 small carrots (2½ oz), cut in thin matchsticks

½ tsp mirin

2 tsp low-sodium soy sauce

Rinse and soak arame in water for 2 to 3 minutes, until just softened. (Do not over soak.) Remove arame from water and squeeze out any excess water. Retain this soaking water. In a medium covered skillet, heat oil, then sauté onions until translucent; add carrots and heat for 1 minute. Add drained arame and sauté for 2 minutes. Then add in the soaking water, except the very last part, which may contain a bit of debris. Cover and cook for 15 minutes over medium-low heat. Add mirin and soy sauce, and cook, covered, for another 3 minutes or until tender. Uncover and simmer until remaining liquid has boiled away.

Yield: 1½ cups (6, ¼-cup servings)

~For gluten free, use tamari in place of soy sauce~

Inspired by Gretchen DeWire

Arame with Carrot and Onion: 1 serving = ¼ cup

Energy (kcal)	27		
Total Fat (g)	0.8	Calcium (mg)	13
Total Carbohydrate (g)	5.0	Phosphorus (mg)	13
Total Protein (g)	0.7	Magnesium (mg)	3
% Calories from Fat	26	Iron (mg)	0.4
% Calories from Carbohydrate	67	Zinc (mg)	0.1
% Calories from Protein	7	Copper (mg)	0.0
Cholesterol (g)	0	Selenium (mcg)	0.2
Total Saturated Fatty Acids (g) (SFA)	0.1	Sodium (mg)	216
Total Monounsaturated Fatty Acids (g) (MUFA)	0.3	Potassium (mg)	82
Total Polyunsaturated Fatty Acids (g) (PUFA)	0.3		
Omega-3 Fatty Acids (g)	0.0		
% Calories from SFA	4.1	Linoleic Acid - PUFA (18:2) (g)	0.3
% Calories from MUFA	10.0	Linolenic Acid – PUFA (18:3) (g)	0.0
% Calories from PUFA	10.9		
Polyunsaturated to Saturated Fat (P:S) Ratio	2.7	Tryptophan (mg)	1
		Threonine (mg)	4
Total Dietary Fiber (g)	1.1	Isoleucine (mg)	3
Soluble Dietary Fiber (g)	0.1	Leucine (mg)	5
Insoluble Dietary Fiber (g)	1.0	Lysine (mg)	4
		Methionine (mg)	1
Total Vitamin A (mcg) (Retinol Activity Equivalents)	113	Phenylalanine (mg)	3
Vitamin D (calciferol) (mcg)	0.0	Valine (mg)	5
Vitamin E (mg) (Total Alpha-Tocopherol)	0.2	Histidine (mg)	1
Vitamin K (mg) (phylloquinone)	2.0		
Vitamin C (mg) (ascorbic acid)	1.1	Daidzein (mg)	0.0
Thiamin (mg) (vitamin B1)	0.0	Genistein (mg)	0.0
Riboflavin (mg) (vitamin B2)	0.0		
Niacin (mg) (vitamin B3)	0.2	Caffeine (mg)	0
Pantothenic Acid (mg)	0.0	Phytic Acid (mg)	2.7
Vitamin B6 (mg)	0.0	Oxalic Acid (mg)	2.4
Total Folate (mcg)	4	Choline (mg)	2.2
Vitamin B12 (mcg) (cobalamin)	0.4		
		Glycemic Index (glucose reference)	83
Beta-Carotene (mcg) (provitamin A carotenoid)	1,154	Glycemic Load (glucose reference)	3
Lutein + Zeaxanthin (mcg)	75		
Lycopene (mcg)	0		

Kombu Ribbons with Carrot (Vegan: GF)

Sweet carrots meld perfectly with the rich and velvety texture of kombu seaweed.

Ingredients

6 strips of dried kombu seaweed (20 g)

2 medium carrots, cut in large diagonal slices about ¼ inch thick

1½ cups water

1 tsp mirin

½ tsp fresh ginger, minced

1 stalk green onions, sliced thinly

Soak kombu in water to cover until kombu is soft (15-20 minutes). Discard this soaking water and squeeze excess water from the soaked kombu. Slice the seaweed into long strips, about ½ inch wide. Tie each in a single knot.

Place seaweed knotted "ribbons" in a medium saucepan, and place carrots in a layer on top of the seaweed. Add water to cover (about 1½ cups), along with mirin cooking wine and minced ginger. Bring to a boil, then simmer until all the water is gone (about 20 minutes). There should be a nice syrupy glaze on the bottom of the pan.

Garnish with sliced fresh green onion.

Yield: 2 cups (4, ½-cup servings)

Kombu Ribbons with Carrot: 1 serving = ½ cup

Energy (kcal)	16		
Total Fat (g)	0.1	Calcium (mg)	22
Total Carbohydrate (g)	3.7	Phosphorus (mg)	12
Total Protein (g)	0.4	Magnesium (mg)	11
% Calories from Fat	5	Iron (mg)	0.3
% Calories from Carbohydrate	89	Zinc (mg)	0.1
% Calories from Protein	6	Copper (mg)	0.0
Cholesterol (g)	0	Selenium (mcg)	0.3
Total Saturated Fatty Acids (g) (SFA)	0.0	Sodium (mg)	43
Total Monounsaturated Fatty Acids (g) (MUFA)	0.0	Potassium (mg)	82
Total Polyunsaturated Fatty Acids (g) (PUFA)	0.0		
Omega-3 Fatty Acids (g)	0.0		
% Calories from SFA	1.2	Linoleic Acid - PUFA (18:2) (g)	0.0
% Calories from MUFA	0.4	Linolenic Acid – PUFA (18:3) (g)	0.0
% Calories from PUFA	1.6		
Polyunsaturated to Saturated Fat (P:S) Ratio	1.4	Tryptophan (mg)	1
		Threonine (mg)	5
Total Dietary Fiber (g)	1.0	Isoleucine (mg)	2
Soluble Dietary Fiber (g)	0.2	Leucine (mg)	3
Insoluble Dietary Fiber (g)	0.8	Lysine (mg)	3
		Methionine (mg)	1
Total Vitamin A (mcg) (Retinol Activity Equivalents)	241	Phenylalanine (mg)	2
Vitamin D (calciferol) (mcg)	0.0	Valine (mg)	2
Vitamin E (mg) (Total Alpha-Tocopherol)	0.4	Histidine (mg)	1
Vitamin K (mg) (phylloquinone)	14.9		
Vitamin C (mg) (ascorbic acid)	1.9	Daidzein (mg)	0.0
Thiamin (mg) (vitamin B1)	0.0	Genistein (mg)	0.0
Riboflavin (mg) (vitamin B2)	0.0		
Niacin (mg) (vitamin B3)	0.2	Caffeine (mg)	0
Pantothenic Acid (mg)	0.1	Phytic Acid (mg)	3.8
Vitamin B6 (mg)	0.0	Oxalic Acid (mg)	8.3
Total Folate (mcg)	15	Choline (mg)	3.4
Vitamin B12 (mcg) (cobalamin)	0.0		
		Glycemic Index (glucose reference)	51
Beta-Carotene (mcg) (provitamin A carotenoid)	2,359	Glycemic Load (glucose reference)	1
Lutein + Zeaxanthin (mcg)	235		
Lycopene (mcg)	0		

Kombu-Daikon-Mushroom (Vegan; GF w/Mod)

A delightful combination of three distinctly different vegetables. It works, because of the intense harmony among them and the true synergy created.

Ingredients

4, 6-inch strips of kombu, soaked in water

7 small shiitake mushrooms, soaked in 1 cup
 hot water (reserve soaking water)

Additional water for cooking (about ½ cup)

1 pound daikon, cut into quarter moons ½-inch thick

1 tsp low-sodium soy sauce

1 tsp mirin

½ tsp ginger

2 scallions, chopped finely

When kombu softens in soaking water, drain and discard water, slice into thin strips. Place at the bottom of a soup pot. When mushrooms are soft, remove from water, squeeze out excess, and save liquid. Slice thinly and place on top of kombu. Layer the daikon over the mushrooms. Add the shiitake soaking water (about 3/4 cup) and enough additional water to give about ½ inch layer of water on the bottom (about another ½ cup, depending on the size of pot). Bring to a boil, cover and simmer on medium-low heat for 8 minutes, then add soy sauce, mirin and ginger and simmer 7 more minutes. Mix, adjust for taste and check that all the vegetables are tender. Remove from heat, mix in chopped scallion and serve.

Yield: 4 cups (4, 1-cup servings)

~For gluten free, use tamari in place of soy sauce~

200

Kombu Daikon Mushroom: 1 serving = 1 cup

Energy (kcal)	46		
Total Fat (g)	0.2	Calcium (mg)	47
Total Carbohydrate (g)	11.0	Phosphorus (mg)	42
Total Protein (g)	1.5	Magnesium (mg)	32
% Calories from Fat	4	Iron (mg)	0.9
% Calories from Carbohydrate	88	Zinc (mg)	0.7
% Calories from Protein	8	Copper (mg)	0.4
Cholesterol (g)	0	Selenium (mcg)	8.7
Total Saturated Fatty Acids (g) (SFA)	0.7	Sodium (mg)	95
Total Monounsaturated Fatty Acids (g) (MUFA)	0.1	Potassium (mg)	323
Total Polyunsaturated Fatty Acids (g) (PUFA)	0.1		
Omega-3 Fatty Acids (g)	0.04		
% Calories from SFA	1.2	Linoleic Acid - PUFA (18:2) (g)	0.04
% Calories from MUFA	0.9	Linolenic Acid – PUFA (18:3) (g)	0.03
% Calories from PUFA	1.3		
Polyunsaturated to Saturated Fat (P:S) Ratio	1.1	Tryptophan (mg)	1
		Threonine (mg)	6
Total Dietary Fiber (g)	2.8	Isoleucine (mg)	6
Soluble Dietary Fiber (g)	0.1	Leucine (mg)	8
Insoluble Dietary Fiber (g)	2.7	Lysine (mg)	6
		Methionine (mg)	2
Total Vitamin A (mcg) (Retinol Activity Equivalents)	4	Phenylalanine (mg)	5
Vitamin D (calciferol) (mcg)	2.4	Valine (mg)	7
Vitamin E (mg) (Total Alpha-Tocopherol)	0.1	Histidine (mg)	3
Vitamin K (mg) (phylloquinone)	19.5		
Vitamin C (mg) (ascorbic acid)	26.6	Daidzein (mg)	0.012
Thiamin (mg) (vitamin B1)	0.0	Genistein (mg)	0.011
Riboflavin (mg) (vitamin B2)	0.1		
Niacin (mg) (vitamin B3)	0.8	Caffeine (mg)	0
Pantothenic Acid (mg)	1.3	Phytic Acid (mg)	39.4
Vitamin B6 (mg)	0.1	Oxalic Acid (mg)	9.5
Total Folate (mcg)	53	Choline (mg)	21.5
Vitamin B12 (mcg) (cobalamin)	0.0		
		Glycemic Index (glucose reference)	58
Beta-Carotene (mcg) (provitamin A carotenoid)	49	Glycemic Load (glucose reference)	5
Lutein + Zeaxanthin (mcg)	85		
Lycopene (mcg)	0.0		

Wakame-Cucumber-Radish salad (Vegan; GF)

A sparkling cucumber presentation, with just a hint of vinegar. Refreshes and cools; it's even better the day after!

Ingredients

½ oz (15 g) dried wakame seaweed

2 cups water, divided

4 medium red radishes (3 oz), sliced in half-moons

½ medium cucumber (4½ oz), sliced in half-moons
 ~1 cup sliced

2 Tbsp apple juice

¼ tsp sesame oil

Pinch salt

(Optional: crushed red pepper)

Rinse and soak wakame in 1 cup of water for ~3 minutes, until just tender. Bring 1 cup of water to a boil. Wash and slice radishes and parboil for 1 minute. Remove and cool. Simmer wakame for about 1 minute. Remove and cool. Mix radishes and wakame with sliced cucumber. In a small bowl, combine apple juice, oil and salt; whisk. Add to vegetables and combine well.

Yield: 1¾ cup (7, ¼-cup servings)

Wakame Cucumber Radish Salad: 1 serving = ¼ cup

Energy (kcal)	10		
Total Fat (g)	0.2	Calcium (mg)	18
Total Carbohydrate (g)	2.1	Phosphorus (mg)	11
Total Protein (g)	0.5	Magnesium (mg)	9
% Calories from Fat	20	Iron (mg)	0.4
% Calories from Carbohydrate	66	Zinc (mg)	0.2
% Calories from Protein	14	Copper (mg)	0.0
Cholesterol (g)	0	Selenium (mcg)	0.2
Total Saturated Fatty Acids (g) (SFA)	0.1	Sodium (mg)	159
Total Monounsaturated Fatty Acids (g) (MUFA)	0.1	Potassium (mg)	85
Total Polyunsaturated Fatty Acids (g) (PUFA)	0.1		
Omega-3 Fatty Acids (g)	0.01		
% Calories from SFA	3.9	Linoleic Acid - PUFA (18:2) (g)	0.1
% Calories from MUFA	6.1	Linolenic Acid – PUFA (18:3) (g)	0.01
% Calories from PUFA	6.6		
Polyunsaturated to Saturated Fat (P:S) Ratio	1.7	Tryptophan (mg)	1
		Threonine (mg)	2
Total Dietary Fiber (g)	0.8	Isoleucine (mg)	2
Soluble Dietary Fiber (g)	0.1	Leucine (mg)	3
Insoluble Dietary Fiber (g)	0.7	Lysine (mg)	2
		Methionine (mg)	1
Total Vitamin A (mcg) (Retinol Activity Equivalents)	14	Phenylalanine (mg)	2
Vitamin D (calciferol) (mcg)	0.0	Valine (mg)	3
Vitamin E (mg) (Total Alpha-Tocopherol)	0.1	Histidine (mg)	1
Vitamin K (mg) (phylloquinone)	3.5		
Vitamin C (mg) (ascorbic acid)	2.7	Daidzein (mg)	0.0
Thiamin (mg) (vitamin B1)	0.0	Genistein (mg)	0.0
Riboflavin (mg) (vitamin B2)	0.0		
Niacin (mg) (vitamin B3)	0.1	Caffeine (mg)	0
Pantothenic Acid (mg)	0.1	Phytic Acid (mg)	0.8
Vitamin B6 (mg)	0.0	Oxalic Acid (mg)	0.5
Total Folate (mcg)	13	Choline (mg)	2.4
Vitamin B12 (mcg) (cobalamin)	0.2		
		Glycemic Index (glucose reference)	49
Beta-Carotene (mcg) (provitamin A carotenoid)	171	Glycemic Load (glucose reference)	1
Lutein + Zeaxanthin (mcg)	5		
Lycopene (mcg)	0		

SOUPS

Barley Vegetable Soup (Vegan; GF w/Mod)

Soulful comfort food ~ perfect for a cold winter's day.

Ingredients

1/3 cup barley (~1 cup cooked)

7 cups water, divided

1 tsp canola oil

¾ cup onion, chopped

¾ cup button mushroom, sliced

½ cup carrot, sliced

½ cup celery, sliced

5 tsp white miso

Wash and drain barley. In a medium soup pot, place 1/3 cup barley and 3 cups water. Bring to a boil and simmer for 1 hour on low heat. (Barley expands greatly, and absorbs a lot of water.) In a medium skillet, heat canola oil and sauté onions over medium heat for 2 minutes, then add the mushrooms, and cook for another 2 minutes, stirring occasionally. Add the carrots and celery, and cook until the carrots start to become tender.

Add these cooked vegetables to the soup pot containing (1 cup of) cooked barley. Add 4 cups water and bring to a boil. Simmer for 20 minutes or more. At the end, dilute miso with a little of the soup broth and mix into the soup (do not boil); heat for another 2 minutes and serve.

Yield: 5 cups (5, 1-cup servings)

Note: Try buying "quick-cooking barley" to shorten the prep time, or place all ingredients in a slow cooker to welcome you home in the evening. Use any on-hand vegetables, and add more barley for a thick stew. A great source of soluble fiber!

~For gluten-free, use brown-rice miso in place of white miso~

Inspired by Gretchen DeWire

Barley Vegetable Soup: 1 serving = 1 cup

Energy (kcal)	74		
Total Fat (g)	1.3	Calcium (mg)	24
Total Carbohydrate (g)	14.2	Phosphorus (mg)	48
Total Protein (g)	2.0	Magnesium (mg)	18
% Calories from Fat	15.5	Iron (mg)	0.6
% Calories from Carbohydrate	75.5	Zinc (mg)	0.5
% Calories from Protein	9	Copper (mg)	0.1
Cholesterol (g)	0	Selenium (mcg)	5.5
Total Saturated Fatty Acids (g) (SFA)	0.1	Sodium (mg)	137
Total Monounsaturated Fatty Acids (g) (MUFA)	0.6	Potassium (mg)	154
Total Polyunsaturated Fatty Acids (g) (PUFA)	0.5		
Omega-3 Fatty Acids (g)	0.1		
% Calories from SFA	1.7	Linoleic Acid - PUFA (18:2) (g)	0.4
% Calories from MUFA	7.6	Linolenic Acid – PUFA (18:3) (g)	0.1
% Calories from PUFA	5.3		
Polyunsaturated to Saturated Fat (P:S) Ratio	3.2	Tryptophan (mg)	3
		Threonine (mg)	8
Total Dietary Fiber (g)	2.8	Isoleucine (mg)	8
Soluble Dietary Fiber (g)	0.5	Leucine (mg)	13
Insoluble Dietary Fiber (g)	2.3	Lysine (mg)	9
		Methionine (mg)	3
Total Vitamin A (mcg) (Retinol Activity Equivalents)	99	Phenylalanine (mg)	9
Vitamin D (calciferol) (mcg)	0.0	Valine (mg)	10
Vitamin E (mg) (Total Alpha-Tocopherol)	0.3	Histidine (mg)	4
Vitamin K (mg) (phylloquinone)	7.5		
Vitamin C (mg) (ascorbic acid)	2.4	Daidzein (mg)	0.4
Thiamin (mg) (vitamin B1)	0.1	Genistein (mg)	0.7
Riboflavin (mg) (vitamin B2)	0.1		
Niacin (mg) (vitamin B3)	1.0	Caffeine (mg)	0
Pantothenic Acid (mg)	0.3	Phytic Acid (mg)	69.0
Vitamin B6 (mg)	0.1	Oxalic Acid (mg)	5.8
Total Folate (mcg)	11	Choline (mg)	10.8
Vitamin B12 (mcg) (cobalamin)	0.0		
		Glycemic Index (glucose reference)	45
Beta-Carotene (mcg) (provitamin A carotenoid)	973	Glycemic Load (glucose reference)	5
Lutein + Zeaxanthin (mcg)	132		
Lycopene (mcg)	0		

Kidney Bean Soup with Kale (Vegan; GF w/Mod)

Multicolored and inviting…Great for leftovers, as the soup thickens up into a yummy stew. Great nutrition never tasted so good!

Ingredients

¾ cup dried kidney beans

7½ cups water, divided (1½ to soak, 2 to cook beans; 4 for soup)

1 tsp sesame oil

1 medium onion, cut in large slices

2 small stalks of celery, but in large slices

1 medium carrot, sliced in large flat squares

2 Tbsp + 1 tsp low-sodium soy sauce

½ tsp olive oil

¼ tsp black pepper

¼ tsp dried Italian seasoning

¼ tsp fresh grated ginger

1/8 tsp curry powder

2 cups kale, sliced thinly

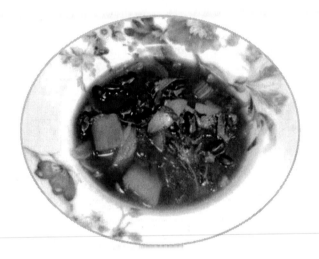

Wash and drain beans, add 1½ cups of water and soak for 5 hours or overnight. Drain and discard soaking water, then add 2 cups of water. Pressure cook for 1 hour. In a large soup pot, heat sesame oil and sauté onion for 3 minutes, then add celery and carrots, cooking for 2 minutes more. Add cooked kidney beans and their liquid (about 1 cup of liquid), plus 4 more cups of water. Bring to a boil and simmer on medium for 15 minutes. Add soy sauce, olive oil, pepper, Italian seasoning, ginger and curry powder; simmer for 5 minutes. [Note: soup can be cooked longer for richer flavor or in winter for a softer soup.] Before serving, add kale and simmer 10-15 minutes until kale is tender, while still bright green.

Note: For this dish, it is best to make the beans from dried, but this step can be done a day in advance to simplify meal prep.

Yield: 7 cups (7, 1-cup servings)

~For gluten free, use tamari in place of soy sauce~

Inspired by Gretchen DeWire

Kidney Bean Soup with Kale: 1 serving = 1 cup

Energy (kcal)	93		
Total Fat (g)	1.4	Calcium (mg)	50
Total Carbohydrate (g)	15.7	Phosphorus (mg)	92
Total Protein (g)	5.4	Magnesium (mg)	33
% Calories from Fat	13	Iron (mg)	1.6
% Calories from Carbohydrate	67	Zinc (mg)	0.7
% Calories from Protein	20	Copper (mg)	0.2
Cholesterol (g)	0	Selenium (mcg)	1.0
Total Saturated Fatty Acids (g) (SFA)	0.2	Sodium (mg)	204
Total Monounsaturated Fatty Acids (g) (MUFA)	0.5	Potassium (mg)	338
Total Polyunsaturated Fatty Acids (g) (PUFA)	0.5		
Omega-3 Fatty Acids (g)	0.1		
% Calories from SFA	1.9	Linoleic Acid - PUFA (18:2) (g)	0.4
% Calories from MUFA	5.0	Linolenic Acid – PUFA (18:3) (g)	0.1
% Calories from PUFA	4.8		
Polyunsaturated to Saturated Fat (P:S) Ratio	2.6	Tryptophan (mg)	7
		Threonine (mg)	21
Total Dietary Fiber (g)	4.3	Isoleucine (mg)	26
Soluble Dietary Fiber (g)	1.2	Leucine (mg)	44
Insoluble Dietary Fiber (g)	3.1	Lysine (mg)	37
		Methionine (mg)	7
Total Vitamin A (mcg) (Retinol Activity Equivalents)	215	Phenylalanine (mg)	31
Vitamin D (calciferol) (mcg)	0.0	Valine (mg)	30
Vitamin E (mg) (Total Alpha-Tocopherol)	0.4	Histidine (mg)	14
Vitamin K (mg) (phylloquinone)	183.5		
Vitamin C (mg) (ascorbic acid)	11.0	Daidzein (mg)	0.0
Thiamin (mg) (vitamin B1)	0.1	Genistein (mg)	0.0
Riboflavin (mg) (vitamin B2)	0.1		
Niacin (mg) (vitamin B3)	0.7	Caffeine (mg)	0
Pantothenic Acid (mg)	0.2	Phytic Acid (mg)	106.1
Vitamin B6 (mg)	0.1	Oxalic Acid (mg)	12.6
Total Folate (mcg)	75	Choline (mg)	19.8
Vitamin B12 (mcg) (cobalamin)	0.0		
		Glycemic Index (glucose reference)	36
Beta-Carotene (mcg) (provitamin A carotenoid)	2,433	Glycemic Load (glucose reference)	4
Lutein + Zeaxanthin (mcg)	3,955		
Lycopene (mcg)	0		

Miso Soup (Vegan; GF w/Mod)

A cup of –pick-me-up!" Endless possibilities for this wonderful flavored broth make tasty soup a cinch. Keeping it simple highlights the flavor complexity.

Ingredients

5½ cups water, divided

2 shiitake mushrooms, dried s
after reconstituted)

2 Tbsp wakame seaweed (~5 g)

2 Tbsp white miso

6 oz of tofu (cut into ½ inch cubes, ~1¼ cups)

1 scallion, chopped

Bring 5 cups of water to a boil and soak 2 medium mushrooms in ½ cup boiling water. Soak wakame in water just to cover. After 3-4 minutes, drain and slice the softened wakame. When mushrooms have softened, slice thinly and add to boiling water along with the mushroom soaking water (about ¼ cup). Simmer for about 10 minutes or until mushrooms are tender. Dilute miso with some of the soup stock, and add back to the broth. Add tofu to soup and bring back to a simmer; quickly add drained wakame. Cook for about 2 minutes, turn off the heat, pour the soup into a soup bowl and garnish with scallions.

Optional: add mung bean sprouts before serving.

Yield: 5 cups (5, 1-cup servings)

~For gluten-free, use brown-rice miso in place of white miso~

Adapted from a recipe by Fukue (Fay) Toyozato (Zen Vegetarian Cooking class)

Miso Soup: 1 serving = 1 cup

Energy (kcal)	52		
Total Fat (g)	2.2	Calcium (mg)	131
Total Carbohydrate (g)	4.7	Phosphorus (mg)	69
Total Protein (g)	4.6	Magnesium (mg)	28
% Calories from Fat	36	Iron (mg)	1.1
% Calories from Carbohydrate	34	Zinc (mg)	0.6
% Calories from Protein	30	Copper (mg)	0.2
Cholesterol (g)	0	Selenium (mcg)	6.8
Total Saturated Fatty Acids (g) (SFA)	0.5	Sodium (mg)	205
Total Monounsaturated Fatty Acids (g) (MUFA)	0.6	Potassium (mg)	108
Total Polyunsaturated Fatty Acids (g) (PUFA)	1.0		
Omega-3 Fatty Acids (g)	0.1		
% Calories from SFA	7.5	Linoleic Acid - PUFA (18:2) (g)	0.9
% Calories from MUFA	10.3	Linolenic Acid – PUFA (18:3) (g)	0.1
% Calories from PUFA	15.7		
Polyunsaturated to Saturated Fat (P:S) Ratio	2.1	Tryptophan (mg)	7
		Threonine (mg)	19
Total Dietary Fiber (g)	1.0	Isoleucine (mg)	22
Soluble Dietary Fiber (g)	0.2	Leucine (mg)	35
Insoluble Dietary Fiber (g)	0.8	Lysine (mg)	29
		Methionine (mg)	6
Total Vitamin A (mcg) (Retinol Activity Equivalents)	8	Phenylalanine (mg)	22
Vitamin D (calciferol) (mcg)	0.5	Valine (mg)	24
Vitamin E (mg) (Total Alpha-Tocopherol)	0.1	Histidine (mg)	13
Vitamin K (mg) (phylloquinone)	9.5		
Vitamin C (mg) (ascorbic acid)	0.8	Daidzein (mg)	5.1
Thiamin (mg) (vitamin B1)	0.0	Genistein (mg)	7.2
Riboflavin (mg) (vitamin B2)	0.1		
Niacin (mg) (vitamin B3)	0.2	Caffeine (mg)	0
Pantothenic Acid (mg)	0.3	Phytic Acid (mg)	250.2
Vitamin B6 (mg)	0.1	Oxalic Acid (mg)	8.4
Total Folate (mcg)	17	Choline (mg)	18.9
Vitamin B12 (mcg) (cobalamin)	0.1		
		Glycemic Index (glucose reference)	54
Beta-Carotene (mcg) (provitamin A carotenoid)	97	Glycemic Load (glucose reference)	2
Lutein + Zeaxanthin (mcg)	34		
Lycopene (mcg)	0		

Squash Soup (Vegan: GF)

The natural sweetness of winter squash, intensified by roasting, is joined by a perfect ginger splash. Splendid consistency which will warm the coldest winter day.

Ingredients

1 buttercup squash, ~3 lbs with seeds removed (baked & mashed: yields ~5 cups)

½ tsp olive oil

½ cube sodium-free vegetable bouillon

4 cups water, divided

1 tsp sesame oil

2 small onions chopped (1¼ cups)

½ tsp salt, divided

3 tsp grated ginger

1 tsp mirin

½ tsp black pepper

2 Tbsp chopped cilantro

Preheat oven to 375°F. Wash and cut squash in half, removing insides with seeds and any pulp. Brush with olive oil and place each half, face down, on a baking sheet. Bake for about 40 minutes, until soft. Let cool.

Dilute bouillon in 1 cup hot water. Heat a small skillet and add sesame oil. Sauté onions thoroughly, adding a pinch of salt at the beginning. When onions start to brown, add diluted bouillon and 3 cups more of water. Bring to a boil. When squash has cooled, carve out the squash from the skin and mash gently. Add to the pot and stir. Simmer over medium-low heat for 20 minutes. Squeeze ginger and add this juice (~3 tsp), along with the mirin, remaining salt (½ tsp salt minus a pinch) and the pepper, and cook 5 minutes more. Using a regular blender or hand-held blender, puree the mixture to make a creamy soup. Garnish with cilantro or parsley.

Yield: 4½ cups soup (4½, 1-cup servings)

Note: This is a very basic version of squash soup. Other herbs or spices can be added for an entirely new taste. You can also cook the squash one day and make soup the next.

Adapted from: Madison D, *Vegetarian Cooking for Everyone*, 1997, p 215 (Winter Squash Soup with Fried Sage Leaves)

Squash Soup: 1 serving = 1 cup

Energy (kcal)	133		
Total Fat (g)	2.5	Calcium (mg)	75
Total Carbohydrate (g)	28.4	Phosphorus (mg)	65
Total Protein (g)	2.9	Magnesium (mg)	42
% Calories from Fat	17	Iron (mg)	1.4
% Calories from Carbohydrate	77	Zinc (mg)	0.7
% Calories from Protein	6	Copper (mg)	0.3
Cholesterol (g)	0	Selenium (mcg)	1.3
Total Saturated Fatty Acids (g) (SFA)	0.4	Sodium (mg)	284
Total Monounsaturated Fatty Acids (g) (MUFA)	0.9	Potassium (mg)	717
Total Polyunsaturated Fatty Acids (g) (PUFA)	0.9		
Omega-3 Fatty Acids (g)	0.3		
% Calories from SFA	2.8	Linoleic Acid - PUFA (18:2) (g)	0.6
% Calories from MUFA	5.6	Linolenic Acid – PUFA (18:3) (g)	0.3
% Calories from PUFA	5.8		
Polyunsaturated to Saturated Fat (P:S) Ratio	2.1	Tryptophan (mg)	4
		Threonine (mg)	9
Total Dietary Fiber (g)	8.0	Isoleucine (mg)	11
Soluble Dietary Fiber (g)	4.3	Leucine (mg)	15
Insoluble Dietary Fiber (g)	3.7	Lysine (mg)	11
		Methionine (mg)	3
Total Vitamin A (mcg) (Retinol Activity Equivalents)	698	Phenylalanine (mg)	11
Vitamin D (calciferol) (mcg)	0.0	Valine (mg)	11
Vitamin E (mg) (Total Alpha-Tocopherol)	0.4	Histidine (mg)	5
Vitamin K (mg) (phylloquinone)	14.1		
Vitamin C (mg) (ascorbic acid)	27.8	Daidzein (mg)	0.0
Thiamin (mg) (vitamin B1)	0.1	Genistein (mg)	0.0
Riboflavin (mg) (vitamin B2)	0.2		
Niacin (mg) (vitamin B3)	1.4	Caffeine (mg)	9
Pantothenic Acid (mg)	0.7	Phytic Acid (mg)	57.2
Vitamin B6 (mg)	0.5	Oxalic Acid (mg)	6.2
Total Folate (mcg)	59	Choline (mg)	31.3
Vitamin B12 (mcg) (cobalamin)	0.9		
		Glycemic Index (glucose reference)	74
Beta-Carotene (mcg) (provitamin A carotenoid)	7,466	Glycemic Load (glucose reference)	15
Lutein + Zeaxanthin (mcg)	3,779		
Lycopene (mcg)	0		

Tofu – Green Pea Soup (Vegan; GF)

Appealing to eyes and taste buds, this is a versatile, all-weather soup that nourishes and soothes.

Ingredients

½ tsp sesame oil

1 scallion, chopped

2 medium white, button mushrooms, sliced

3 1/8 cups water, divided

1 sodium-free vegan bouillon cube

¼ cup frozen green peas (or fresh, if available)

½ medium carrot, cut in cubes (1 cup)

6 oz tofu, cut into small, ¼" cubes

¼ tsp salt

Pinch white pepper

2 Tbsp kuzu (or arrowroot flour)

In a medium soup pot, heat the oil and sauté scallions for about 1 minute. Add mushroom slices and cook another minute. Add 3 cups of water and bring to a boil. In a small bowl, add ½ cup of boiling water to the bouillon cube and whisk until completely dissolved before adding to the soup. Mix in the peas and carrots; simmer for 5 minutes. Add tofu; season with salt and white pepper to taste. Dissolve kuzu in 1/8 cup water; add this mixture to soup, and stir soup frequently until thickened (1-2 minutes). Remove from heat and serve.

Yield: 3 cups (3, 1-cup servings)

Tofu Green Pea Soup: 1 serving = 1 cup

Energy (kcal)	83		
Total Fat (g)	3.2	Calcium (mg)	133
Total Carbohydrate (g)	9.3	Phosphorus (mg)	90
Total Protein (g)	5.6	Magnesium (mg)	29
% Calories from Fat	33	Iron (mg)	1.4
% Calories from Carbohydrate	44	Zinc (mg)	0.7
% Calories from Protein	23	Copper (mg)	0.2
Cholesterol (g)	0	Selenium (mcg)	6.9
Total Saturated Fatty Acids (g) (SFA)	0.6	Sodium (mg)	125
Total Monounsaturated Fatty Acids (g) (MUFA)	1.0	Potassium (mg)	166
Total Polyunsaturated Fatty Acids (g) (PUFA)	1.4		
Omega-3 Fatty Acids (g)	0.1		
% Calories from SFA	6.2	Linoleic Acid - PUFA (18:2) (g)	1.3
% Calories from MUFA	10.2	Linolenic Acid – PUFA (18:3) (g)	0.1
% Calories from PUFA	14.1		
Polyunsaturated to Saturated Fat (P:S) Ratio	2.2	Tryptophan (mg)	8
		Threonine (mg)	24
Total Dietary Fiber (g)	1.7	Isoleucine (mg)	27
Soluble Dietary Fiber (g)	0.4	Leucine (mg)	41
Insoluble Dietary Fiber (g)	1.3	Lysine (mg)	36
		Methionine (mg)	7
Total Vitamin A (mcg) (Retinol Activity Equivalents)	97	Phenylalanine (mg)	26
Vitamin D (calciferol) (mcg)	0.0	Valine (mg)	28
Vitamin E (mg) (Total Alpha-Tocopherol)	0.1	Histidine (mg)	16
Vitamin K (mg) (phylloquinone)	15.6		
Vitamin C (mg) (ascorbic acid)	2.8	Daidzein (mg)	5.4
Thiamin (mg) (vitamin B1)	0.1	Genistein (mg)	7.6
Riboflavin (mg) (vitamin B2)	0.1		
Niacin (mg) (vitamin B3)	0.7	Caffeine (mg)	0
Pantothenic Acid (mg)	0.3	Phytic Acid (mg)	295.1
Vitamin B6 (mg)	0.1	Oxalic Acid (mg)	11.5
Total Folate (mcg)	24	Choline (mg)	24.6
Vitamin B12 (mcg) (cobalamin)	0.0		
		Glycemic Index (glucose reference)	81
Beta-Carotene (mcg) (provitamin A carotenoid)	983	Glycemic Load (glucose reference)	6
Lutein + Zeaxanthin (mcg)	375		
Lycopene (mcg)	0		

Vegetable Miso Soup for Noodles (Vegan; GF w/Mod)

A gentle, sweet soup that complements any noodle dish. Fun to eat all by itself too!

Ingredients

1 Tbsp olive oil

1 medium onion, diced in large chunks, 1 cup

2 stalks celery, sliced on diagonal, ½ cup

1/8 head medium green cabbage, sliced, 2 cups

1 medium turnip, diced, 1 1/3 cups

2 small carrots, sliced on diagonal, about ½ cup

8 cups water

3 Tbsp white miso

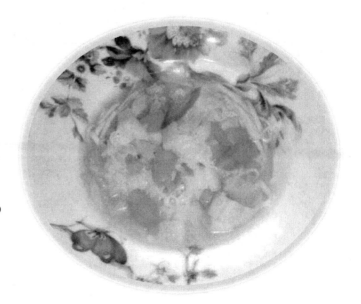

Heat oil in soup pot, add onions and sauté until tender. Add in celery, then cabbage, turnip and carrots, each time coating with oil and mixing well. Add water and bring to a boil. Simmer for about 20 minutes, until all vegetables are very tender. Dilute miso with a small amount (1/4 cup) of soup broth. Add to soup and heat for 2 minutes (do not reboil).

Serve one cup of soup over about 1 cup of noodles of your choice.

Yield: 8 cups (8, 1-cup servings)

~ For gluten-free, use brown-rice miso in place of white miso and place over rice noodles~

Vegetable Miso Soup for Noodles: 1 serving = 1 cup of soup

Energy (kcal)	43		
Total Fat (g)	1.9	Calcium (mg)	31
Total Carbohydrate (g)	6.1	Phosphorus (mg)	24
Total Protein (g)	1.0	Magnesium (mg)	11
% Calories from Fat	39	Iron (mg)	0.2
% Calories from Carbohydrate	54	Zinc (mg)	0.2
% Calories from Protein	7	Copper (mg)	0.1
Cholesterol (g)	0	Selenium (mcg)	0.6
Total Saturated Fatty Acids (g) (SFA)	0.3	Sodium (mg)	149
Total Monounsaturated Fatty Acids (g) (MUFA)	1.3	Potassium (mg)	131
Total Polyunsaturated Fatty Acids (g) (PUFA)	0.3		
Omega-3 Fatty Acids (g)	0.04		
% Calories from SFA	5.6	Linoleic Acid - PUFA (18:2) (g)	0.3
% Calories from MUFA	26.0	Linolenic Acid – PUFA (18:3) (g)	0.04
% Calories from PUFA	6.2		
Polyunsaturated to Saturated Fat (P:S) Ratio	1.1	Tryptophan (mg)	1
		Threonine (mg)	4
Total Dietary Fiber (g)	1.4	Isoleucine (mg)	4
Soluble Dietary Fiber (g)	0.3	Leucine (mg)	5
Insoluble Dietary Fiber (g)	1.1	Lysine (mg)	4
		Methionine (mg)	1
Total Vitamin A (mcg) (Retinol Activity Equivalents)	62	Phenylalanine (mg)	3
Vitamin D (calciferol) (mcg)	0.0	Valine (mg)	4
Vitamin E (mg) (Total Alpha-Tocopherol)	0.4	Histidine (mg)	2
Vitamin K (mg) (phylloquinone)	23.9		
Vitamin C (mg) (ascorbic acid)	10.0	Daidzein (mg)	0.5
Thiamin (mg) (vitamin B1)	0.0	Genistein (mg)	0.8
Riboflavin (mg) (vitamin B2)	0.0		
Niacin (mg) (vitamin B3)	0.2	Caffeine (mg)	0
Pantothenic Acid (mg)	0.1	Phytic Acid (mg)	10.8
Vitamin B6 (mg)	0.1	Oxalic Acid (mg)	4.3
Total Folate (mcg)	12	Choline (mg)	9.4
Vitamin B12 (mcg) (cobalamin)	0		
		Glycemic Index (glucose reference)	60
Beta-Carotene (mcg) (provitamin A carotenoid)	616	Glycemic Load (glucose reference)	3
Lutein + Zeaxanthin (mcg)	76		
Lycopene (mcg)	0		

White Bean Soup with Escarole (Vegan; GF)

A delicate soup and a lovely way to enjoy white beans with melt-in-your-mouth escarole.

Ingredients

1 Tbsp olive oil

2 large cloves of garlic, sliced, about 4 tsp

4 cups water

2 bay leaves

1 can (15 oz) great northern beans, rinsed and drained (about 1½ cups)

1/8 tsp pepper

½ tsp Kosher salt

1/8 tsp dried oregano

¼ head escarole, chopped coarsely (about 3½ oz by weight, 2½ cups chopped)

In a medium soup pot, heat oil, and then stir-fry garlic for about a minute, just to flavor the oil. Add water and bay leaves and bring to a boil. In the meantime, take ¼ cup of the beans and mash them with a fork. Add these and the remaining whole beans to the pot and simmer over medium heat for about 20 minutes, or until beans are tender.

Remove bay leaves. Add pepper, salt, and oregano. Stir. Just before serving, add in escarole and cook about 5 minutes, until escarole has wilted and is tender.

Yield: 4 cups soup (4, 1-cup servings)

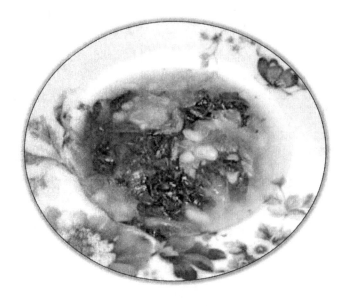

White Bean Soup with Escarole: 1 serving =1 cup

Energy (kcal)	131		
Total Fat (g)	3.7	Calcium (mg)	86
Total Carbohydrate (g)	18.5	Phosphorus (mg)	86
Total Protein (g)	7.0	Magnesium (mg)	49
% Calories from Fat	25	Iron (mg)	2.8
% Calories from Carbohydrate	57	Zinc (mg)	1.2
% Calories from Protein	18	Copper (mg)	0.2
Cholesterol (g)	0	Selenium (mcg)	1.3
Total Saturated Fatty Acids (g) (SFA)	0.5	Sodium (mg)	312
Total Monounsaturated Fatty Acids (g) (MUFA)	2.5	Potassium (mg)	463
Total Polyunsaturated Fatty Acids (g) (PUFA)	0.5		
Omega-3 Fatty Acids (g)	0.1		
% Calories from SFA	3.6	Linoleic Acid - PUFA (18:2) (g)	0.4
% Calories from MUFA	16.8	Linolenic Acid – PUFA (18:3) (g)	0.1
% Calories from PUFA	3.2		
Polyunsaturated to Saturated Fat (P:S) Ratio	0.9	Tryptophan (mg)	8
		Threonine (mg)	29
Total Dietary Fiber (g)	5.0	Isoleucine (mg)	31
Soluble Dietary Fiber (g)	0.2	Leucine (mg)	55
Insoluble Dietary Fiber (g)	4.8	Lysine (mg)	47
		Methionine (mg)	10
Total Vitamin A (mcg) (Retinol Activity Equivalents)	27	Phenylalanine (mg)	37
Vitamin D (calciferol) (mcg)	0.0	Valine (mg)	36
Vitamin E (mg) (Total Alpha-Tocopherol)	1.2	Histidine (mg)	19
Vitamin K (mg) (phylloquinone)	62.0		
Vitamin C (mg) (ascorbic acid)	2.5	Daidzein (mg)	0.0
Thiamin (mg) (vitamin B1)	0.1	Genistein (mg)	0.0
Riboflavin (mg) (vitamin B2)	0.1		
Niacin (mg) (vitamin B3)	0.2	Caffeine (mg)	0
Pantothenic Acid (mg)	0.4	Phytic Acid (mg)	159.1
Vitamin B6 (mg)	0.1	Oxalic Acid (mg)	88.1
Total Folate (mcg)	89	Choline (mg)	28.2
Vitamin B12 (mcg) (cobalamin)	0.0		
		Glycemic Index (glucose reference)	30
Beta-Carotene (mcg) (provitamin A carotenoid)	324	Glycemic Load (glucose reference)	4
Lutein + Zeaxanthin (mcg)	517		
Lycopene (mcg)	0		

DESSERTS

Azuki-Chestnut-Raisin-Apple Dessert (Vegan; GF)

A textural wonder of contrast and sweetness. Who said dessert couldn't be nutritious as well as delicious?!

Ingredients

1 cup azuki beans, uncooked (3 cups cooked)

1 cup dried chestnuts

5 cups water, divided

½ cup raisins

1 medium apple, peeled, cored and chopped

1/8 tsp salt

Wash and drain beans and the chestnuts. In two separate bowls, soak beans in 2 cups of water and chestnuts in 1 cup of water for ~5 hours or overnight. Retain chestnut water, but discard bean soaking water. In a pressure cooker, combine beans and chestnuts with soaking water. Add 2 more cups of plain water. Add raisins and apples. Pressure cook beans for 1 hour. When pressure has come down, remove lid, add salt and simmer for 2 more minutes. Break up any large chunks of chestnuts with spoon. Serve hot as is, or pureed in a food processor and served with chopped nuts, berries, and rice- or soy-whipped topping.

Yield: 4 3/4 cups (4 3/4, 1-cup servings)

Based on a recipe by Aveline Kushi and Wendy Esko, from the *Changing Seasons Macrobiotic Cookbook,* 2003, with permission of Wendy Esko

Azuki-Chestnut-Raisin Dessert: 1 serving = 1 cup

Energy (kcal)	359		
Total Fat (g)	1.4	Calcium (mg)	72
Total Carbohydrate (g)	76.0	Phosphorus (mg)	304
Total Protein (g)	13.0	Magnesium (mg)	105
% Calories from Fat	3	Iron (mg)	3.9
% Calories from Carbohydrate	84	Zinc (mg)	2.7
% Calories from Protein	13	Copper (mg)	0.7
Cholesterol (g)	0	Selenium (mcg)	2.4
Total Saturated Fatty Acids (g) (SFA)	0.3	Sodium (mg)	93
Total Monounsaturated Fatty Acids (g) (MUFA)	0.4	Potassium (mg)	1216
Total Polyunsaturated Fatty Acids (g) (PUFA)	0.5		
Omega-3 Fatty Acids (g)	0.1		
% Calories from SFA	0.7	Linoleic Acid - PUFA (18:2) (g)	0.5
% Calories from MUFA	1.0	Linolenic Acid – PUFA (18:3) (g)	0.1
% Calories from PUFA	1.2		
Polyunsaturated to Saturated Fat (P:S) Ratio	1.8	Tryptophan (mg)	13
		Threonine (mg)	44
Total Dietary Fiber (g)	15.1	Isoleucine (mg)	51
Soluble Dietary Fiber (g)	2.1	Leucine (mg)	103
Insoluble Dietary Fiber (g)	13.0	Lysine (mg)	93
		Methionine (mg)	15
Total Vitamin A (mcg) (Retinol Activity Equivalents)	1	Phenylalanine (mg)	67
Vitamin D (calciferol) (mcg)	0	Valine (mg)	66
Vitamin E (mg) (Total Alpha-Tocopherol)	0.2	Histidine (mg)	34
Vitamin K (mg) (phylloquinone)	7.1		
Vitamin C (mg) (ascorbic acid)	6.3	Daidzein (mg)	0.5
Thiamin (mg) (vitamin B1)	0.3	Genistein (mg)	0.7
Riboflavin (mg) (vitamin B2)	0.1		
Niacin (mg) (vitamin B3)	1.4	Caffeine (mg)	0
Pantothenic Acid (mg)	0.9	Phytic Acid (mg)	752.8
Vitamin B6 (mg)	0.4	Oxalic Acid (mg)	70.7
Total Folate (mcg)	210	Choline (mg)	61.9
Vitamin B12 (mcg) (cobalamin)	0		
		Glycemic Index (glucose reference)	32
Beta-Carotene (mcg) (provitamin A carotenoid)	12	Glycemic Load (glucose reference)	20
Lutein + Zeaxanthin (mcg)	6		
Lycopene (mcg)	0		

Almond Miso Dip <small>(Vegan)</small>

This rich, tasty —frostig" adds zest to a basic fruit plate or as a nutty vegetable accompaniment. A little goes a long way..

Ingredients

¼ cup almond butter, unsalted

2¼ tsp barley miso

2 Tbsp maple syrup

2 Tbsp water

1½ Tbsp brown rice syrup

1½ Tbsp chopped walnuts

Pinch of cinnamon

Pinch of nutmeg

In a medium mixing bowl, hand-combine almond butter, miso, maple syrup, water, brown rice syrup, walnuts, cinnamon and nutmeg. If a thinner sauce is desired, more water can be added.

Serve with your favorite slices of fruit or raw vegetables.

Yield: 9 Tbsp (9, 1-Tbsp servings)

From Marilyn Moser-Waxman, *The Nourishing Well*, Havertown, PA, www.thenourishingwell.com.

Almond Miso Dip: 1 serving = 1 Tbsp.

Energy (kcal)	78		
Total Fat (g)	5.0	Calcium (mg)	25
Total Carbohydrate (g)	8.0	Phosphorus (mg)	43
Total Protein (g)	1.4	Magnesium (mg)	25
% Calories from Fat	54	Iron (mg)	0.4
% Calories from Carbohydrate	40	Zinc (mg)	0.5
% Calories from Protein	6	Copper (mg)	0.1
Cholesterol (g)	0	Selenium (mcg)	0.5
Total Saturated Fatty Acids (g) (SFA)	0.5	Sodium (mg)	61
Total Monounsaturated Fatty Acids (g) (MUFA)	2.8	Potassium (mg)	72
Total Polyunsaturated Fatty Acids (g) (PUFA)	1.5		
Omega-3 Fatty Acids (g)	0.1		
% Calories from SFA	5.2	Linoleic Acid - PUFA (18:2) (g)	1.3
% Calories from MUFA	30.0	Linolenic Acid – PUFA (18:3) (g)	0.1
% Calories from PUFA	15.9		
Polyunsaturated to Saturated Fat (P:S) Ratio	3.1	Tryptophan (mg)	2
		Threonine (mg)	5
Total Dietary Fiber (g)	0.4	Isoleucine (mg)	6
Soluble Dietary Fiber (g)	0.1	Leucine (mg)	11
Insoluble Dietary Fiber (g)	0.3	Lysine (mg)	5
		Methionine (mg)	2
Total Vitamin A (mcg) (Retinol Activity Equivalents)	0	Phenylalanine (mg)	7
Vitamin D (calciferol) (mcg)	0	Valine (mg)	7
Vitamin E (mg) (Total Alpha-Tocopherol)	2.0	Histidine (mg)	4
Vitamin K (mg) (phylloquinone)	0.5		
Vitamin C (mg) (ascorbic acid)	0.1	Daidzein (mg)	0.231
Thiamin (mg) (vitamin B1)	0.0	Genistein (mg)	0.352
Riboflavin (mg) (vitamin B2)	0.0		
Niacin (mg) (vitamin B3)	0.2	Caffeine (mg)	0
Pantothenic Acid (mg)	0.0	Phytic Acid (mg)	77.6
Vitamin B6 (mg)	0.0	Oxalic Acid (mg)	34.1
Total Folate (mcg)	6	Choline (mg)	5.4
Vitamin B12 (mcg) (cobalamin)	0		
		Glycemic Index (glucose reference)	60
Beta-Carotene (mcg) (provitamin A carotenoid)	1	Glycemic Load (glucose reference)	5
Lutein + Zeaxanthin (mcg)	0		
Lycopene (mcg)	0		

Baked Apples (Vegan: GF)

An easy, satisfying dessert to celebrate the wonders of this simple fruit.

Ingredients

4 medium apples

4 tsp raisins

4 tsp chopped walnuts

2 tsp maple syrup, divided

1/8 tsp cinnamon

1/3 cup water

Preheat oven to 400°F. Wash and core the apples, but leave about ½ inch of apple at the bottom to hold the filling. In a small bowl, mix raisins, walnuts, 1 tsp maple syrup and the cinnamon. Fill each apple with a quarter of this mixture. Place apples in a square 8 x 8" glass baking pan and add water. Drizzle 1 tsp of maple syrup on top of the filling in each apple. Bake for 30 to 45 minutes or until apples are tender.

Serve as is, or with Caramel Sauce.

Yield: 4 servings

Baked Apples: 1 serving = 1 apple

Energy (kcal)	129		
Total Fat (g)	1.9	Calcium (mg)	18
Total Carbohydrate (g)	30.2	Phosphorus (mg)	32
Total Protein (g)	0.9	Magnesium (mg)	15
% Calories from Fat	13	Iron (mg)	0.4
% Calories from Carbohydrate	85	Zinc (mg)	0.3
% Calories from Protein	2	Copper (mg)	0.1
Cholesterol (g)	0	Selenium (mcg)	0.2
Total Saturated Fatty Acids (g) (SFA)	0.2	Sodium (mg)	3
Total Monounsaturated Fatty Acids (g) (MUFA)	0.2	Potassium (mg)	235
Total Polyunsaturated Fatty Acids (g) (PUFA)	1.2		
Omega-3 Fatty Acids (g)	0.2		
% Calories from SFA	1.3	Linoleic Acid - PUFA (18:2) (g)	1.0
% Calories from MUFA	1.5	Linolenic Acid – PUFA (18:3) (g)	0.2
% Calories from PUFA	8.1		
Polyunsaturated to Saturated Fat (P:S) Ratio	6.1	Tryptophan (mg)	1
		Threonine (mg)	3
Total Dietary Fiber (g)	4.6	Isoleucine (mg)	3
Soluble Dietary Fiber (g)	1.4	Leucine (mg)	6
Insoluble Dietary Fiber (g)	3.2	Lysine (mg)	4
		Methionine (mg)	1
Total Vitamin A (mcg) (Retinol Activity Equivalents)	5	Phenylalanine (mg)	3
Vitamin D (calciferol) (mcg)	0	Valine (mg)	4
Vitamin E (mg) (Total Alpha-Tocopherol)	0.4	Histidine (mg)	2
Vitamin K (mg) (phylloquinone)	4.2		
Vitamin C (mg) (ascorbic acid)	8.5	Daidzein (mg)	0.0
Thiamin (mg) (vitamin B1)	0.0	Genistein (mg)	0.0
Riboflavin (mg) (vitamin B2)	0.1		
Niacin (mg) (vitamin B3)	0.2	Caffeine (mg)	0
Pantothenic Acid (mg)	0.1	Phytic Acid (mg)	135.0
Vitamin B6 (mg)	0.1	Oxalic Acid (mg)	5.8
Total Folate (mcg)	8	Choline (mg)	7.5
Vitamin B12 (mcg) (cobalamin)	0		
		Glycemic Index (glucose reference)	42
Beta-Carotene (mcg) (provitamin A carotenoid)	50	Glycemic Load (glucose reference)	11
Lutein + Zeaxanthin (mcg)	53		
Lycopene (mcg)	0		

Banana Peanut Roll (Vegan: GF w/Mod)

A honey of a snack: fortifying and rich. Requires no baking, just a steamer. You can vary it up with different nut (or seed) butters, or other dried fruits. Hearty finger-food that won't linger!

Ingredients

Cooking spray (about 3 seconds)

1 lb of whole wheat pizza dough

7/8 cup chunky peanut butter (smooth is also fine)

3/8 cup raisins

2 medium, ripe bananas, sliced on the diagonal

¼ cup brown rice syrup

Boil water in a large steamer. Spray cooking oil onto the steamer base.

Roll out the pizza dough on a lightly floured surface. Leaving 2 inches free on either end of the dough, layer peanut butter, raisins, sliced bananas and finally drizzle brown rice syrup. Roll up the dough carefully from one end, and pinch edges to seal. Place inside the steamer base, bending into an arc to fit. Make light knife strokes to divide the strudel into slices, but stay close to the surface, to prevent any tears.

Let steam for 30 minutes. Remove and cool before slicing into wedges.

Yield: 12, 1"-wide wedges

~For gluten-free, use a gluten-free pizza dough in place of whole wheat dough~

Banana Peanut Roll: 1 serving = 1-inch wedge

Energy (kcal)	237		
Total Fat (g)	10.2	Calcium (mg)	42
Total Carbohydrate (g)	34.1	Phosphorus (mg)	112
Total Protein (g)	8.3	Magnesium (mg)	50
% Calories from Fat	36	Iron (mg)	1.6
% Calories from Carbohydrate	51	Zinc (mg)	1.0
% Calories from Protein	13	Copper (mg)	0.2
Cholesterol (g)	0	Selenium (mcg)	13.8
Total Saturated Fatty Acids (g) (SFA)	2.1	Sodium (mg)	288
Total Monounsaturated Fatty Acids (g) (MUFA)	4.6	Potassium (mg)	270
Total Polyunsaturated Fatty Acids (g) (PUFA)	3.0		
Omega-3 Fatty Acids (g)	0.1		
% Calories from SFA	7.3	Linoleic Acid - PUFA (18:2) (g)	2.9
% Calories from MUFA	16.3	Linolenic Acid – PUFA (18:3) (g)	0.1
% Calories from PUFA	10.6		
Polyunsaturated to Saturated Fat (P:S) Ratio	1.4	Tryptophan (mg)	9
		Threonine (mg)	21
Total Dietary Fiber (g)	6.2	Isoleucine (mg)	25
Soluble Dietary Fiber (g)	2.3	Leucine (mg)	53
Insoluble Dietary Fiber (g)	3.9	Lysine (mg)	23
		Methionine (mg)	11
Total Vitamin A (mcg) (Retinol Activity Equivalents)	1	Phenylalanine (mg)	40
Vitamin D (calciferol) (mcg)	0.0	Valine (mg)	30
Vitamin E (mg) (Total Alpha-Tocopherol)	1.8	Histidine (mg)	19
Vitamin K (mg) (phylloquinone)	0.6		
Vitamin C (mg) (ascorbic acid)	1.9	Daidzein (mg)	0.2
Thiamin (mg) (vitamin B1)	0.2	Genistein (mg)	0.3
Riboflavin (mg) (vitamin B2)	0.2		
Niacin (mg) (vitamin B3)	4.1	Caffeine (mg)	0
Pantothenic Acid (mg)	0.5	Phytic Acid (mg)	107.6
Vitamin B6 (mg)	0.2	Oxalic Acid (mg)	39.8
Total Folate (mcg)	52	Choline (mg)	20.9
Vitamin B12 (mcg) (cobalamin)	0.0		
		Glycemic Index (glucose reference)	67
Beta-Carotene (mcg) (provitamin A carotenoid)	5	Glycemic Load (glucose reference)	19
Lutein + Zeaxanthin (mcg)	20		
Lycopene (mcg)	0		

Blueberry Tarts (Vegan)

Little cups of fruity goodness. Crunchy, creamy, sweet and rich all rolled into one. Experiment with other favorite fruits. Although the recipe seems complicated, it really has just 4 basic parts (the 4th-- tofu topping-- is optional) and each part can be prepared well in advance.

Ingredients

1. <u>Crumb Topping</u>

1/8 cup maple syrup

1 Tbsp canola oil

½ Tbsp almond butter (unsalted)

3/4 tsp vanilla

1/8 tsp sea salt

½ cup + 2 Tbsp whole wheat pastry flour

Preheat oven to 350°F. Brush a cookie sheet with canola oil. Whisk together wet ingredients of maple syrup, oil, almond butter and vanilla. In a separate bowl, add salt to flour and mix. Add wet ingredients to flour and mix gently with fork. Use hands to create a crumbly mixture. Place on cookie sheet and bake for 15-20 minutes until brown color and nutty fragrance start to develop.

Yield: 1 cup (1 serving = ~2 Tbsp; so provides crumb topping for ~8 tarts)

2. <u>Tart Shells (Prepare while crumb topping is baking) - 6 tart shells</u>

2 Tbsp canola oil

Phyllo dough, 4 sheets 12" x 16" each, thawed (4 oz total)

In a 12-cup muffin pan, brush the insides and rims of 6 cups with oil.
Unwrap phyllo dough and place one sheet on a piece of waxed paper, which is placed atop a cutting board. Brush this generously with oil. Layer the 2nd piece of dough on top and repeat oil brushing. Continue until 4 sheets have been oiled, including top sheet. Cut this stack of phyllo sheets in 12 even 4" x 4" squares (3 columns and 4 rows). Place one square stack into a muffin cup, to cover half the bottom, while the extra is hanging over the side. Press into the cup gently. Take another stack and place it on the other half, slightly overlapping, to make a complete cup. Repeat this in the 5 other oiled cups. Fill the remaining, empty cups with water.

Bake at 350°F for 10-12 minutes, or until golden brown. Remove, gently loosen each and cool on a wire rack. Set aside and prepare the filling.

3. Blueberry filling

4 cups blueberries (fresh or frozen)

2 tbsp maple syrup

1 tsp vanilla

2 Tbsp corn starch

¼ cup water

1 tsp fresh-squeezed lemon juice

Place blueberries in a medium saucepan, add maple syrup and vanilla. Simmer over medium high heat until tender: a minute or two for fresh blueberries or several minutes if frozen.

Dilute cornstarch in water, then add to the blueberries, stirring constantly as the mixture thickens quickly. Add in lemon juice and remove from heat.

Yield: 3 cups (6, ½-cup per servings)

4. Tofu Topping (optional) – this recipe makes 1½ cups (24 Tbsp); use 2 Tbsp for each tart
     Note: topping is best made several hours ahead for the best taste & texture.

1 package silken tofu, soft, 12.3 oz

2 tsp vanilla

¼ cup maple syrup

2 tsp tahini

Place tofu, vanilla, maple syrup and tahini in a food processor and blend until smooth. Best if chilled for at least 3 hours before serving.

For each tart shell, use ½ cup blueberry mixture, 2 Tbsp crumb topping, and (optional) 2 Tbsp tofu topping.

Blueberry Tart: 1 serving = 1 tart

Energy (kcal)	330*		
Total Fat (g)	9.5	Calcium (mg)	48
Total Carbohydrate (g)	57.0	Phosphorus (mg)	119
Total Protein (g)	6.3	Magnesium (mg)	45
% Calories from Fat	25.1	Iron (mg)	2.2
% Calories from Carbohydrate	66.1	Zinc (mg)	1.6
% Calories from Protein	7.3	Copper (mg)	0.2
Cholesterol (g)	0	Selenium (mcg)	17.9
Total Saturated Fatty Acids (g) (SFA)	0.9	Sodium (mg)	118
Total Monounsaturated Fatty Acids (g) (MUFA)	4.8	Potassium (mg)	264
Total Polyunsaturated Fatty Acids (g) (PUFA)	3.1		
Omega-3 Fatty Acids (g)	0.8		
% Calories from SFA	2.2	Linoleic Acid - PUFA (18:2) (g)	2.3
% Calories from MUFA	12.9	Linolenic Acid – PUFA (18:3) (g)	0.8
% Calories from PUFA	8.2		
Polyunsaturated to Saturated Fat (P:S) Ratio	3.7	Tryptophan (mg)	8
		Threonine (mg)	21
Total Dietary Fiber (g)	6.4	Isoleucine (mg)	26
Soluble Dietary Fiber (g)	0.9	Leucine (mg)	46
Insoluble Dietary Fiber (g)	5.5	Lysine (mg)	24
		Methionine (mg)	10
Total Vitamin A (mcg) (Retinol Activity Equivalents)	4	Phenylalanine (mg)	32
Vitamin D (calciferol) (mcg)	0	Valine (mg)	30
Vitamin E (mg) (Total Alpha-Tocopherol)	2.3	Histidine (mg)	14
Vitamin K (mg) (phylloquinone)	30.5		
Vitamin C (mg) (ascorbic acid)	4.2	Daidzein (mg)	3.2
Thiamin (mg) (vitamin B1)	0.3	Genistein (mg)	4.5
Riboflavin (mg) (vitamin B2)	0.2		
Niacin (mg) (vitamin B3)	2.7	Caffeine (mg)	0
Pantothenic Acid (mg)	0.4	Phytic Acid (mg)	196.4
Vitamin B6 (mg)	0.2	Oxalic Acid (mg)	25.4
Total Folate (mcg)	50	Choline (mg)	23.2
Vitamin B12 (mcg) (cobalamin)	0		
		Glycemic Index (glucose reference)	55
Beta-Carotene (mcg) (provitamin A carotenoid)	44	Glycemic Load (glucose reference)	28
Lutein + Zeaxanthin (mcg)	138		
Lycopene (mcg)	0		

*Calories from alcohol in vanilla, so % calories do not add to 100% from CHO, FAT and PRO.

Blueberry Tofu Cheesecake (Vegan)

This is a cholesterol-free cheesecake that can satisfy any sweet tooth. Try substituting blueberries with cherries or strawberries for a change of pace. Any granola can be used for the crust, or you can simply use a pre-made graham-cracker crust.

Ingredients

Pie Crust (Note: this amount of granola is enough for 3 single pie crusts)

3½ cups rolled oats

1½ cups walnuts, chopped very coarsely*

1 cup whole wheat pastry flour

½ tsp salt

½ tsp cinnamon

½ cup + 1 Tbsp safflower (or canola) oil

½ cup maple syrup

¼ cup apple juice (for moisture)

3/4 tsp vanilla

Additional ingredient

3 Tbsp apple juice (to hold the crust together)

Filling

½ cup apple juice

2 tsp agar powder (8 tsp agar flakes)

2 cakes of extra firm silken tofu (12.3 oz each)

½ cup maple syrup

¼ cup almond butter (smooth, unsalted)

2 Tbsp lemon juice

1 tsp vanilla

¼ tsp salt

Fruit topping

2 cups apple juice

2 cups blueberries

1/8 tsp salt

3 Tbsp kuzu

¼ cup water

1 tsp lemon juice

Pie Crust

Preheat oven to 350°F. In a large mixing bowl, mix rolled oats, walnuts, flour, salt and cinnamon. Set aside. In a medium bowl, whisk together the oil, maple syrup, ¼ cup of apple juice and vanilla. Add wet ingredients to dry and mix together. Place on cookie sheet about ½-inch thick layer. Bake for 45 minutes to one hour with frequent turning (at least every 15 minutes) to turn a nice brown color. Let cool.

This makes 6 3/4 cups of granola. Take about a third of this granola (~2¼ cups) and blend in a food processor (or blender) until it is in fine crumbs. In a medium bowl, add ~3 Tbsp of apple juice so crumbs hold together. Oil a 9-inch spring-form pan and press the crumbs into the bottom. Bake for 10 minutes.

Filling

Turn oven down to 325°F. Heat ½ cup of apple juice to a boil in a small saucepan. Turn heat down to low, dissolve agar powder, stirring continuously, for 1 minute. Cool. In food processor, combine tofu, maple syrup, almond butter, lemon juice, vanilla and salt. Blend until smooth. Add cooled apple juice mixture and blend 1 more minute. Pour into cooled crust. Bake 30 minutes. Check cake to see if tofu is set. When center is firm, turn off the heat and let cake remain in the oven for another 30 minutes. Remove from oven and let sit for at least 6 hours before removing from the pan, waiting at least 2 hours before covering with topping.

Topping

Bring 2 cups of apple juice to a boil in a medium saucepan. Add blueberries and salt; simmer for 2 minutes. In a small bowl, dilute kuzu in water and stir to dissolve completely. Add to the apple juice mixture, stirring constantly, until thickened; then simmer for one more minute. Turn off heat and mix in lemon juice. Let cool. After cake has cooled pour on top of cheesecake. After refrigeration, topping will become more set and cake will become firmer.

Yield: 12 servings

Blueberry Tofu Cheesecake: 1 serving = 1 slice

Energy (kcal)	285		
Total Fat (g)	12.5	Calcium (mg)	68
Total Carbohydrate (g)	36.6	Phosphorus (mg)	170
Total Protein (g)	8.8	Magnesium (mg)	69
% Calories from Fat	38	Iron (mg)	2.0
% Calories from Carbohydrate	50	Zinc (mg)	2.0
% Calories from Protein	12	Copper (mg)	0.4
Cholesterol (g)	0	Selenium (mcg)	13.6
Total Saturated Fatty Acids (g) (SFA)	1.2	Sodium (mg)	134
Total Monounsaturated Fatty Acids (g) (MUFA)	3.5	Potassium (mg)	376
Total Polyunsaturated Fatty Acids (g) (PUFA)	6.9		
Omega-3 Fatty Acids (g)	0.6		
% Calories from SFA	3.8	Linoleic Acid - PUFA (18:2) (g)	6.3
% Calories from MUFA	10.5	Linolenic Acid – PUFA (18:3) (g)	0.6
% Calories from PUFA	21.0		
Polyunsaturated to Saturated Fat (P:S) Ratio	5.6	Tryptophan (mg)	11
		Threonine (mg)	33
Total Dietary Fiber (g)	2.9	Isoleucine (mg)	40
Soluble Dietary Fiber (g)	0.9	Leucine (mg)	70
Insoluble Dietary Fiber (g)	2.0	Lysine (mg)	47
		Methionine (mg)	13
Total Vitamin A (mcg) (Retinol Activity Equivalents)	1	Phenylalanine (mg)	47
Vitamin D (calciferol) (mcg)	0	Valine (mg)	47
Vitamin E (mg) (Total Alpha-Tocopherol)	3.0	Histidine (mg)	21
Vitamin K (mg) (phylloquinone)	6.9		
Vitamin C (mg) (ascorbic acid)	4.4	Daidzein (mg)	8.6
Thiamin (mg) (vitamin B1)	0.2	Genistein (mg)	12.0
Riboflavin (mg) (vitamin B2)	0.1		
Niacin (mg) (vitamin B3)	0.9	Caffeine (mg)	0
Pantothenic Acid (mg)	0.3	Phytic Acid (mg)	315.8
Vitamin B6 (mg)	0.1	Oxalic Acid (mg)	37.3
Total Folate (mcg)	50	Choline (mg)	34.6
Vitamin B12 (mcg) (cobalamin)	0		
		Glycemic Index (glucose reference)	48
Beta-Carotene (mcg) (provitamin A carotenoid)	9	Glycemic Load (glucose reference)	16
Lutein + Zeaxanthin (mcg)	54		
Lycopene (mcg)	0		

Brown Rice Crispy Snacks (Vegan)

Hearty, simple, portable energy squares—crunchy, creamy, chewy, sweet and satisfying. Make a double batch and freeze to save time. Experiment with different shapes, butters and dried fruit. Watch them disappear!

Ingredients

1 cup raisins

5 cups crispy brown rice cereal

3/8 cup (6 Tbsp) brown rice syrup *

1/4 cup barley malt *

1 cup crunchy peanut butter

In a large bowl, mix raisins together with 4 cups of crispy cereal. In a small saucepan, blend the brown rice syrup and barley malt over low heat. Remove from heat and stir in peanut butter until smooth. Slowly add this mixture to the cereal and raisins until it is well incorporated, using your hands to help. Finally, add in the remaining cup of cereal.

Press mixture, with slightly wet hands, to gently flatten into an 8 x 12" pan. Chill for 15 minutes or more until firm. Cut into squares.

Yield: 24 squares, 2 x 2" (about ¾" high)

*Any combination of brown rice syrup and barley malt can be used (or only one) – whichever you prefer. The measurements also are just approximate. Optional - ½ cup of non-dairy, grain-sweetened chocolate chips; these would be mixed in with the cereal and raisins at the beginning. A few tablespoons of ground flax seed can also be added; do not use too much (up to ½ cup only) or the snack will have a funny aftertaste.

The final mixture could also be rolled into small balls and another shape, then chilled.

Brown Rice Crispy Snacks = 1 serving= 1 square (2 x 2 inches)

Energy (kcal)	131		
Total Fat (g)	5.6	Calcium (mg)	11
Total Carbohydrate (g)	18.5	Phosphorus (mg)	74
Total Protein (g)	3.5	Magnesium (mg)	28
% Calories from Fat	36	Iron (mg)	0.5
% Calories from Carbohydrate	55	Zinc (mg)	0.5
% Calories from Protein	9	Copper (mg)	0.1
Cholesterol (g)	0	Selenium (mcg)	1.6
Total Saturated Fatty Acids (g) (SFA)	1.2	Sodium (mg)	93
Total Monounsaturated Fatty Acids (g) (MUFA)	2.7	Potassium (mg)	147
Total Polyunsaturated Fatty Acids (g) (PUFA)	1.6		
Omega-3 Fatty Acids (g)	0.0		
% Calories from SFA	7.4	Linoleic Acid - PUFA (18:2) (g)	1.6
% Calories from MUFA	16.9	Linolenic Acid – PUFA (18:3) (g)	0.0
% Calories from PUFA	10.1		
Polyunsaturated to Saturated Fat (P:S) Ratio	1.4	Tryptophan (mg)	4
		Threonine (mg)	8
Total Dietary Fiber (g)	1.1	Isoleucine (mg)	9
Soluble Dietary Fiber (g)	0.1	Leucine (mg)	22
Insoluble Dietary Fiber (g)	1.0	Lysine (mg)	1
		Methionine (mg)	4
Total Vitamin A (mcg) (Retinol Activity Equivalents)	0	Phenylalanine (mg)	17
Vitamin D (calciferol) (mcg)	0	Valine (mg)	12
Vitamin E (mg) (Total Alpha-Tocopherol)	1.0	Histidine (mg)	8
Vitamin K (mg) (phylloquinone)	0.4		
Vitamin C (mg) (ascorbic acid)	.1	Daidzein (mg)	0
Thiamin (mg) (vitamin B1)	0.0	Genistein (mg)	0
Riboflavin (mg) (vitamin B2)	0.0		
Niacin (mg) (vitamin B3)	2.2	Caffeine (mg)	0
Pantothenic Acid (mg)	0.2	Phytic Acid (mg)	100.0
Vitamin B6 (mg)	0.1	Oxalic Acid (mg)	19.7
Total Folate (mcg)	10	Choline (mg)	9.4
Vitamin B12 (mcg) (cobalamin)	0		
		Glycemic Index (glucose reference)	71
Beta-Carotene (mcg) (provitamin A carotenoid)	0	Glycemic Load (glucose reference)	12
Lutein + Zeaxanthin (mcg)	0		
Lycopene (mcg)	0		

Caramel Corn with Peanuts (Vegan)

A carnival at home! Simple popcorn gets a makeover with this festive addition of nuts and syrup.
A fiber-rich way to add crunch and fun to a familiar snack.

Ingredients

4 cups of cooked popcorn (plain)*

1/3 cup roasted, unsalted peanuts

2 Tbsp maple syrup

2 Tbsp barley malt

½ tsp olive oil (to brush baking pan)

Preheat oven to 300°F.

In a large mixing bowl, mix peanuts with popcorn. In a small saucepan, add maple syrup and barley malt and stir over medium heat until mixture becomes well blended and thin. (Do not overheat.)

Pour mixture over popcorn-peanuts and mix to coat well. Spread on a baking sheet lightly brushed with olive oil. Bake for 20 minutes, turning every 5 minutes. Be very careful not to overcook and keep an eye on it as it is easy for the syrups to get dark. Remove from oven and let sit for about 1 hour before serving. Mixture will initially be somewhat moist, but becomes drier upon standing.

Note: Try mixing up the nuts (almonds are especially good) and adding some seeds. For added sweetness, try including raisins or another dried fruit.

*Popcorn may also be prepared in a popcorn maker, using canola oil and a pinch of salt. A half cup of raw popcorn with 1 tsp canola oil yields about 6½ cups of cooked.

Yield: 3½ cups of caramel corn (3½ 1-cup servings)

Caramel Corn with Peanuts: 1 serving = 1 cup

Energy (kcal)	187		
Total Fat (g)	7.9	Calcium (mg)	23
Total Carbohydrate (g)	25.8	Phosphorus (mg)	109
Total Protein (g)	5.1	Magnesium (mg)	47
% Calories from Fat	36	Iron (mg)	0.9
% Calories from Carbohydrate	55	Zinc (mg)	1.2
% Calories from Protein	9	Copper (mg)	0.1
Cholesterol (g)	0	Selenium (mcg)	2.5
Total Saturated Fatty Acids (g) (SFA)	1.1	Sodium (mg)	7
Total Monounsaturated Fatty Acids (g) (MUFA)	4.0	Potassium (mg)	180
Total Polyunsaturated Fatty Acids (g) (PUFA)	2.5		
Omega-3 Fatty Acids (g)	0.0		
% Calories from SFA	5.0	Linoleic Acid - PUFA (18:2) (g)	2.5
% Calories from MUFA	17.9	Linolenic Acid – PUFA (18:3) (g)	0.0
% Calories from PUFA	11.1		
Polyunsaturated to Saturated Fat (P:S) Ratio	2.2	Tryptophan (mg)	5
		Threonine (mg)	18
Total Dietary Fiber (g)	2.4	Isoleucine (mg)	18
Soluble Dietary Fiber (g)	0.0	Leucine (mg)	39
Insoluble Dietary Fiber (g)	2.4	Lysine (mg)	18
		Methionine (mg)	8
Total Vitamin A (mcg) (Retinol Activity Equivalents)	1	Phenylalanine (mg)	25
Vitamin D (calciferol) (mcg)	0	Valine (mg)	23
Vitamin E (mg) (Total Alpha-Tocopherol)	1.1	Histidine (mg)	13
Vitamin K (mg) (phylloquinone)	0.5		
Vitamin C (mg) (ascorbic acid)	0	Daidzein (mg)	0.0
Thiamin (mg) (vitamin B1)	0.1	Genistein (mg)	0.0
Riboflavin (mg) (vitamin B2)	0.1		
Niacin (mg) (vitamin B3)	3.0	Caffeine (mg)	0
Pantothenic Acid (mg)	0.3	Phytic Acid (mg)	117.8
Vitamin B6 (mg)	0.1	Oxalic Acid (mg)	22.4
Total Folate (mcg)	24	Choline (mg)	9.7
Vitamin B12 (mcg) (cobalamin)	0		
		Glycemic Index (glucose reference)	73
Beta-Carotene (mcg) (provitamin A carotenoid)	8	Glycemic Load (glucose reference)	17
Lutein + Zeaxanthin (mcg)	133		
Lycopene (mcg)	0		

Caramel Sauce (Vegan)

Extra-sweet and sticky sauce, ready for an apple on a stick!

Ingredients

2 Tbsp kuzu

4 tsp agar agar flakes (or 1 tsp agar powder)

1 tsp arrowroot flour

¼ tsp sea salt

1¼ cup + 1 Tbsp water

1 Tbsp safflower oil

1 cup barley malt

3 Tbsp maple syrup

1 tsp vanilla

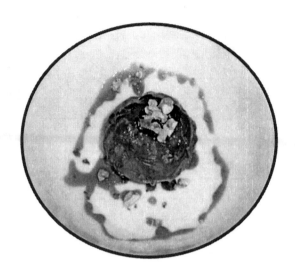

In a medium saucepan, combine the kuzu, agar, arrowroot and salt. Using a small wire whisk, add in water slowly to dissolve kuzu. Over medium heat and stirring constantly, dissolve agar flakes completely. In a separate small bowl, combine oil, barley malt and maple syrup. Add to saucepan and blend well. Bring mixture to a boil, stirring frequently. Simmer over low heat for 10 minutes, stirring regularly. Remove from heat and stir in vanilla.

Use as a topping for desserts, such as baked apples. Store in refrigerator. Reheat as needed to loosen up the caramel once it has gelled.

Yield: 2 cups of sauce (16, 2-Tbsp servings)

Adapted from: Sandra Lynn Shuman's *Macrobiotic Desserts*, 1981 (Dictionart, Los Angeles, CA)

Caramel Sauce: 1 serving = 2 Tbsp.

Energy (kcal)	85		
Total Fat (g)	0.9	Calcium (mg)	15
Total Carbohydrate (g)	17.7	Phosphorus (mg)	47
Total Protein (g)	1.2	Magnesium (mg)	15
% Calories from Fat	9	Iron (mg)	0.2
% Calories from Carbohydrate	85	Zinc (mg)	0.2
% Calories from Protein	6	Copper (mg)	0.0
Cholesterol (g)	0	Selenium (mcg)	2.5
Total Saturated Fatty Acids (g) (SFA)	0.1	Sodium (mg)	45
Total Monounsaturated Fatty Acids (g) (MUFA)	0.1	Potassium (mg)	71
Total Polyunsaturated Fatty Acids (g) (PUFA)	0.6		
Omega-3 Fatty Acids (g)	0.0		
% Calories from SFA	0.6	Linoleic Acid - PUFA (18:2) (g)	0.6
% Calories from MUFA	1.3	Linolenic Acid – PUFA (18:3) (g)	0.0
% Calories from PUFA	6.6		
Polyunsaturated to Saturated Fat (P:S) Ratio	11.8	Tryptophan (mg)	2
		Threonine (mg)	4
Total Dietary Fiber (g)	0.1	Isoleucine (mg)	4
Soluble Dietary Fiber (g)	0.1	Leucine (mg)	8
Insoluble Dietary Fiber (g)	0.0	Lysine (mg)	5
		Methionine (mg)	2
Total Vitamin A (mcg) (Retinol Activity Equivalents)	0	Phenylalanine (mg)	5
Vitamin D (calciferol) (mcg)	0.0	Valine (mg)	6
Vitamin E (mg) (Total Alpha-Tocopherol)	0.3	Histidine (mg)	3
Vitamin K (mg) (phylloquinone)	0.1		
Vitamin C (mg) (ascorbic acid)	0.0	Daidzein (mg)	0.0
Thiamin (mg) (vitamin B1)	0.0	Genistein (mg)	0.0
Riboflavin (mg) (vitamin B2)	0.1		
Niacin (mg) (vitamin B3)	1.6	Caffeine (mg)	0
Pantothenic Acid (mg)	0.0	Phytic Acid (mg)	0.0
Vitamin B6 (mg)	0.1	Oxalic Acid (mg)	0.1
Total Folate (mcg)	2	Choline (mg)	0.1
Vitamin B12 (mcg) (cobalamin)	0.0		
		Glycemic Index (glucose reference)	98
Beta-Carotene (mcg) (provitamin A carotenoid)	0	Glycemic Load (glucose reference)	17
Lutein + Zeaxanthin (mcg)	0		
Lycopene (mcg)	0		

Cherry Kanten (Vegan; GF)

A light & cooling, refreshing summer dessert. This recipe is simple to prepare and can be varied endlessly, with different combinations of fruits, juices and additions of slivered nuts.

Ingredients

½ cup defrosted, (previously frozen) cherries (pitted)

1¾ cups apple juice

¼ cup cherry juice (or black cherry juice)

1 Tbsp orange juice

1 Tbsp agar flakes

Defrost frozen cherries in the refrigerator the night before. (Fresh pitted cherries could also be used.) In a medium saucepan, combine apple, cherry and orange juice and stir in the agar flakes until they are well dissolved. Bring to a boil, stirring occasionally; add cherries and simmer for 5 minutes. Place in small custard cups. Let cool, and then refrigerate to set completely.

Yield: 5, ½-cup servings

Cherry Kanten: 1 serving = ½ cup

Energy (kcal)	57		
Total Fat (g)	0.1	Calcium (mg)	10
Total Carbohydrate (g)	14.3	Phosphorus (mg)	10
Total Protein (g)	0.3	Magnesium (mg)	7
% Calories from Fat	2	Iron (mg)	0.2
% Calories from Carbohydrate	96	Zinc (mg)	0.0
% Calories from Protein	2	Copper (mg)	0.0
Cholesterol (g)	0	Selenium (mcg)	0.1
Total Saturated Fatty Acids (g) (SFA)	0.0	Sodium (mg)	4
Total Monounsaturated Fatty Acids (g) (MUFA)	0.0	Potassium (mg)	130
Total Polyunsaturated Fatty Acids (g) (PUFA)	0.0		
Omega-3 Fatty Acids (g)	0.0		
% Calories from SFA	0.4	Linoleic Acid - PUFA (18:2) (g)	0.0
% Calories from MUFA	0.2	Linolenic Acid – PUFA (18:3) (g)	0.0
% Calories from PUFA	0.7		
Polyunsaturated to Saturated Fat (P:S) Ratio	1.8	Tryptophan (mg)	0.1
		Threonine (mg)	1
Total Dietary Fiber (g)	0.7	Isoleucine (mg)	0.4
Soluble Dietary Fiber (g)	0.4	Leucine (mg)	1
Insoluble Dietary Fiber (g)	0.4	Lysine (mg)	1
		Methionine (mg)	0.3
Total Vitamin A (mcg) (Retinol Activity Equivalents)	2	Phenylalanine (mg)	1
Vitamin D (calciferol) (mcg)	0	Valine (mg)	1
Vitamin E (mg) (Total Alpha-Tocopherol)	0.1	Histidine (mg)	0.2
Vitamin K (mg) (phylloquinone)	0.4		
Vitamin C (mg) (ascorbic acid)	4.0	Daidzein (mg)	0
Thiamin (mg) (vitamin B1)	0.0	Genistein (mg)	0
Riboflavin (mg) (vitamin B2)	0.0		
Niacin (mg) (vitamin B3)	0.1	Caffeine (mg)	0
Pantothenic Acid (mg)	0.1	Phytic Acid (mg)	0.2
Vitamin B6 (mg)	0.0	Oxalic Acid (mg)	1.0
Total Folate (mcg)	1	Choline (mg)	2.9
Vitamin B12 (mcg) (cobalamin)	0		
		Glycemic Index (glucose reference)	38
Beta-Carotene (mcg) (provitamin A carotenoid)	22	Glycemic Load (glucose reference)	5
Lutein + Zeaxanthin (mcg)	34		
Lycopene (mcg)	0		

Fruit Smoothie (Vegan; GF w/Mod)

Luscious and complex, this is a basic smoothie recipe with endless possibilities. As chock-full of nutrients as it is with flavor!

Ingredients

1½ cups vanilla soymilk

1 cup frozen cherries

1 cup frozen blueberries

½ cup orange juice

1 Tbsp almond butter

1 Tbsp ground flaxseed

1 Tbsp brown rice syrup

Place soymilk, cherries, blueberries, juice, almond butter, flaxseed and brown rice syrup in high-speed blender and blend until velvety smooth.

Note: Fresh fruits can be used whenever available.

Yield: 3½ cups (3½, 1-cup servings)

~For gluten-free, use soymilk which does not contain malted wheat or barley~

Fruit Smoothie: 1 serving = 1 cup

Energy (kcal)	201		
Total Fat (g)	5.8	Calcium (mg)	161
Total Carbohydrate (g)	3.4	Phosphorus (mg)	130
Total Protein (g)	5.8	Magnesium (mg)	57
% Calories from Fat	24	Iron (mg)	1.7
% Calories from Carbohydrate	66	Zinc (mg)	0.5
% Calories from Protein	10	Copper (mg)	0.2
Cholesterol (g)	0	Selenium (mcg)	3.6
Total Saturated Fatty Acids (g) (SFA)	0.6	Sodium (mg)	73
Total Monounsaturated Fatty Acids (g) (MUFA)	2.3	Potassium (mg)	380
Total Polyunsaturated Fatty Acids (g) (PUFA)	2.3		
Omega-3 Fatty Acids (g)	0.7		
% Calories from SFA	2.6	Linoleic Acid - PUFA (18:2) (g)	1.6
% Calories from MUFA	9.7	Linolenic Acid – PUFA (18:3) (g)	0.7
% Calories from PUFA	9.6		
Polyunsaturated to Saturated Fat (P:S) Ratio	3.7	Tryptophan (mg)	8
		Threonine (mg)	22
Total Dietary Fiber (g)	4.5	Isoleucine (mg)	24
Soluble Dietary Fiber (g)	1.2	Leucine (mg)	41
Insoluble Dietary Fiber (g)	3.3	Lysine (mg)	30
		Methionine (mg)	8
Total Vitamin A (mcg) (Retinol Activity Equivalents)	70	Phenylalanine (mg)	27
Vitamin D (calciferol) (mcg)	1.1	Valine (mg)	27
Vitamin E (mg) (Total Alpha-Tocopherol)	3.1	Histidine (mg)	14
Vitamin K (mg) (phylloquinone)	15.4		
Vitamin C (mg) (ascorbic acid)	22.5	Daidzein (mg)	5.2
Thiamin (mg) (vitamin B1)	0.1	Genistein (mg)	5.3
Riboflavin (mg) (vitamin B2)	0.2		
Niacin (mg) (vitamin B3)	1.6	Caffeine (mg)	0
Pantothenic Acid (mg)	0.3	Phytic Acid (mg)	159.2
Vitamin B6 (mg)	0.2	Oxalic Acid (mg)	33.1
Total Folate (mcg)	31	Choline (mg)	21.1
Vitamin B12 (mcg) (cobalamin)	1.3		
		Glycemic Index (glucose reference)	60
Beta-Carotene (mcg) (provitamin A carotenoid)	45	Glycemic Load (glucose reference)	18
Lutein + Zeaxanthin (mcg)	132		
Lycopene (mcg)	0		

Lemon Soy Pudding (Vegan; GF w/Mod)

Smooth tartness in contrast to crunchy walnuts and chewy dried fruit elevate this yummy pudding.
For a change of pace, try adding key lime juice or orange instead of lemon. Good any time of year!

Ingredients

2 cups apple juice

2 Tbsp agar flakes

2 cups vanilla soymilk

¼ cup brown rice syrup

Pinch salt

4 Tbsp kuzu, diluted in 6 Tbsp. of water

¼ cup fresh lemon juice

1 tsp lemon zest

¼ cup roasted walnuts

¼ cup dried cranberries

In a medium saucepan, mix juice with agar flakes, and stir well Using medium-high heat, cook the mixture, stirring frequently, until agar flakes are completely dissolved. Add soymilk, brown rice syrup and salt; mix well and heat gently for 5 minutes, stirring occasionally. In the meantime, dilute kuzu in water and prepare lemon juice and zest. Add kuzu/water mixture gently to saucepan, stirring continuously to prevent lumps from forming. Simmer until the mixture thickens. Turn off heat, then stir in the lemon juice and zest. Pour into individual bowls, sprinkle each with walnuts and dried cranberries.

Yield: 4 cups (8, ½-cup servings)

~For gluten-free, use soymilk which does not contain malted wheat or barley~

Adapted from a recipe by Luchi Baranda, Kushi Institute cooking class, www.kushiinstitute.org

Lemon Soy Pudding: 1 serving = ½ cup

Energy (kcal)	155		
Total Fat (g)	3.5	Calcium (mg)	87
Total Carbohydrate (g)	29.5	Phosphorus (mg)	61
Total Protein (g)	2.9	Magnesium (mg)	25
% Calories from Fat	19	Iron (mg)	0.9
% Calories from Carbohydrate	74	Zinc (mg)	0.3
% Calories from Protein	7	Copper (mg)	0.1
Cholesterol (g)	0	Selenium (mcg)	2.0
Total Saturated Fatty Acids (g) (SFA)	0.4	Sodium (mg)	74
Total Monounsaturated Fatty Acids (g) (MUFA)	0.6	Potassium (mg)	171
Total Polyunsaturated Fatty Acids (g) (PUFA)	2.3		
Omega-3 Fatty Acids (g)	0.4		
% Calories from SFA	2.1	Linoleic Acid - PUFA (18:2) (g)	1.9
% Calories from MUFA	3.0	Linolenic Acid – PUFA (18:3) (g)	0.4
% Calories from PUFA	12.7		
Polyunsaturated to Saturated Fat (P:S) Ratio	6.0	Tryptophan (mg)	4
		Threonine (mg)	12
Total Dietary Fiber (g)	1.6	Isoleucine (mg)	13
Soluble Dietary Fiber (g)	0.7	Leucine (mg)	22
Insoluble Dietary Fiber (g)	0.9	Lysine (mg)	16
		Methionine (mg)	4
Total Vitamin A (mcg) (Retinol Activity Equivalents)	37	Phenylalanine (mg)	14
Vitamin D (calciferol) (mcg)	0.6	Valine (mg)	14
Vitamin E (mg) (Total Alpha-Tocopherol)	0.9	Histidine (mg)	7
Vitamin K (mg) (phylloquinone)	2.4		
Vitamin C (mg) (ascorbic acid)	4.6	Daidzein (mg)	3.0
Thiamin (mg) (vitamin B1)	0.0	Genistein (mg)	3.1
Riboflavin (mg) (vitamin B2)	0.1		
Niacin (mg) (vitamin B3)	0.7	Caffeine (mg)	0
Pantothenic Acid (mg)	0.1	Phytic Acid (mg)	70.5
Vitamin B6 (mg)	0.1	Oxalic Acid (mg)	11.0
Total Folate (mcg)	11	Choline (mg)	8.4
Vitamin B12 (mcg) (cobalamin)	0.8		
		Glycemic Index (glucose reference)	74
Beta-Carotene (mcg) (provitamin A carotenoid)	1	Glycemic Load (glucose reference)	21
Lutein + Zeaxanthin (mcg)	12		
Lycopene (mcg)	0		

Oatmeal Cookies with Orange and Ginger (Vegan)

Oatmeal cookies with sparkle! The surprising flavors of orange and ginger add zip to a wholesome treat.

Ingredients

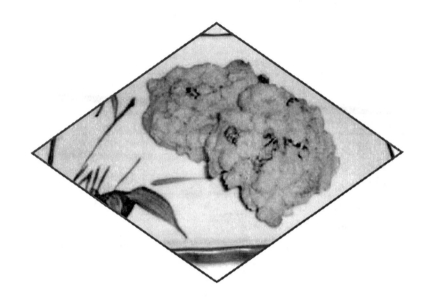

¾ cup rolled oats

¾ cup whole wheat pastry flour

½ cup raisins

½ cup chopped walnuts

½ tsp baking powder

¼ tsp sea salt

¼ cup walnut oil

¼ cup orange juice

2 Tbsp barley malt

2 Tbsp pure maple syrup

1½ tsp grated fresh ginger

½ tsp vanilla

½ tsp orange zest (from organic orange)

Line a baking sheet with parchment paper. In a medium mixing bowl, combine oats, flour, raisins, walnuts, baking powder and salt. In a separate bowl, whisk together oil, orange juice, barley malt, maple syrup, ginger, vanilla and orange zest. Add the wet ingredients to the dry and combine to moisten well. Mixture will be wet.

Preheat oven to 350°F. Let cookie mixture sit for 10 minutes, so oats can absorb some of the liquid. Transfer heaping tablespoons of dough to baking sheet and press the center lightly with a fork. Cookies will be about 2" in diameter. Bake for 15 to 20 minutes, until cookies become a deep golden brown.

Yield: 1½ dozen (18), 2-inch-diameter cookies

Recipe adapted from *Sweet and Natural* by Meredith McCarty, www.healingcuisine.com

Oatmeal Cookies with Orange and Ginger: 1 serving = 1 cookie

Energy (kcal)	105		
Total Fat (g)	5.5	Calcium (mg)	20
Total Carbohydrate (g)	13.1	Phosphorus (mg)	55
Total Protein (g)	1.9	Magnesium (mg)	20
% Calories from Fat	45	Iron (mg)	0.6
% Calories from Carbohydrate	48	Zinc (mg)	0.5
% Calories from Protein	7	Copper (mg)	0.1
Cholesterol (g)	0	Selenium (mcg)	5.0
Total Saturated Fatty Acids (g) (SFA)	0.5	Sodium (mg)	48
Total Monounsaturated Fatty Acids (g) (MUFA)	1.1	Potassium (mg)	96
Total Polyunsaturated Fatty Acids (g) (PUFA)	3.6		
Omega-3 Fatty Acids (g)	0.6		
% Calories from SFA	4.5	Linoleic Acid - PUFA (18:2) (g)	3.0
% Calories from MUFA	8.8	Linolenic Acid – PUFA (18:3) (g)	0.6
% Calories from PUFA	29.4		
Polyunsaturated to Saturated Fat (P:S) Ratio	6.5	Tryptophan (mg)	3
		Threonine (mg)	6
Total Dietary Fiber (g)	1.3	Isoleucine (mg)	7
Soluble Dietary Fiber (g)	0.4	Leucine (mg)	13
Insoluble Dietary Fiber (g)	0.9	Lysine (mg)	6
		Methionine (mg)	3
Total Vitamin A (mcg) (Retinol Activity Equivalents)	0	Phenylalanine (mg)	9
Vitamin D (calciferol) (mcg)	0	Valine (mg)	9
Vitamin E (mg) (Total Alpha-Tocopherol)	0.1	Histidine (mg)	4
Vitamin K (mg) (phylloquinone)	0.8		
Vitamin C (mg) (ascorbic acid)	1.9	Daidzein (mg)	0
Thiamin (mg) (vitamin B1)	0.1	Genistein (mg)	0
Riboflavin (mg) (vitamin B2)	0.0		
Niacin (mg) (vitamin B3)	0.6	Caffeine (mg)	0
Pantothenic Acid (mg)	0.1	Phytic Acid (mg)	82.8
Vitamin B6 (mg)	0.1	Oxalic Acid (mg)	7.2
Total Folate (mcg)	8	Choline (mg)	5.0
Vitamin B12 (mcg) (cobalamin)	0		
		Glycemic Index (glucose reference)	59
Beta-Carotene (mcg) (provitamin A carotenoid)	2	Glycemic Load (glucose reference)	7
Lutein + Zeaxanthin (mcg)	21		
Lycopene (mcg)	0		

Peaches in Sauce (Vegan; GF)

Peaches at their sweetest -- this is an incredibly delicious way to enjoy summer fruit. A great stand-alone dessert, it is also nice with accompaniments such as nuts or granola topping, soy ice cream or parfaits.

Ingredients

4 medium peaches, sliced (~4 cups)

2 cups peach juice, divided

3 Tbsp kuzu or cornstarch

½ tsp cinnamon (optional)

1/8 tsp salt

Wash and peel peaches (unless they are organic, then reserve the peel); slice into medium slices and place in a medium saucepan. In a separate small saucepan, bring 1½ cups of juice to a boil. Add the juice to the pan of peaches and simmer, covered, for 5 minutes. Add cinnamon and salt; stir gently. Dilute kuzu or cornstarch with ½ cup water, and add to the softened peaches. Cook for 1 minute longer, until the mixture thickens.

Yield: 4½ cups (9, ½-cup servings)

Adapted from a recipe by Harriet McNear, Kushi Institute cooking class, www.kushiinstitute.org

Peaches in Sauce: 1 serving = ½ cup

Energy (kcal)	67		
Total Fat (g)	0.2	Calcium (mg)	8
Total Carbohydrate (g)	16.8	Phosphorus (mg)	17
Total Protein (g)	0.8	Magnesium (mg)	9
% Calories from Fat	2	Iron (mg)	0.3
% Calories from Carbohydrate	94	Zinc (mg)	0.2
% Calories from Protein	4	Copper (mg)	0.1
Cholesterol (g)	0	Selenium (mcg)	0.3
Total Saturated Fatty Acids (g) (SFA)	0.00	Sodium (mg)	38
Total Monounsaturated Fatty Acids (g) (MUFA)	0.1	Potassium (mg)	153
Total Polyunsaturated Fatty Acids (g) (PUFA)	0.1		
Omega-3 Fatty Acids (g)	0.0		
% Calories from SFA	0.2	Linoleic Acid - PUFA (18:2) (g)	0.1
% Calories from MUFA	0.6	Linolenic Acid – PUFA (18:3) (g)	0.0
% Calories from PUFA	0.8		
Polyunsaturated to Saturated Fat (P:S) Ratio	4.4	Tryptophan (mg)	1
		Threonine (mg)	2
Total Dietary Fiber (g)	1.4	Isoleucine (mg)	2
Soluble Dietary Fiber (g)	0.74	Leucine (mg)	3
Insoluble Dietary Fiber (g)	0.65	Lysine (mg)	3
		Methionine (mg)	1
Total Vitamin A (mcg) (Retinol Activity Equivalents)	18	Phenylalanine (mg)	2
Vitamin D (calciferol) (mcg)	0	Valine (mg)	3
Vitamin E (mg) (Total Alpha-Tocopherol)	0.7	Histidine (mg)	1
Vitamin K (mg) (phylloquinone)	2.4		
Vitamin C (mg) (ascorbic acid)	7.5	Daidzein (mg)	0
Thiamin (mg) (vitamin B1)	0.0	Genistein (mg)	0
Riboflavin (mg) (vitamin B2)	0.0		
Niacin (mg) (vitamin B3)	0.7	Caffeine (mg)	0
Pantothenic Acid (mg)	0.1	Phytic Acid (mg)	0
Vitamin B6 (mg)	0.0	Oxalic Acid (mg)	3.0
Total Folate (mcg)	3	Choline (mg)	5.5
Vitamin B12 (mcg) (cobalamin)	0		
		Glycemic Index (glucose reference)	52
Beta-Carotene (mcg) (provitamin A carotenoid)	182	Glycemic Load (glucose reference)	8
Lutein + Zeaxanthin (mcg)	83		
Lycopene (mcg)	0		

Pear Crunch <small>(Vegan)</small>

One of the best desserts ever! Incredibly sweet fruit with a fabulously crunchy topping – look no further for a serving of sheer delight. Experiment with other fruit alone or in combination; in summer, strawberries are great, and require only brief stovetop cooking.

~For this recipe, both the fruit and the granola topping can be made ahead of time~

<u>Ingredients</u>

<u>Baked Sliced Pears</u>

6 Bosc pears, peeled, cored, sliced & cut into
   bite-size pieces (~4 cups of sliced pears)

1½ c. unsweetened apple juice

6 T maple syrup*

Juice of 2 lemons (4 Tbsp)

2 Tbsp cornstarch (organic)

1 tsp cinnamon

¼ tsp salt

1/8 tsp nutmeg

*Syrup is optional; it gives the pears a much sweeter taste.

Preheat oven to 350°F. In a large mixing bowl, combine pears, apple juice, maple syrup, lemon, cornstarch, cinnamon, salt and nutmeg. Spoon into a glass baking pan, cover with foil, poking holes in the top to prevent juice overflow.

Cook for 1 hour or more until fruit is soft.

Yield for Pears: 6 cup (12, ½-cup servings)

NOTE: You can serve with the following crunch topping (use about 3 Tbsp of topping for each ½-cup serving of fruit.)

Crunchy granola *(Makes 6¾ cups)*

3½ cups rolled oats

1½ cups walnuts, chopped very coarsely, (another kind of nut can also be substituted here)

1 cup whole wheat pastry flour

1/3 cup raisins

½ tsp salt

½ tsp cinnamon

½ cup + 1 Tbsp safflower (or canola) oil

½ cup maple syrup

¼ cup apple juice (for moisture)

3/4 tsp vanilla

Preheat oven to 350°F. In a large mixing bowl, mix rolled oats, walnuts, flour, raisins, salt and cinnamon. Set aside. In a medium bowl, whisk together the oil, maple syrup, apple juice and vanilla.

Add wet ingredients to dry and mix together. Spread onto a cookie sheet. Bake 45-60 minutes, with frequent turning (at least every 15 minutes) until a nice brown color develops.

Serve on top of cooked fruit, or as granola.

This topping can be saved for up to a couple of weeks if covered tightly.

Yield of topping: 6 3/4 cups; (for a serving of cooked fruit, use about 3 Tbsp)

Thanks to Hiroshi Hayashi, *The Monadnock School of Natural Cooking and Philosophy* (Peterborough, NH)

Pear Crunch: 1 serving = ½ cup

Energy (kcal)	225		
Total Fat (g)	7.4	Calcium (mg)	35
Total Carbohydrate (g)	39.7	Phosphorus (mg)	81
Total Protein (g)	2.9	Magnesium (mg)	36
% Calories from Fat	38	Iron (mg)	1.1
% Calories from Carbohydrate	67	Zinc (mg)	1.3
% Calories from Protein	5	Copper (mg)	0.2
Cholesterol (g)	0	Selenium (mcg)	6.3
Total Saturated Fatty Acids (g) (SFA)	0.6	Sodium (mg)	87
Total Monounsaturated Fatty Acids (g) (MUFA)	1.1	Potassium (mg)	256
Total Polyunsaturated Fatty Acids (g) (PUFA)	5.1		
Omega-3 Fatty Acids (g)	0.5		
% Calories from SFA	2.4	Linoleic Acid - PUFA (18:2) (g)	4.7
% Calories from MUFA	4.3	Linolenic Acid – PUFA (18:3) (g)	0.5
% Calories from PUFA	19.6		
Polyunsaturated to Saturated Fat (P:S) Ratio	8.0	Tryptophan (mg)	4
		Threonine (mg)	9
Total Dietary Fiber (g)	4.8	Isoleucine (mg)	11
Soluble Dietary Fiber (g)	1.4	Leucine (mg)	20
Insoluble Dietary Fiber (g)	3.3	Lysine (mg)	11
		Methionine (mg)	4
Total Vitamin A (mcg) (Retinol Activity Equivalents)	1	Phenylalanine (mg)	13
Vitamin D (calciferol) (mcg)	0	Valine (mg)	14
Vitamin E (mg) (Total Alpha-Tocopherol)	1.5	Histidine (mg)	6
Vitamin K (mg) (phylloquinone)	4.8		
Vitamin C (mg) (ascorbic acid)	6.5	Daidzein (mg)	0.0
Thiamin (mg) (vitamin B1)	0.1	Genistein (mg)	0.0
Riboflavin (mg) (vitamin B2)	0.1		
Niacin (mg) (vitamin B3)	0.7	Caffeine (mg)	0
Pantothenic Acid (mg)	0.2	Phytic Acid (mg)	123.6
Vitamin B6 (mg)	0.1	Oxalic Acid (mg)	12.1
Total Folate (mcg)	16	Choline (mg)	12.5
Vitamin B12 (mcg) (cobalamin)	0		
		Glycemic Index (glucose reference)	46
Beta-Carotene (mcg) (provitamin A carotenoid)	13	Glycemic Load (glucose reference)	16
Lutein + Zeaxanthin (mcg)	72		
Lycopene (mcg)	0		

Teff Peanut Butter Cookies (Vegan; GF w/Mod)

Pour yourself a cup of tea and enjoy the chocolaty taste of teff in a memorable, rich peanut-butter snack.

Ingredients

¾ cups teff flour

¼ tsp sea salt

½ cup peanut butter (crunch or smooth)

¼ cup maple syrup

¼ cup canola oil

2 Tbsp soymilk

1 tsp vanilla

Preheat oven to 350°F. Combine flour and sea salt; set aside. In a food processor, blend peanut butter, maple syrup, oil, soymlk and vanilla until well mixed. Add mixture to flour and blend thoroughly. Form dough into small rounds. Place them on an ungreased cookie sheet. Using a fork, gently press down twice, the second time at right angles to the first press. Bake from 12-14 minutes.

Note: If you have teff, it only takes a minute to grind into flour using a standard coffee grinder.

Yield: 1 dozen cookies

~For gluten-free, use soymilk which does not contain malted wheat or barley~

Adapted from: Leslie Cerier, www.lesliecerier.com, *The Organic Gourmet*

Teff Peanut Butter Cookies: 1 serving = 1 cookie

Energy (kcal)	166		
Total Fat (g)	10.3	Calcium (mg)	33
Total Carbohydrate (g)	15.3	Phosphorus (mg)	90
Total Protein (g)	4.3	Magnesium (mg)	39
% Calories from Fat	53	Iron (mg)	1.2
% Calories from Carbohydrate	37	Zinc (mg)	1.0
% Calories from Protein	10	Copper (mg)	0.2
Cholesterol (g)	0	Selenium (mcg)	1.2
Total Saturated Fatty Acids (g) (SFA)	1.5	Sodium (mg)	102
Total Monounsaturated Fatty Acids (g) (MUFA)	5.6	Potassium (mg)	136
Total Polyunsaturated Fatty Acids (g) (PUFA)	3.0		
Omega-3 Fatty Acids (g)	0.4		
% Calories from SFA	7.8	Linoleic Acid - PUFA (18:2) (g)	2.5
% Calories from MUFA	28.9	Linolenic Acid – PUFA (18:3) (g)	0.4
% Calories from PUFA	15.3		
Polyunsaturated to Saturated Fat (P:S) Ratio	1.9	Tryptophan (mg)	4
		Threonine (mg)	12
Total Dietary Fiber (g)	1.6	Isoleucine (mg)	13
Soluble Dietary Fiber (g)	0.1	Leucine (mg)	29
Insoluble Dietary Fiber (g)	1.5	Lysine (mg)	12
		Methionine (mg)	8
Total Vitamin A (mcg) (Retinol Activity Equivalents)	2	Phenylalanine (mg)	21
Vitamin D (calciferol) (mcg)	0.0	Valine (mg)	17
Vitamin E (mg) (Total Alpha-Tocopherol)	1.8	Histidine (mg)	10
Vitamin K (mg) (phylloquinone)	3.6		
Vitamin C (mg) (ascorbic acid)	0.0	Daidzein (mg)	0.1
Thiamin (mg) (vitamin B1)	0.1	Genistein (mg)	0.1
Riboflavin (mg) (vitamin B2)	0.05		
Niacin (mg) (vitamin B3)	1.9	Caffeine (mg)	0
Pantothenic Acid (mg)	0.2	Phytic Acid (mg)	110.6
Vitamin B6 (mg)	0.1	Oxalic Acid (mg)	23.1
Total Folate (mcg)	18	Choline (mg)	8.6
Vitamin B12 (mcg) (cobalamin)	0.0		
		Glycemic Index (glucose reference)	48
Beta-Carotene (mcg) (provitamin A carotenoid)	1	Glycemic Load (glucose reference)	7
Lutein + Zeaxanthin (mcg)	8		
Lycopene (mcg)	0		

Tofu Topping (Vegan: GF)

This is a vegan version of whipped topping. Very satisfying!

Ingredients

1 package silken tofu, soft, 12.3 oz

2 tsp vanilla

¼ cup maple syrup

2 tsp tahini

Place tofu, vanilla, maple syrup and tahini in a food processor and blend until smooth. Chill for at least 3 hours before serving.

Yield: 1½ cups (2 Tbsp per serving = 12 servings)

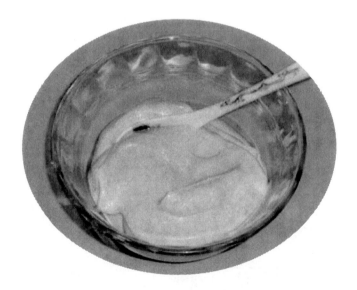

Tofu Topping: 1 serving = 2 Tbsp.

Energy (kcal)	43*		
Total Fat (g)	1.2	Calcium (mg)	17
Total Carbohydrate (g)	5.5	Phosphorus (mg)	32
Total Protein (g)	2.1	Magnesium (mg)	10
% Calories from Fat	26	Iron (mg)	0.5
% Calories from Carbohydrate	50	Zinc (mg)	0.5
% Calories from Protein	20	Copper (mg)	0.1
Cholesterol (g)	0	Selenium (mcg)	2.8
Total Saturated Fatty Acids (g) (SFA)	0.2	Sodium (mg)	12
Total Monounsaturated Fatty Acids (g) (MUFA)	0.3	Potassium (mg)	75
Total Polyunsaturated Fatty Acids (g) (PUFA)	0.6		
Omega-3 Fatty Acids (g)	0.1		
% Calories from SFA	3.8	Linoleic Acid - PUFA (18:2) (g)	0.6
% Calories from MUFA	6.7	Linolenic Acid – PUFA (18:3) (g)	0.1
% Calories from PUFA	13.1		
Polyunsaturated to Saturated Fat (P:S) Ratio	3.5	Tryptophan (mg)	3
		Threonine (mg)	9
Total Dietary Fiber (g)	0.1	Isoleucine (mg)	11
Soluble Dietary Fiber (g)	0.03	Leucine (mg)	18
Insoluble Dietary Fiber (g)	0.07	Lysine (mg)	14
		Methionine (mg)	4
Total Vitamin A (mcg) (Retinol Activity Equivalents)	0	Phenylalanine (mg)	12
Vitamin D (calciferol) (mcg)	0	Valine (mg)	12
Vitamin E (mg) (Total Alpha-Tocopherol)	0.1	Histidine (mg)	5
Vitamin K (mg) (phylloquinone)	0.6		
Vitamin C (mg) (ascorbic acid)	0	Daidzein (mg)	3.2
Thiamin (mg) (vitamin B1)	0.0	Genistein (mg)	4.5
Riboflavin (mg) (vitamin B2)	0.0		
Niacin (mg) (vitamin B3)	0.1	Caffeine (mg)	0
Pantothenic Acid (mg)	0.0	Phytic Acid (mg)	68.2
Vitamin B6 (mg)	0.0	Oxalic Acid (mg)	4.9
Total Folate (mcg)	14	Choline (mg)	8.7
Vitamin B12 (mcg) (cobalamin)	0		
		Glycemic Index (glucose reference)	49
Beta-Carotene (mcg) (provitamin A carotenoid)	0	Glycemic Load (glucose reference)	3
Lutein + Zeaxanthin (mcg)	0		
Lycopene (mcg)	0		

*Calories from alcohol in vanilla, so % calories does not add to 100% from CHO, FAT and PRO.

Vegan Chocolate Pudding (Vegan; GF w/Mod)

Velvety pudding with a subtle sweetness in a rich, full chocolate base ~ Amazingly easy to make ~ Delicious warm or cold.

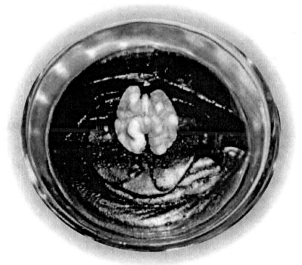

Ingredients

2 cups plain soymilk, divided

½ cup brown rice syrup

2 oz unsweetened chocolate, chopped

1/8 tsp salt

3 Tbsp cornstarch

1 tsp vanilla

In a medium saucepan, combine 1¾ cup soymilk, brown rice syrup, chocolate and salt. Heat over medium, stirring occasionally, until chocolate melts; blend with a whisk until mixture becomes smooth.

Dilute cornstarch with ¼ cup soymilk. Add to blended cocoa mix, stir well. Bring to a boil, then turn to low and simmer for 1 minute, stirring constantly. Add vanilla and remove from heat.

Yield: 2 cups (4, ½-cup servings)

~For gluten-free, use soymilk which does not contain malted wheat or barley~

Adapted from recipe for *Old Fashioned Chocolate Pudding* in Rombauer IS, Becker MR & Becker E, *Joy of Cooking, 75th Anniversary*, NY: Scribner, 2006 (page 807)

Vegan Chocolate Pudding: 1 serving = ½ cup

Energy (kcal)	302		
Total Fat (g)	9.4	Calcium (mg)	171
Total Carbohydrate (g)	54.4	Phosphorus (mg)	135
Total Protein (g)	6.1	Magnesium (mg)	75
% Calories from Fat	26.1	Iron (mg)	3.9
% Calories from Carbohydrate	66.9	Zinc (mg)	1.6
% Calories from Protein	6.1	Copper (mg)	0.6
Cholesterol (g)	0	Selenium (mcg)	4.3
Total Saturated Fatty Acids (g) (SFA)	4.9	Sodium (mg)	220
Total Monounsaturated Fatty Acids (g) (MUFA)	2.7	Potassium (mg)	279
Total Polyunsaturated Fatty Acids (g) (PUFA)	1.4		
Omega-3 Fatty Acids (g)	0.2		
% Calories from SFA	13.5	Linoleic Acid - PUFA (18:2) (g)	1.2
% Calories from MUFA	7.6	Linolenic Acid – PUFA (18:3) (g)	0.2
% Calories from PUFA	3.8		
Polyunsaturated to Saturated Fat (P:S) Ratio	0.3	Tryptophan (mg)	8
		Threonine (mg)	23
Total Dietary Fiber (g)	3.8	Isoleucine (mg)	26
Soluble Dietary Fiber (g)	0.8	Leucine (mg)	44
Insoluble Dietary Fiber (g)	3.0	Lysine (mg)	34
		Methionine (mg)	8
Total Vitamin A (mcg) (Retinol Activity Equivalents)	74	Phenylalanine (mg)	29
Vitamin D (calciferol) (mcg)	1.3	Valine (mg)	31
Vitamin E (mg) (Total Alpha-Tocopherol)	1.8	Histidine (mg)	14
Vitamin K (mg) (phylloquinone)	5.7		
Vitamin C (mg) (ascorbic acid)	0.4	Daidzein (mg)	6.0
Thiamin (mg) (vitamin B1)	0.1	Genistein (mg)	6.2
Riboflavin (mg) (vitamin B2)	0.1		
Niacin (mg) (vitamin B3)	1.0	Caffeine (mg)	11
Pantothenic Acid (mg)	0.1	Phytic Acid (mg)	241.4
Vitamin B6 (mg)	0.1	Oxalic Acid (mg)	33.0
Total Folate (mcg)	18	Choline (mg)	17.1
Vitamin B12 (mcg) (cobalamin)	1.5		
		Glycemic Index (glucose reference)	86
Beta-Carotene (mcg) (provitamin A carotenoid)	1	Glycemic Load (glucose reference)	44
Lutein + Zeaxanthin (mcg)	5		
Lycopene (mcg)	0		

SELECTED NUTRIENT TABLES

Grains: Major Energy Components and Total Fiber
~All information listed in the following tables is per serving~

Recipe Name	Serving Size Description	Energy (kcal)	Total Fat (g)	CHO (g)	PRO (g)	Chol (mg)	Sat'd Fat (g)	MUFA (g)	PUFA (g)	Total Fiber (g)
Banana Nut Bread	1 square	325	12.4	50.7	7.8	0	1.2	1.7	8.7	6.6
Blueberry Pancakes	1 pancake	180	5.6	29.5	5.0	35	0.7	2.9	1.6	3.7
Brown Rice Pilaf	1/2 cup	110	2.5	19.8	2.5	0	0.4	0.9	1.0	3.0
Brown Rice Sushi	4 slices	170	3.5	31.5	4.1	0	0.6	1.9	0.7	6.0
Buckwheat and sprouts	1 cup	135	5.8	19.0	4.1	0	0.9	2.2	2.4	2.9
Chestnut Sweet Rice with Hazelnuts	1/2 cup	195	4.7	34.5	4.2	0	0.5	2.9	1.0	5.4
Cold Sesame Noodles	1 cup	303	5.1	55.0	9.1	0	0.7	1.8	2.2	6.5
Corn Bread with Raisins	1 square (2x2 inches)	173	6.6	26.5	3.8	27	0.7	3.7	1.9	2.7
Fried Brown Rice	1 cup	290	11.7	39.3	7.2	85	2.1	7.2	1.7	5.7
Fried Noodles	1.5 cups	168	4.3	28.2	7.3	0	0.7	1.7	1.8	5.4
Granola	1/4 cup	167	9.6	18.6	3.3	0	0.8	1.5	6.8	2.4
Millet Stew	1 cup	138	1.8	26.4	4.2	0	0.3	0.4	0.9	3.5
Pasta Fagiole	1 cup	231	5.4	36.3	9.0	0	0.8	3.4	0.8	4.9
Penne with Avocado and Tomato	1 cup	212	10.1	27.8	5.7	0	1.4	6.7	1.3	4.6
Polenta pan fry	4 x 2 x 3/4-inch slices	62	0.5	12.6	1.4	0	0.0	0.3	0.2	0.3
Polenta w/Mushroom Gravy	4 x 2 x 3/4-inch slices	80	1.4	14.9	2.0	0	0.2	0.6	0.5	0.5
Quinoa Stuffed Peppers	1 pepper	270	8.5	34.4	16.1	0	1.1	4.4	2.3	4.2
Rice Salad	1 cup	205	7.6	27.5	8.3	0	1.3	4.0	1.9	4.8
Spiral Pasta Salad	1 cup	110	6.8	11.4	2.5	0	0.9	4.7	0.8	2.7
Steamed Onion Strudel	1 wedge	120	2.9	23.2	4.7	0	0.4	1.4	0.7	6.1
Tabouli Salad	1 cup	152	6.0	23.8	3.5	0	0.8	3.6	1.0	5.9
Vegetable-brown rice medley	1 cup	329	5.4	61.3	9.5	0	1.0	1.9	2.1	9.1
Recommendations for ages 19-50 Men/Women (if different)		**	**	130	56/46	**	**	**	**	38/25

CHO=Carbohydrates; PRO = Protein; Chol = Cholesterol; Sat'd fat=Saturated fat; MUFA = Monounsaturated fat; PUFA = Polyunsaturated fat

** See Appendix A for detailed recommendations at each life stage

Selected Mineral Content of Grain Recipes

Recipe Name	Serving Size Description	Calcium (mg)	P (mg)	Mg (mg)	Iron (mg)	Zinc (mg)	Cu (mg)	Se (mcg)	Na (mg)	K (mg)
Banana Nut Bread	1 square	64	228	86	2.3	2.4	0.4	29.3	161	417
Blueberry Pancakes	1 pancake	80	123	40	1.4	1.2	0.1	19.1	184	173
Brown Rice Pilaf	1/2 cup	14	84	36	0.4	0.6	0.1	8.9	82	117
Brown Rice Sushi	4 slices	32	121	59	1.0	1.0	0.2	12.2	180	212
Buckwheat and sprouts	1 cup	21	89	58	1.2	0.9	0.2	2.2	187	166
Chestnut Sweet Rice with Hazelnuts	1/2 cup	25	123	65	0.9	0.9	0.3	11.4	64	185
Cold Sesame Noodles	1 cup	67	130	21	1.9	0.9	0.2	21.7	132	239
Corn Bread with Raisins	1 square (2x2 inches)	60	101	33	1.1	0.7	0.1	11.4	159	153
Fried Brown Rice	1 cup	36	178	74	1.2	1.3	0.2	21.7	169	155
Fried Noodles	1.5 cups	27	67	25	1.1	0.5	0.1	4.2	318	216
Granola	1/4 cup	20	91	36	1.0	1.0	0.2	8.1	46	122
Millet Stew	1 cup	41	107	44	1.3	0.7	0.3	1.2	207	214
Pasta Fagiole	1 cup	73	109	51	3.3	1.1	0.3	19.0	94	536
Penne with Avocado and Tomato	1 cup	23	101	38	1.3	1.0	0.2	24.4	62	199
Polenta pan fry	4 x 2 x 3/4-inch slices	3	13	5	0.6	0.1	0.0	2.7	107	24
Polenta with Mushroom Gravy	4 x 2 x 3/4-inch slices	10	34	8	0.7	0.3	0.1	6.5	99	106
Quinoa Stuffed Peppers	1 pepper	69	302	85	4.1	2.1	0.7	15.2	256	718
Rice Salad	1 cup	143	168	71	2.0	1.3	0.3	15.8	258	195
Spiral Pasta Salad	1 cup	36	58	23	1.0	0.5	0.1	5.8	108	256
Steamed Onion Strudel	1 wedge	48	60	23	1.6	0.6	0.1	14.0	307	134
Tabouli Salad	1 cup	29	90	48	1.1	0.7	0.2	1.1	115	311
Vegetable-brown rice medley	1 cup	93	260	125	1.8	2.0	0.4	29.3	199	217
Recommendations for ages 19-50 Men/Women (if different)		1000	700	400/310	8/18	11/8	0.9	55	1,500	4,700

P=Phosphorus; Mg=Magnesium; Cu=Copper; Se=Selenium; Na=Sodium; K=Potassium

Beans and Bean Products: Energy Nutrients and Types of Fat

Recipe Name	Serving Size Description	Energy (kcal)	Total Fat (g)	CHO (g)	PRO (g)	Chol (mg)	Sat'd Fat (g)	MUFA (g)	PUFA (g)
Beans									
Azuki Beans and Squash	1/2 cup	203	0.4	40.6	11.0	0	0.1	0	0.1
Baked azuki beans	1 cup	256	1.4	51	11.8	0	0.2	0.9	0.2
Bean Burgers	1 burger 3-inch diameter	151	4.5	23.1	5.1	0	0.7	2.9	0.8
Bean Stew	1 cup	205	2.1	31.2	17.7	0	0.3	0.9	0.7
Black bean soup	1 1/2 cups	251	4.2	43.5	11.9	0	0.7	2.5	0.7
Curry Chickpeas	1 cup	208	4.7	36.9	6.8	0	0.6	2.5	1.1
Lentil Soup	1 cup	179	2.2	30.6	10.2	0	0.3	1.2	0.5
Quick Red Lentil Spread	1/4 cup	82	4.6	7.7	3.7	0	0.5	0.8	3.2
Red Pepper Hummus	1/4 cup	124	6.5	4.4	4.2	0	0.9	3.8	1.4
Split Pea Soup	1 cup	148	0.9	27.3	9.1	0	0.1	0.2	0.4
Warm Bean Salad	1 cup	325	4.6	57.3	13.9	0	0.7	2.4	0.9
Soy Products									
Deep Fried Tempeh	1/4 cup	88	6.5	3.3	5.4	0	0.9	3	2
Scrambled Tofu + Egg-beaters and Mushrooms	1/2 cup	111	7.1	5	9.2	0	0.8	4.3	1.6
Scrambled Tofu with Onion	1/2 cup	111	7	5.5	8.7	0	0.8	4.4	1.4
Scrambled tofu with shiitake mushrooms	1/2 cup	97	5.9	5.1	8.1	0	0.6	3.9	1
Spicy Simmered Tofu	1/2 cup	92	6.6	3.7	5.8	0	0.9	3.3	2.3
Tempeh Salad with Mayo	1/2 cup	127	8.9	6.9	6.6	2	1.5	2.4	4
Tempeh Salad-vegan	1/2 cup	79	3.9	6.2	6.1	0	0.8	1.2	1.4
Tempeh with Orange Glaze	2 ounce portion	229	13.9	18.3	10.7	0	2.3	7.4	2.9
Tofu Burgers	1 3-oz burger 2-inch diameter	121	6.8	8.8	7.8	0	1.2	3.0	2.2
Tofu Cream Cheese	2 Tbsp	26	1.7	1	2.1	0	0.2	0.5	0.9
Tofu lunchmeat	2 slices	87	5.5	2.1	9.4	0	1	1.9	2.2
Recommendations for ages 19-50 Men/Women (if different)		**	**	130	56/46	**	**	**	**

CHO=Carbohydrates; PRO = Protein; Chol = Cholesterol; Sat'd fat=Saturated fat; MUFA = Monounsaturated fat; PUFA = Polyunsaturated fat

** See Appendix A for detailed recommendations at each life stage

Beans and Bean Products: Energy and Fiber Components

Recipe Name	Serving Size Description	Energy (kcal)	Total Fiber (g)	Soluble Fiber (g)	Insoluble Fiber (g)
Beans					
Azuki Beans and Squash	1/2 cup	203	12.1	2.8	9.3
Baked azuki beans	1 cup	256	12.0	1.9	10.2
Bean Burgers	1 burger 3-inch diameter	151	5.9	0.8	5.1
Bean Stew	1 cup	205	8.9	2.9	6.1
Black bean soup	1 1/2 cups	251	12.2	1.1	11.1
Curry Chickpeas	1 cup	208	6.2	0.9	4.5
Lentil Soup	1 cup	179	6.7	0.7	5.9
Quick Red Lentil Spread	1/4 cup	82	2.2	0.2	2.0
Red Pepper Hummus	1/4 cup	124	3.0	0.4	2.6
Split Pea Soup	1 cup	148	11.6	0.2	11.2
Warm Bean Salad	1 cup	325	7.7	1.8	5.8
Soy Products					
Deep Fried Tempeh	1/4 cup	88	1.0	0.4	0.5
Scrambled Tofu + Eggbeaters and Mushrooms	1/2 cup	111	1.1	0.3	0.8
Scrambled Tofu with Onion	1/2 cup	111	0.9	0.3	0.6
Scrambled tofu with shiitake mushrooms	1/2 cup	97	1.1	0.2	0.9
Spicy Simmered Tofu	1/2 cup	92	0.8	0.3	0.5
Tempeh Salad with Mayo	1/2 cup	127	1.8	0.6	1.2
Tempeh Salad-vegan	1/2 cup	79	1.6	0.5	1.1
Tempeh with Orange Glaze	2 ounce portion	229	2.2	1.0	1.2
Tofu Burgers	1 3-oz burger 2-inch diameter	121	1.6	0.6	1.0
Tofu Cream Cheese	2 Tbsp	26	0.3	0.1	0.2
Tofu lunchmeat	2 slices	87	1.0	0.5	0.6
Recommendations for ages 19-50 Men/Women (if different)			38/25	#	#

Specific requirements for each type of fiber have not been established.

269

Beans and Bean Products: Selected Mineral Content

Recipe Name	Serving Size Description	Calcium (mg)	P (mg)	Mg (mg)	Iron (mg)	Zinc (mg)	Cu (mg)	Se (mcg)	Na (mg)	K (mg)
Azuki Beans and Squash	1/2 cup	58	246	82	3.1	2.6	0.5	1.9	137	909
Baked azuki beans	1 cup	62	27	86	3.1	2.7	0.5	2.5	176	927
Bean Burgers	1 burger 3-inch diameter	40	115	44	1.4	0.9	0.2	5.7	75	236
Bean Stew	1 cup	69	237	57	4.0	1.6	0.4	6.7	185	555
Black bean soup	1 1/2 cups	62	205	99	3.1	1.6	0.4	2.3	356	740
Curry Chickpeas	1 cup	64	143	50	2.8	1.2	0.4	3.3	84	466
Lentil Soup	1 cup	42	191	45	3.8	1.4	0.3	10.6	219	447
Quick Red Lentil Spread	1/4 cup	16	77	22	1.2	0.6	0.2	1.2	131	152
Red Pepper Hummus	1/4 cup	36	50	25	1.6	0.8	0.2	1.7	105	93
Split Pea Soup	1 cup	61	119	49	1.7	1.2	0.2	1.2	157	472
Warm Bean Salad	1 cup	56	187	59	3.6	1.5	0.3	32.7	215	457
Soy Products										
Deep Fried Tempeh	1/4 cup	32	79	24	0.8	0.3	0.2	0.0	108	123
Scrambled Tofu + Eggbeaters and Mushrooms	1/2 cup	138	109	45	1.9	1.2	0.3	15.9	99	178
Scrambled Tofu with Onion	1/2 cup	150	128	47	1.7	1.1	0.2	12.3	78	186
Scrambled tofu with shiitake mushrooms	1/2 cup	142	114	46	1.7	1.1	0.3	13.7	73	163
Spicy Simmered Tofu	1/2 cup	139	89	28	1.3	0.6	0.2	6.8	171	131
Tempeh Salad with Mayo	1/2 cup	51	102	32	1.1	0.5	0.2	0.3	160	224
Tempeh Salad-vegan	1/2 cup	47	93	30	1.0	0.4	0.2	0.2	118	208
Tempeh with Orange Glaze	2 ounce portion	74	161	55	1.8	0.8	0.3	0.4	139	399
Tofu Burgers	1 3-oz burger 2-inch diameter	170	125	40	1.8	0.9	0.2	10.4	228	159
Tofu Cream Cheese	2 Tbsp	39	36	10	0.5	0.3	0.1	2.6	77	48
Tofu lunchmeat	2 slices	228	40	43	1.9	1.0	0.2	11.2	102	173
Recommendations for ages 19-50 Men/Women (if different)		1000	700	400/310	8/18	11/8	0.9	55	1,500	4,700

P=Phosphorus; Mg=Magnesium; Cu=Copper; Se=Selenium; Na=Sodium; K=Potassium

Vegetables: Energy Nutrients and Types of Fat

Recipe Name	Serving Size Description	Energy (kcal)	Total Fat (g)	CHO (g)	PRO (g)	Chol. (mg)	Sat'd Fat (g)	MUFA (g)	PUFA (g)	Total Fiber (g)
Bok choy	1/2 cup	86	6.3	5.8	3.2	0	0.9	3.4	1.7	1.8
Broccoli Rabe	1/2 cup	61	3.8	3.9	3.0	0	0.5	2.5	0.5	2.1
Brussels Sprouts Sauté	1/2 cup	52	2.3	7.2	2.3	0	0.4	0.8	1.0	2.3
Burdock and Carrots	1/3 cup	91	3.6	14.3	1.5	0	0.5	1.4	1.5	2.1
Cabbage with Ginger	1/2 cup	49	3.5	4.4	1.0	0	0.5	1.4	1.4	1.5
Carrots with Parsnips	1/2 cup	67	2.8	10.4	1.1	0	0.4	1.4	0.8	2.6
Cole Slaw	1/2 cup	46	3.4	4.0	0.5	2	0.5	0.8	1.8	0.9
Green Beans + Soy Crumbles	1 cup	160	6.6	12.9	14.6	0	0.9	4.3	1.0	4.3
Home Fry Pancake	1/4 pancake	129	2.4	25.3	2.2	0	0.3	1.6	0.3	2.6
Kale with Sunflower Seeds	1 cup	87	5.4	8.9	3.1	0	0.7	1.7	2.6	2.9
Kohlrabi with Peppercorn	1/2 cup	35	1.9	4.4	1.2	0	0.3	1.3	0.2	2.5
Lotus Root with Lemons	1/3 cup	36	1.2	6.4	0.6	0	0.2	0.5	0.5	1.2
Onion Rings	6 rings	208	12.5	22.2	3.6	0	1.0	7.6	3.6	3.3
Pan Fried Zucchini	3 pieces	121	6.6	13.6	2.8	0	1.0	4.4	1.0	2.0
Roasted Potatoes	1 cup	173	4.1	32.0	3.0	0	0.6	2.8	0.5	3.7
Salad with Green Beans	2 cups	50	2.9	5.6	1.8	0	0.4	1.0	1.3	2.1
Seasoned Broccoli	1 cup	80	5.5	7.1	2.3	0	0.8	3.7	0.7	3.3
Spinach Sauté	1/2 cup	55	3.3	5.2	2.9	0	0.5	2.2	0.4	2.2
Squash-Cabbage-Onion Medley	1 cup	45	0.3	10.7	1.6	0	0.0	0.0	0.1	3.0
Steamed Cauliflower with Sesame-Miso-Scallion Dressing	1 cup	64	3.4	7.1	3.3	0	0.5	1.1	1.5	3.5
Steamed Collards with Pine Nut Dressing	1/2 cup	86	6.4	6.0	3.3	0	0.5	1.7	3.2	3.0
Watercress with garlic	.75 cup	70	5.8	3.2	2.8	0	0.8	3.7	1.0	0.6
Recommendations for ages 19-50 Men/Women (if different)		**	**	130	56/46	**	**	**	**	38/25

CHO=Carbohydrates; PRO = Protein; Chol = Cholesterol; Sat'd fat=Saturated fat; MUFA = Monounsaturated fat; PUFA = Polyunsaturated fat

** See Appendix A for detailed recommendations at each life stage

271

Vegetables: Fat-Soluble Vitamin and Phytochemical Content

Recipe Name	Serving Size Description	Vitamin A(mcg) (RAE)+	Lutein + Zeaxanthin (mcg)	Lycopene (mcg)	Vitamin D (calciferol) (mcg)	Vitamin E (mg)++	Vitamin K (mcg)
Bok choy	1/2 cup	361	66	0	0.0	0.6	60.1
Broccoli Rabe	1/2 cup	163	1,212	0	0.0	2.3	186.4
Brussels Sprouts Sauté	1/2 cup	33	1,087	0	0.0	0.4	118.6
Burdock and Carrots	1/3 cup	359	289	0	0.0	0.7	7.2
Cabbage with Ginger	1/2 cup	3	20	0	0.0	0.2	82.0
Carrots with Parsnips	1/2 cup	302	341	0	0.0	0.9	36.7
Cole Slaw	1/2 cup	48	31	0	.013	0.3	25.7
Green Beans + Soy Crumbles	1 cup	43	873	0	0.0	1.4	24.0
Home Fry Pancake	1/4 pancake	0	11	0	0.0	0.4	4.1
Kale with Sunflower Seeds	1 cup	885	23,720	0	0.0	1.9	1062.8
Kohlrabi with Peppercorn	1/2 cup	1	0	0	0.0	0.6	1.5
Lotus Root with Lemons	1/3 cup	1	14	0	0.0	0.0	2.8
Onion Rings	6 rings	1	100	0	0.0	2.3	9.1
Pan Fried Zucchini	3 pieces	33	491	0	.167	1.2	6.5
Roasted Potatoes	1 cup	729	2	0	0.0	1.1	4.8
Salad with Green Beans	2 cups	118	531	86	0.0	0.2	23.2
Seasoned Broccoli	1 cup	77	1,056	0	0.0	2.7	140.6
Spinach Sauté	1/2 cup	472	10,178	0	0.0	2.3	446.1
Squash-Cabbage-Onion Medley	1 cup	143	779	0	0.0	0.2	67.1
Steamed Cauliflower with Sesame-Miso-Scallion Dressing	1 cup	4	107	0	0.0	0.2	30.3
Steamed Collards with Pine Nut Dressing	1/2 cup	387	7,344	0	0.0	1.7	425.2
Watercress with garlic	.75 cup	164	5,926	0	0.0	1.7	259.8
Recommendations for ages 19-50 Men/Women (if different)		900/700	#	#	15	15	90/120

= specific recommendations have not been established; + RAE = Retinol Activity Equivalents; ++ vitamin E in the form of α-Tocopherol

Vegetables: Selected Water-Soluble Vitamin Content

Recipe Name	Serving Size Description	Thiamin (mg)	Riboflavin (mg)	Niacin (mg)	Vitamin B6 (mg)	Folate (mcg)	Vitamin B12 (mcg)	Vitamin C (mg)	Choline (mg)
Bok choy	1/2 cup	0.1	0.1	0.9	0.4	70	0.0	46.0	23.1
Broccoli Rabe	1/2 cup	0.1	0.1	1.5	0.2	51	0.0	27.6	25.3
Brussels Sprouts Sauté	1/2 cup	0.1	0.1	0.6	0.2	51	0.0	52.8	35.0
Burdock and Carrots	1/3 cup	0.0	0.1	0.6	0.2	16	0.0	2.7	11.7
Cabbage with Ginger	1/2 cup	0.0	0.0	0.2	0.1	23	0.0	28.2	15.7
Carrots with Parsnips	1/2 cup	0.1	0.0	0.7	0.1	31	0.0	8.7	14.6
Cole Slaw	1/2 cup	0.0	0.0	0.1	0.1	15	0.0	12.0	5.0
Green Beans + Soy Crumbles	1 cup	0.1	0.1	1.0	0.1	67	0.0	13.0	35.5
Home Fry Pancake	1/4 pancake	0.1	0.0	1.7	0.3	11	0.0	9.4	16.7
Kale with Sunflower Seeds	1 cup	0.1	0.1	0.8	0.2	24	0.0	53.7	2.5
Kohlrabi with Peppercorn	1/2 cup	0.0	0.0	0.3	0.1	11	0.0	41.9	8.7
Lotus Root with Lemons	1/3 cup	0.1	0.0	0.1	0.1	4	0.0	11.2	10.0
Onion Rings	6 rings	0.1	0.1	1.5	0.1	14	0.0	1.1	9.8
Pan Fried Zucchini	3 pieces	0.1	0.1	1.3	0.1	24	0.2	2.0	8.6
Roasted Potatoes	1 cup	0.2	0.1	2.2	0.4	12	0.0	24.5	20.8
Salad with Green Beans	2 cups	0.1	0.1	0.6	0.1	38	0.0	8.9	9.3
Seasoned Broccoli	1 cup	0.1	0.1	0.5	0.2	105	0.0	63.1	39.0
Spinach Sauté	1/2 cup	0.1	0.2	0.5	0.3	132	0.0	9.8	18.7
Squash-Cabbage-Onion Medley	1 cup	0.1	0.1	0.5	0.2	33	0.0	28.8	19.5
Steamed Cauliflower with Sesame-Miso-Scallion Dressing	1 cup	0.1	0.1	0.8	0.2	64	0.0	56.1	50.6
Steamed Collards with Pine Nut Dressing	1/2 cup	0.1	0.1	0.9	0.1	92	0.0	17.6	35.3
Watercress with garlic	.75 cup	0.1	0.1	0.4	0.2	10	0.0	31.8	11.3
Recommendations for ages 19-50 Men/Women (if different)		1.2/1.1	1.3/1.1	16/14	1.3	400	2.4	75/90	550/425

Vegetables: Selected Mineral Content

Recipe Name	Serving Size Description	Calcium (mg)	Magnesium (mg)	Iron (mg)	Zinc (mg)	Selenium (mcg)	Sodium (mg)	Potassium (mg)
Bok choy	1/2 cup	169	21	2.0	0.4	1.5	188	660
Broccoli Rabe	1/2 cup	91	21	1.0	0.4	1.4	96	261
Brussels Sprouts Sauté	1/2 cup	34	18	1.1	0.3	1.5	91	277
Burdock and Carrots	1/3 cup	36	24	0.6	0.3	0.8	170	275
Cabbage with Ginger	1/2 cup	36	12	0.1	0.2	0.5	82	154
Carrots with Parsnips	1/2 cup	30	19	0.6	0.3	0.9	127	239
Cole Slaw	1/2 cup	16	5	0.2	0.1	0.2	61	78
Green Beans + Soy Crumbles	1 cup	82	28	3.0	0.9	3.9	133	212
Home Fry Pancake	1/4 pancake	10	25	0.4	0.3	0.4	82	415
Kale with Sunflower Seeds	1 cup	97	28	1.3	0.5	3.3	106	331
Kohlrabi with Peppercorn	1/2 cup	17	14	0.4	0.0	0.5	49	241
Lotus Root with Lemons	1/3 cup	12	9	0.4	0.1	0.2	96	146
Onion Rings	6 rings	14	37	1.0	0.8	16.6	151	138
Pan Fried Zucchini	3 pieces	41	26	1.0	0.4	7.4	94	169
Roasted Potatoes	1 cup	34	40	0.9	0.5	0.4	158	656
Salad with Green Beans	2 cups	44	16	0.9	0.4	0.3	56	160
Seasoned Broccoli	1 cup	42	21	0.7	0.4	1.6	187	289
Spinach Sauté	1/2 cup	128	79	3.3	0.7	1.8	155	433
Squash-Cabbage-Onion Medley	1 cup	48	19	0.4	0.3	0.7	42	290
Steamed Cauliflower with Sesame-Miso-Scallion Dressing	1 cup	46	18	1.0	0.5	0.9	53	215
Steamed Collards with Pine Nut Dressing	1/2 cup	135	42	1.6	0.8	0.6	81	167
Watercress with garlic	.75 cup	129	24	0.4	0.2	1.4	186	358
Recommendations for ages 19-50 Men/Women (if different)		1000	400/310	8/18	11/8	55	1,500	4,700

Desserts: Major Energy Components and Total Fiber

Recipe Name	Serving Size Description	Energy (kcal)	Total Fat (g)	CHO (g)	PRO (g)	Chol (mg)	Sat'd Fat (g)	MUFA (g)	PUFA (g)	Total Fiber (g)
Azuki-Chestnut-Raisin-Dessert	1 cup	359	1.4	76.0	13.0	0	0.3	0.4	0.5	15.1
Almond Miso Dip	1 Tbsp	78	5.0	8.0	1.4	0	0.5	2.8	1.5	0.4
Baked Apples	1 apple	129	1.9	30.2	0.9	0	0.2	0.2	1.2	4.7
Banana Peanut Roll	1-inch wedge	237	10.2	34.1	8.3	0	2.1	4.6	3.0	6.3
Blueberry Tart	1 tart	330	9.5	57.0	6.3	0	0.9	4.8	3.1	6.5
Blueberry Tofu Cheesecake	Slice	285	12.5	36.6	8.8	0	1.2	3.5	6.9	2.9
Brown Rice Crispy Snacks	2 x 2 inch square	131	5.6	18.5	3.5	0	1.2	2.7	1.6	1.1
Caramel corn with Peanuts	1 cup	187	7.9	25.8	5.1	0	1.1	4.0	2.5	2.4
Cherry Kanten	1/2 cup	57	0.1	14.3	0.3	0	0.0	0.0	0.0	0.7
Crumb Topping	2 Tbsp	83	2.6	13.8	2.1	0	0.2	1.5	0.7	1.8
Fruit Smoothie	1 cup	201	5.8	34.4	5.8	0	0.6	2.3	2.3	4.6
Lemon Soy Pudding	1/2 cup	155	3.5	29.5	2.9	0	0.4	0.6	2.3	1.6
Oatmeal Cookies with Orange & Ginger	1 cookie	105	5.5	13.1	1.9	0	0.5	1.1	3.6	1.3
Peaches in Sauce	1/2 cup	67	0.2	16.8	0.8	0	0.0	0.1	0.1	1.5
Pear Crunch	1/2 cup	225	7.4	39.7	2.9	0	0.6	1.1	5.1	4.8
Pumpkin-Carrot-Walnut Muffin	1 muffin	239	5.0	45.9	5.6	0	0.5	1.3	2.8	4.2
Teff Peanut Butter Cookies	1 cookie	166	10.3	15.3	4.3	0	1.5	5.6	3.0	1.6
Tofu Topping	2 Tbsp	43	1.2	5.5	2.1	0	0.2	0.3	0.6	0.1
Vegan Chocolate Pudding	1/2 cup	302	9.4	54.4	6.1	0	4.9	2.7	1.4	3.8
Recommendations for ages 19-50 Men/Women (if different)		**	**	130	56/46	**	**	**	**	38/25

CHO=Carbohydrates; PRO = Protein; Chol = Cholesterol; Sat'd fat=Saturated fat; MUFA = Monounsaturated fat; PUFA = Polyunsaturated fat

** See Appendix A for detailed recommendations at each life stage

275

Desserts: Selected Mineral Content

Recipe Name	Serving Size Description	Mg (mg)	Iron (mg)	Zinc (mg)	Se (mcg)	Na (mg)	K (mg)
Azuki-Chestnut-Raisin-Dessert	1 cup	105	3.9	2.7	2.4	93	1216
Almond Miso Dip	1 Tbsp	25	0.4	0.5	0.5	61	72
Baked Apples	1 apple	15	0.4	0.3	0.2	3	235
Banana Peanut Roll	1-inch wedge	50	1.6	1.0	12.8	288	270
Blueberry Tart	1 tart	45	2.1	1.6	17.9	118	264
Blueberry Tofu Cheesecake	Slice	69	2.0	2.0	13.6	134	376
Brown Rice Crispy Snacks	2 x 2 inch square	28	0.5	0.5	1.6	93	147
Caramel corn with Peanuts	1 cup	47	0.9	1.2	2.5	7	180
Cherry Kanten	1/2 cup	7	0.2	0.0	0.1	4	130
Crumb Topping	2 Tbsp	23	0.6	0.7	10.0	38	75
Fruit Smoothie	1 cup	57	1.7	0.5	3.6	73	380
Lemon Soy Pudding	1/2 cup	25	0.9	0.3	2.0	74	171
Oatmeal Cookies with Orange & Ginger	1 cookie	20	0.6	0.5	5.0	48	96
Peaches in Sauce	1/2 cup	9	0.3	0.2	0.3	38	153
Pear Crunch	1/2 cup	36	1.1	1.3	6.3	87	256
Pumpkin-Carrot-Walnut Muffin	1 muffin	57	1.8	0.9	19.0	181	275
Teff Peanut Butter Cookies	1 cookie	39	1.2	1.0	1.2	102	136
Tofu Topping	2 Tbsp	10	0.5	0.5	2.8	12	75
Vegan Chocolate Pudding	1/2 cup	75	3.9	1.6	4.3	220	279
Recommendations for ages 19-50 Men/Women (if different)		400/310	8/18	11/8	55	1,500	4,700

Mg=Magnesium, Se=Selenium; Na=Sodium; K=Potassium

REFERENCES

Alford J, Duguid N, *Seductions of Rice*, NY: Artisan Publishers, 1998.

Bellame J, Bellame J. *Japanese Foods that Heal.* North Clarendon, VT: Tuttle Publishing, 2007.

*Brown SG. *Modern-Day Macrobiotics.* Berkeley, CA: North Atlantic Books, 2005.

Gibson RS, Yeudall F, Drost N, et al. Dietary interventions to prevent zinc deficiency. Am J Clin Nutr 1998;68(suppl):484S-7S.

Gropper SS, Smith JL, Groff JL. *Advanced Nutrition and Human Metabolism*, 5th edition. Belmont, CA: Wadsworth/Cengage Learning, 2009.

Grus T (2011). How to use xanthan gum and guar gum in gluten-free cooking. *About.com. Gluten-free cooking.* http://glutenfreecooking.about.com/od/glutenfreecookingbasics/a/xanthan guargums.htm. (5 Jan 2011).

Institute of Medicine. *Dietary Reference Intakes: The Essential Guide to Nutrient Requirements.* Washington, DC: National Academies Press, 2006.

Institute of Medicine. *Dietary Reference Intakes for Calcium and Vitamin D.* Washington, DC: National Academies Press, 2011.

Jacobson MF. Six Arguments for a Greener Diet. Washington, DC: Center for Science in the Public Interest, 2006.

Katzen M: *The Vegetable Dishes I Can't Live Without.* NY: Hyperion, 2007.

Kushi A, Wendy E: *Changing Seasons Macrobiotic Cookbook*, NY: Avery, 2003.

Kushi A, Esko W: *The Good Morning Macrobiotic Breakfast Book*, NY: Avery, 1991.

Kushi A: *How to Cook with Miso*, Tokyo: Japan Publications, Inc., 1978.

*Kushi M, Jack A: *The Macrobiotic Path to Total Health*, NY: Ballantine Books, 2003.

Madison D: *Vegetarian Cooking for Everyone*, New York: Broadway Books, 1997.

Madison D. *This Can't Be Tofu!* NY: Broadway Books, 2000.

Madison D, McFarlin P: *What We Eat When We Eat Alone*, Layton, UT: Gibbs Smith, 2009.

McGee H. *On Food and Cooking: The Science and Lore of the Kitchen.* New York: Scribner, 2004.

Melina V, Davis B. *The New Becoming Vegetarian.* Summertown, TN: Healthy Living Publications, 2003.

Nutrition Coordinating Center (NCC), University of Minnesota: Nutrition Data System for Research (NDSR) User Manual, version 2009, Regents of the University of Minnesota, 2009.

Ohsawa L. *The Art of Just Cooking,* Hayama, Japan: Autumn Press, 1974.

Pollan M. *The Omnivore's Dilemma: A Natural History of Four Meals.* NY: Penguin Press, 2006.

Position Paper of the American Dietetic Association: Vegetarian Diets. J Am Diet Assoc 2009;109:1266-1282.

Rombauer IS, Becker MR, Becker E, *Joy of Cooking*, 75th Anniversary. NY: Scribner, 2006.

Sandstroöm B, Almgren A, Kivistö B, Cederblad A. Effect of protein level and protein source on zinc absorption in humans. J Nutr 1989;119:48-53.

Shuman S, *Macrobiotic Desserts*, Los Angeles, CA: Dictionart, 1981.

Stepaniak J, Melina V. *Raising Vegetarian Children.* NY: McGraw Hill, 2003.

Szafranski M, Whittington JA, Bessinger C. Pureed cannellini beans can be substituted for shortening in brownies. J Am Diet Assoc 2005;105:1295-1298.

U.S. Department of Agriculture and U.S. Department of Human Services. *Dietary Guidelines for Americans, 2010.* 7th Edition, Washington, DC: U.S. Government Printing Office, December, 2010.

*Varona V, *Macrobiotics for Dummies*, Indianapolis, IN: Wiley Publishing, Inc., 2009.

Weaver CM, Proulx WR, Heaney R. Choices for achieving adequate calcium with a vegetarian diet. Am J Clin Nutr 1999;70(suppl):543S-548S.

Whitney E, Rolfes SR. *Understanding Nutrition*, 12th edition, Belmont, CA: Wadsworth, Cengage Learning, 2011.

World Health Organization, *Trace Minerals in Human Health and Nutrition, India: WHO, 1996, Chapter 5: Zinc (p 77).*

*Excellent books on the subject of Macrobiotics

APPENDIX A

RECOMMENDATIONS FOR SELECTED NUTRIENTS

The amounts listed in the following tables reflect those considered to be the advisable amount for each life stage category, by gender. Those values in **bold** are the Recommended Dietary Allowances (RDAs), and have a good deal of supportive scientific evidence behind them. Those with an "*" represent "Adequate Intakes," (AIs) for which less definitive scientific data is available. Both values, however, can be useful in comparing food intake in terms of those amounts which will optimize health and well being.

The following information has been adapted and reprinted with permission from *Dietary Reference Intakes: The Essential Guide to Nutrient Requirements*, 2006, and *Dietary Reference Intakes for Calcium and Vitamin D*, 2011, by the Institute of Medicine, National Academy of Sciences, Courtesy of National Academies Press, Washington, DC.

Carbohydrate (CHO) Recommendations by Age and Gender Group

Life Stage Group	CHO, g/day MALES	CHO, g/day FEMALES
Infants 0-6 mo	60*	
7-12 mo	95*	
Children 1-3 y	**130**	
4-8 y	**130**	
9-13 y	**130**	**130**
14-18 y	**130**	**130**
19-30 y	**130**	**130**
31-50 y	**130**	**130**
50-70 y	**130**	**130**
>70 y	**130**	**130**
Pregnancy All ages	-----	**175**
Lactation All ages	-----	**210**

Protein Recommendations by Age and Gender Group

Life Stage Group	Protein, g/day MALES	Protein, g/day FEMALES
Infants 0-6 mo	9.1*	
7-12 mo	**11**	
Children 1-3 y	**13**	
4-8 y	**19**	
9-13 y	**34**	**34**
14-18 y	**52**	**46**
19-30 y	**56**	**46**
31-50 y	**56**	**46**
50-70 y	**56**	**46**
>70 y	**56**	**46**
Pregnancy + Lactation All ages	-----	**71**

Bold type indicates Recommended Dietary Allowances;
"*" represents "Adequate Intakes"

Note: These recommendations are based upon body weight for a reference (average) individual in each group. For example, the recommended protein intake for adults is 0.8 grams per kilogram daily.

Amino Acid Recommendations by Age and Gender Group

Amino Acids per day mg/kg body weight								
Life Stage Group	Histidine	Isoleucine	Leucine	Lysine	Methionine & cysteine	Phenylalanine & Tyrosine	Threonine	Tryptophan	Valine
Infants 0-6 mo	36*	88*	156*	107*	59*	135*	73*	28*	87*
7-12 mo	32	43	93	89	43	84	49	13	58
Children 1-3 y	21	28	63	58	28	54	32	8	37
4-8 y	16	22	49	46	22	41	24	6	28
MALES 9-13 y	17	22	49	46	22	41	24	6	28
14-18 y	15	21	47	43	21	38	22	6	27
19 and older	14	19	42	38	19	33	20	5	24
FEMALES 9-13 y	15	21	47	43	21	38	22	6	27
14-18 y	14	19	44	40	19	35	21	5	24
19 and older	14	19	42	38	19	33	20	5	24
Pregnancy All ages	18	25	56	51	25	44	26	7	31
Lactation All ages	19	30	62	52	26	51	30	9	35

Bold type indicates Recommended Dietary Allowances;
"*" represents "Adequate Intakes"

Note: 1 kg = 2.2 lbs (kg=kilogram; lbs = pounds)

Dietary Fat Recommendations by Age and Gender Group

A. <u>Total Fat:</u> Only for infants has an adequate intake been determined, as shown in the following table. For all the other age groups, a range of fat in terms of percentage of the total calories has been set, known as the "Acceptable Macronutrient Distribution Range" (AMDR). AMDR which is the "range of intake for a particular energy source that is associated with reduced risk of chronic disease while providing intakes of essential nutrients" (Institute of Medicine, 2006). Recommendations for the essential fatty acids (Part B below) have been set for all age groups.

Life Stage Group: Infants	Total Fat g/day MALES and FEMALES
0-6 mo	31*
7-12 mo	30*

"*" represents "Adequate Intakes"

B. <u>Essential Fatty Acids:</u> Linoleic and Alpha-Linolenic (α-Linolenic acid) Acids

Life Stage Group	Linoleic acid (n-6), g/day MALES	Linoleic acid (n-6), g/day FEMALES	α-Linolenic acid (n-6), g/day MALES	α-Linolenic acid (n-6), g/day FEMALES
Infants 0-6 mo	4.4*		0.5*	
7-12 mo	4.6*		0.5*	
Children 1-3 y	7.0*		0.7*	
4-8 y	10*		0.9*	
9-13 y	12*	10*	1.2*	1.0*
14-18 y	16*	11*	1.6*	1.1*
19-30 y	17*	12*	1.6*	1.1*
31-50 y	17*	12*	1.6*	1.1*
50-70 y	14*	11*	1.6*	1.1*
>70 y	14*	11*	1.6*	1.1*
Pregnancy All ages	-----	13*	-----	1.4*
Lactation All ages	-----	13*	-----	1.3*

"*" represents "Adequate Intakes"

C. <u>Saturated Fat and Cholesterol:</u> Individuals are encouraged to select diets as low as possible in dietary cholesterol and saturated fat, provided their overall diets are nutritional sound. [11]

---

[11] The latest Dietary Guidelines for Americans (2010) recommends consuming <u>less than 10% of calories</u> from saturated fat, and choosing mono- and polyunsaturated fat instead. Individuals are encouraged to consume <u>less than 300 mg</u> of cholesterol per day.

Acceptable Macronutrient Distribution Ranges for Protein, Fat and Carbohydrate

Acceptable Macronutrient Distribution Ranges (AMDR) is the "range of intake for a particular energy source that is associated with reduced risk of chronic disease while providing intakes of essential nutrients" (Institute of Medicine, 2006). Energy is based on total daily calories (kcal). [12] Specific recommendations for total daily calories depend upon age, gender, body size, physical activity level as well as weight management goals. Figures are based on reference (average-sized) individuals for each age group. Online *calorie calculators* are available to determine more specific, individualized, daily energy requirements.

Life Stage Group	AMDR, % of daily total calories		
	Protein	Total Fat	Total Carbohydrates
Infants 0-12 mo	ND	#	ND
Children 1-3 y	5-20	30-40	45-65 *(for all groups)*
4-8 y	10-30	25-35	
Males and Females 9-13 y	10-30	25-35	
14-18 y	10-30	25-35	
19 and older	10-35	20-35	
Pregnancy & Lactation All ages	10-35	20-35	

ND = "not determinable due to lack of data of adverse effects in this age group and concern with regard to lack of ability to handle excess amounts. Source of intake should be from food only to prevent high levels of intake."
"#" For healthy, breastfed infants, the AI is used (see previous page).

---

[12] The estimated numbers of calories (rounded to the nearest 200 calories) needed to maintain weight at varying genders, ages and activity levels are listed below (USDA and USDHHS, 2010).

Average calories to maintain body weight (kcal/day) ranging from sedentary to active lifestyle		
Age (yrs)	Females	Males
2-3	1000-1400	1000-1400
4-8	1200-1800	1200-2000
9-13	1400-2200	1600-2600
14-18	1800-2400	2000-3200
19-30	1800-2400	2400-3000
31-50	1800-2200	2200-3000
51+	1600-2200	2000-2800

Total Fiber - Recommendations by Age and Gender Group

Life Stage Group	Total Fiber, g/day MALES	Total Fiber, g/day FEMALES
Infants 0-6 mo	ND	
7-12 mo	ND	
Children 1-3 y	19*	
4-8 y	25*	
9-13 y	31*	26*
14-18 y	38*	26*
19-30 y	38*	25*
31-50 y	38*	25*
50-70 y	30*	21*
>70 y	30*	21*
Pregnancy all ages	-----	28*
Lactation all ages	-----	29*

ND ="not determinable due to lack of data of adverse effects in this age group and concern with regard to lack of ability to handle excess amounts. Source of intake should be from food only to prevent high levels of intake."

"*" represents "Adequate Intakes"

Recommended Intakes of Fat-Soluble Vitamins for Individuals

Life Stage Group	Vit A (mcg/d)	Vit D (mcg)	Vit E (mg/d)	Vit K (mcg/d)
Infants				
0-6 mo	400*	10 (400 IU)*	4*	2.0*
7-12 mo	500*	10 (400 IU)*	5*	2.5*
Children				
1-3 y	**300**	**15 (600 IU)**	**6**	30*
4-8 y	**400**	**15 (600 IU)**	**7**	55*
Males				
9-13 y	**600**	**15 (600 IU)**	**11**	60*
14-18 y	**900**	**15 (600 IU)**	**15**	75*
19-30 y	**900**	**15 (600 IU)**	**15**	120*
31-50 y	**900**	**15 (600 IU)**	**15**	120*
51-70 y	**900**	**15 (600 IU)**	**15**	120*
>70 y	**900**	**20 (800 IU)**	**15**	120*
Females				
9-13 y	**600**	**15 (600 IU)**	**11**	60*
14-18 y	**700**	**15 (600 IU)**	**15**	75*
19-30 y	**700**	**15 (600 IU)**	**15**	90*
31-50 y	**700**	**15 (600 IU)**	**15**	90*
51-70 y	**700**	**15 (600 IU)**	**15**	90*
>70 y	**700**	**20 (800 IU)**	**15**	90*
Pregnancy				
14-18 y	**750**	**15 (600 IU)**	**15**	75*
19-30 y	**770**	**15 (600 IU)**	**15**	90*
31-50 y	**770**	**15 (600 IU)**	**15**	90*
Lactation				
14-18 y	**1,200**	**15 (600 IU)**	**19**	75*
19-30 y	**1,300**	**15 (600 IU)**	**19**	90*
31-50 y	**1,300**	**15 (600 IU)**	**19**	90*

Bold type indicates Recommended Dietary Allowances; "*" represents "Adequate Intakes"

Recommended Intakes of Selected Water-Soluble Vitamins for Individuals

Life Stage Group	Thiamin (mg/d)	Riboflavin (mg/d)	Niacin (mg/d)	Vit B6 (mg/d)	Vit B12 (mcg/d)	Folate (mcg/d)	Vit C (mg/d)	Panto-Thenic acid (mg/day)	Choline (mg/d)
Infants									
0-6 mo	0.2*	0.3*	2*	0.1*	0.4*	65*	40*	1.7*	125*
7-12 mo	0.3*	0.4*	4*	0.3*	0.5*	80*	50*	1.8*	150*
Children									
1-3 y	**0.5**	**0.5**	**6**	**0.5**	**0.9**	**150**	**15**	2*	200*
4-8 y	**0.6**	**0.6**	**8**	**0.6**	**1.2**	**200**	**25**	3*	250*
Males									
9-13 y	**0.9**	**0.9**	**12**	**1.0**	**1.8**	**300**	**45**	4*	375*
14-18 y	**1.2**	**1.3**	**16**	**1.3**	**2.4**	**400**	**75**	5*	550*
19-30 y	**1.2**	**1.3**	**16**	**1.3**	**2.4**	**400**	**90**	5*	550*
31-50 y	**1.2**	**1.3**	**16**	**1.3**	**2.4**	**400**	**90**	5*	550*
51-70 y	**1.2**	**1.3**	**16**	**1.7**	**2.4**	**400**	**90**	5*	550*
>70 y	**1.2**	**1.3**	**16**	**1.7**	**2.4**	**400**	**90**	5*	550*
Females									
9-13 y	**0.9**	**0.9**	**12**	**1.0**	**1.8**	**300**	**45**	4*	375*
14-18 y	**1.0**	**1.0**	**14**	**1.2**	**2.4**	**400**	**65**	5*	400*
19-30 y	**1.1**	**1.1**	**14**	**1.3**	**2.4**	**400**	**75**	5*	425*
31-50 y	**1.1**	**1.1**	**14**	**1.3**	**2.4**	**400**	**75**	5*	425*
51-70 y	**1.1**	**1.1**	**14**	**1.5**	**2.4**	**400**	**75**	5*	425*
>70 y	**1.1**	**1.1**	**14**	**1.5**	**2.4**	**400**	**75**	5*	425*
Pregnancy									
14-18 y	**1.4**	**1.4**	**18**	**1.9**	**2.6**	**600**	**80**	6*	450*
19-30 y	**1.4**	**1.4**	**18**	**1.9**	**2.6**	**600**	**85**	6*	450*
31-50 y	**1.4**	**1.4**	**18**	**1.9**	**2.6**	**600**	**85**	6*	450*
Lactation									
14-18 y	**1.4**	**1.6**	**17**	**2.0**	**2.8**	**500**	**115**	7*	550*
19-30 y	**1.4**	**1.6**	**17**	**2.0**	**2.8**	**500**	**120**	7*	550*
31-50 y	**1.4**	**1.6**	**17**	**2.0**	**2.8**	**500**	**120**	7*	550*

Bold type indicates Recommended Dietary Allowances; "*" represents "Adequate Intakes"

Recommended Intakes of Selected Minerals for Individuals

Life Stage Group	Calcium (mg/d)	P (mg/d)	Mg (mg/d)	Iron (mg/d)	Zinc (mg/d)	Copper (mcg/d)	Se (mcg/d)	Sodium (mg/d)	K (mg/d)
Infants									
0-6 mo	200*	100*	30*	0.27*	2*	200*	15*	120*	400*
7-12 mo	260*	275*	75*	**11**	**3**	220*	20*	370*	700*
Children									
1-3 y	**700**	**460**	**80**	**7**	**3**	**340**	**20**	1,000*	3,000*
4-8 y	**1,000**	**500**	**130**	**10**	**5**	**440**	**30**	1,200*	3,800*
Males									
9-13 y	**1,300**	**1,250**	**240**	**8**	**8**	**700**	**40**	1,500*	4,500*
14-18 y	**1,300**	**1,250**	**410**	**11**	**11**	**890**	**55**	1,500*	4,700*
19-30 y	**1,000**	**700**	**400**	**8**	**11**	**900**	**55**	1,500*	4,700*
31-50 y	**1,000**	**700**	**420**	**8**	**11**	**900**	**55**	1,500*	4,700*
51-70 y	**1,000**	**700**	**420**	**8**	**11**	**900**	**55**	1,300*	4,700*
>70 y	**1,200**	**700**	**420**	**8**	**11**	**900**	**55**	1,200*	4,700*
Females									
9-13 y	**1,300**	**1,250**	**240**	**8**	**8**	**700**	**40**	1,500*	4,500*
14-18 y	**1,300**	**1,250**	**360**	**15**	**9**	**890**	**55**	1,500*	4,700*
19-30 y	**1,000**	**700**	**310**	**18**	**8**	**900**	**55**	1,500*	4,700*
31-50 y	**1,000**	**700**	**320**	**18**	**8**	**900**	**55**	1,500*	4,700*
51-70 y	**1,200**	**700**	**320**	**8**	**8**	**900**	**55**	1,300*	4,700*
>70 y	**1,200**	**700**	**320**	**8**	**8**	**900**	**55**	1,200*	4,700*
Pregnancy									
14-18 y	**1,300**	**1,250**	**400**	**27**	**12**	**1,000**	**60**	1,500*	4,700*
19-30 y	**1,000**	**700**	**350**	**27**	**11**	**1,000**	**60**	1,500*	4,700*
31-50 y	**1,000**	**700**	**360**	**27**	**11**	**1,000**	**60**	1,500*	4,700*
Lactation									
14-18 y	**1,300**	**1,250**	**360**	**10**	**13**	**1,300**	**70**	1,500*	5,100*
19-30 y	**1,000**	**700**	**310**	**9**	**12**	**1,300**	**70**	1,500*	5,100*
31-50 y	**1,000**	**700**	**320**	**9**	**12**	**1,300**	**70**	1,500*	5,100*

Bold type indicates Recommended Dietary Allowances; "*" represents "Adequate Intakes"
P=Phosphorus; Mg = Magnesium; Se=Selenium; K=Potassium

APPENDIX B

SHOPPING LIST

SHOPPING LIST	Vegetables	Nuts and seeds / butters	Fruit
Grains	Avocado	Almonds	Apples
Bagels	Bean sprouts	Almond butter	Juice
Bread	Bok choy	Hazelnuts (filberts)	Jam
Bread crumbs	Broccoli	Peanuts	Lemons–organic
Corn	Burdock	Peanut butter	Limes
Flour, brown rice	Cabbage	Pecans	Pears
Flour, tapioca	Carrots	Pine Nuts	Pineapple chunks
Macaroni	Cauliflower	Sesame butter (roasted)	Raisins
Pasta – soba/udon	Celery	Sesame seeds	Tangerines
Pastry flour (ww)	Cucumber	Sunflower seeds	*OTHER FRUIT:*
Potato starch	Daikon	Tahini (raw sesame butter)	
Rice, brown	Garlic	Walnuts	*Herbs*
Rice, white	Ginger		Basil
Spaghetti / linguini	Green beans	*Oils:*	Cilantro
Guar / Xanthan gum	Green onions	Canola	Mint
	Greens	Sesame	Oregano
Beans/Tofu	Mushrooms	Olive	Parsley – regular
Chickpeas	Onion–red	Safflower	Parsley - Italian
Kidney	Onion – yellow	Walnut	Thyme
Pinto	Parsnips		
Soybeans, black	Pepper-fresh	*Condiments*	
Soy creamer	Pepper – roasted red	Broth - vegetable	*Spices:*
Soy crumbles	Potatoes	Bouillon (veg) cubes	
Soymilk	Radishes	Miso	
Tempeh	Salad greens / lettuce	Mustard	*Sweeteners*
Tofu	Tomatoes	Soy sauce, low-sodium	Apple butter
		Soy sauce, wheat-free (Tamari)	Barley malt
Beverages		Tomato Sauce	Brown rice syrup
Coffee	*Sea vegetables*	Umeboshi plums	Maple syrup
Tea	Agar	Vinegar: Balsamic	
	Arame	Red wine	*OTHER:*
Eggs	Kombu	Rice	
Eggs	Nori	Wine, cooking	
Egg whites	Wakame	Mirin	

ABOUT THE AUTHOR

Janet M. Lacey, DrPH, RD, is a registered dietitian with a doctorate in Public Health Nutrition from UNC-Chapel Hill and master's degrees in Nutrition and Food Science (MS), and Counseling and School Psychology (MEd) from the University of Massachusetts Amherst and Boston, respectively. Currently, she is a professor of nutrition and dietetics at West Chester University of Pennsylvania. Dr. Lacey is the past-chair of the Vegetarian Nutrition Dietetic Practice Group of the American Dietetic Association. A college educator since 1992, Dr. Lacey has analyzed diets and recipes in a number of research studies and has provided weight loss programs for morbidly obese individuals. She has studied and participated in osteoporosis prevention programs in Japan. Her longstanding interest in plant-based diets began in Boston in the mid-1970s, when she worked and pursued studies of complementary medicine, macrobiotic philosophy and cooking with Michio and Aveline Kushi.

CPSIA information can be obtained
at www.ICGtesting.com
Printed in the USA
FFOW01n1114130218
44323520-45280FF